STUDIES IN THE LABOUR PRO

General Editors: David Knights, Se
Sciences, University of Manchester ....
Technology, Manchester; and Hugh Willmott, Lecturer in the
Management Centre, University of Aston, Birmingham

Since the appearance of Braverman's *Labor and Monopoly Capital*,
the impact of labour-process analysis has been experienced in the
fields of industrial sociology, organisation theory, industrial
relations, labour economics, politics and business studies. The
annual UMIST–ASTON Labour Process conferences have been
influential in providing a regular forum for advancing empirical and
theoretical analysis in these fields. By combining a selection of
papers delivered at these conferences with specially commissioned
contributions, the series examines diverse aspects of the employment
relationship across the range of productive and service industries.
Some volumes explore further the established terrain of management
control, the intensification of work, the deskilling of labour. Others
are attentive to associated topics such as gender relations at work,
new technology, workplace democracy and the international dimensions of the labour process.

STUDIES IN THE LABOUR PROCESS

New Technology and the Labour Process

Edited by

David Knights
Senior Lecturer in Management Sciences
UMIST, Manchester

and

Hugh Willmott
Lecturer
Management Centre
Aston University, Birmingham

First published 1988

Published by
THE MACMILLAN PRESS LTD
Houndmills, Basingstoke, Hampshire RG21 2XS
and London
Companies and representatives
throughout the world

Phototypeset by
STYLESET LIMITED, Warminster, Wiltshire

Printed in Hong Kong

British Library Cataloguing in Publication Data
New technology and the labour process.—
(Studies in the labour process).
1. Labour supply—Effect of technological
innovations on
I. Knights, David   II. Willmott, Hugh
III. Series
331.12'5   HD6331
ISBN 0-333-42912-5 (hardcover)
ISBN 0-333-42913-3 (paperback)

To UMIST/ASTON Labour Process conference participants

Contents

Notes on the Contributors

Martin Beirne is a researcher at Paisley College of Technology. He has previously worked in the Departments of Information Science and of Industrial Relations in the University of Strathclyde. His work has focused on the philosophy, strategy and practices of management in the introduction of new technology, with particular current attention to employee involvement techniques in the design and implementation of computerised information systems. He is the editor of *New Technology and Workplace Democracy*.

Bernard Burnes is a Research Officer in the Department of Management Sciences at UMIST. He worked in the engineering industry for eleven years and holds a degree in economics and social history and a PhD in organisational psychology. For the past five years he has been researching into issues relating to new technology and is currently involved with the National Economic Development Council in a project examining the introduction and use of Advanced Manufacturing Technology. Among his various publications are *New Technology, Old Jobs* (1984), *The Use of CNC Machine Tools* (1986) and *New Technology in Context* (1987).

Patrick Dawson is Lecturer in Organisational Behaviour at the University of Edinburgh. He is currently examining the application of expert systems technology to the design of socially useful computers; in particular, to the development of community-based systems to provide the public with advice and information about welfare benefits.

Lorraine Giordano is completing her doctoral dissertation, 'Beyond Taylorism: Computerization and Cooperation in Production', at the Department of Sociology, New York University. She has been an adjunct lecturer at New York University, the College of New Rochelle – School of New Resources, and Queen's College, City University of New York (1978–85). She has also served as Scholar-in-Residence to Mass Transit Street Theater, New York City, for a play on occupational safety and health entitled, *Hasn't Hurt Me Yet*, funded by the New York Council for the Humanities (1983–4).

Eckart Hildebrandt is a research co-ordinator at the Science Center Berlin, Research Unit Labour Policy. He is a skilled engineer and taught Political Sciences at the Freie Universität Berlin. Subsequently he published *Internationale Beschäftigungskonkurrenz* in 1986. For ten years he has been doing empirical research on rationalisation in steel industries, Trade Union politics, and introduction of information technologies. He has published a range of research reports and is co-author of the yearbook *Kritisches Gewerkschaftsjahrbuch*.

David Knights is Senior Lecturer in Management Sciences, UMIST. He works closely with Hugh Willmott in organising the annual Labour Process Conferences and publishing an edited series from them including *Job Redesign* (1985), *Gender and the Labour Process* (1986) and *Managing the Labour Process* (1986). His current research interests are focused on the financial services and are funded by ICAEW, ESRC and TSB. He has also been actively involved with colleagues in establishing and managing an ESRC Research Centre on Information Technology in the Department of Management Sciences at UMIST.

Lothar Lappe, PhD, social scientist and researcher, is currently at the Max Planck Institute for Human Development and Education, Berlin (since 1977). From 1972 to 1977 he was at the Sociological Research Institute, SOFI, Göttingen. He undertakes empirical studies on labour market process and conditions of work, i.e. women's working conditions, the development of skilled labour in industry and socialisation as a function of work. He is the author of *Die Arbeitssituation erwebstätiger Frauen* (1981) and the co-author of *Konzeptionen zur Analyse der Sozialisation durch Arbeit: Theoretische Vorstudien für eine empirische Untersuchung* (1979) and *Arbeitsbiographie und Persönlichkeitsentwicklung* (1985).

Gloria L. Lee is Director of Postgraduate Studies, Aston University Management Centre. Her research includes organisational analysis; the study of executive careers; labour market segmentation and industrial accidents; youth labour markets, apprenticeship and training; equal opportunity policy and practice; trade unionism and race. Her current research on Engineers and IT is in association with the ESRC Work Organisation Research Council and her publications include: *Who Gets to the Top: A Sociological Study of Business Executives* (1981); *Skill Seekers: black youth apprenticeships* *and disadvantage* (with John Wrench) (1983); *Race and Trade Unionsim*, (1984); *The Manufacture of Disadvantage: Stigma and Social Closure* (as joint editor with R. Loveridge) (1987).

Wanda J. Orlikowski is currently completing a doctorate in Information Systems at the New York University Graduate School of Business Administration. Her dissertation research examines the role played by information technology in mediating and facilitating individual and organisational responses to conditions of post-industrialisation.

Harvie Ramsay lectures in industrial relations at the University of Strathclyde. His current research interests include worker participation, international capital and labour, profit-sharing, and the impact of computerisation on work organisation and control. He has published widely on the first area, including a forthcoming book for Macmillan, *The Myths of Participation*, and is currently involved in co-writing a book on profit-sharing. He is also author of *Transnational Corporations in Australia: Issues for Industrial Democracy*, and co-author of *Socialist Construction and Marxist Theory* and *For Mao: Essays in Historical Materialism*.

Steve Smith lectures in sociology at Kingston Polytechnic and is an honorary research fellow at the Open University's Faculty of Technology. He is co-author of *Managers and Corporate Social Policy; Private Solutions To Public Problems?* (1984). He has also published a number of papers or consultant reports in the sociology of management, technology, training, employment and urban politics. He is continuing to research managerial strategies for new technology in the service sector.

Hugh Willmott is Lecturer and Chair of the Doctoral Programme in the Management Centre, Aston University. He has published widely in management, sociology and accounting journals. Together with David Knights, he has organised the UMIST/ASTON Labour Process Conferences and edited a series of volumes in this area including *Job Redesign* (1985), *Gender and the Labour Process* (1986) and *Managing the Labour Process* (1986). He is currently engaged in research into management control within the life insurance industry (ICAEW/ESRC) and in an international study of the regulation of accounting (ESRC).

1 Introduction

Bernard Burnes, David Knights and
Hugh Willmott

It is no coincidence that the last decade has seen the widespread
adoption of new, microelectronic-based technology and a renewed
interest in the Labour Process. In response to a number of crises (e.g.
energy, inflation, fiscal) the restructuring of companies, industries
and, to some degree, even entire economies has facilitated these
developments. Clearly, the dynamics of technological change are
more wide-ranging than an analysis of the labour process at the
point of production can encompass (Littler and Salaman, 1982). Yet
production is both a starting point and end result of technological
innovation and, therefore, the labour process remains a relevant, if
partial, focus for its analysis.

A crucial question to be asked before examining the labour
process as both a condition and consequence of new technology is
what constitutes its novelty and, thereby, the proliferation of dis-
courses surrounding its development. Conventionally, the technology is seen as new because advanced micro-electronic computerisation
allows for the processing of large volumes of data at speeds way
beyond the capacity of previous more mechanical technologies. In
its early development, the micro-technology was used primarily for
the computerisation of records and especially the pay-roll. Any
impact on employment tended to be counteracted by the general
growth of the non-manual labour force as a result of an affluent
society demanding more services. Consequently, the social impact of
new technology, except for a few fears about the effect on privacy of a
potentially all-embracing computerised surveillance, was minimal.
However, afraid of suffering a competitive disadvantage but also
cajoled by speciality sales staff, corporations soon began to invest
heavily in computer hardware and a new and more diverse set of
uses for the technology rapidly emerged. This was specifically
enhanced by expanding secondary markets in custom-designed
software and an increasing sophistication of data processing staff
and other areas within the user companies.

As long as the economy was expanding, the substitution of capital for labour reflected in the dramatic advances in the uses of new technology was not immediately and directly manifested in the unemployment statistics. But once state-induced recessions accompanied the expansion of new technology, employment began to suffer badly. It was at this point that the literature on new technology really proliferated. Indeed, some of this literature was stimulated by governments themselves in the late 1970s as they became anxious about the impact of new technology on employment levels.

One of the earliest of these government-commissioned researches was 'The Computerisation of Society: A Report to the President of France' (Nora and Minc, 1980) which drew special attention to the potential of microelectronics to reduce employment levels drastically. Within a few years, a trickle of interest had turned into a flood of material as the mass media began examining the potential benefits of new technology in terms of productivity and growth, and academics responded to the release of funds for the study of the effects of new technology, including their impact on employment. One widely-held view (e.g. Rathenau Commission 1980) is that whilst the introduction of new technology might lead to job losses, the failure to use the most advanced technological systems in any one country would be devastating on all economic criteria,including employment, because of the erosion of international competitiveness. This expectation has been echoed in the argument that those who introduce it first will gain the greatest benefits from new technology by stealing a march on their competitors (Wakeham and Beresford-Knox 1980).

These two – the speed of technological innovation and application and its impact on employment – have tended to dominate the general debate on new technology. Though not unexpected, it is regrettable that governments, organisations and even trade unions have failed to compliment this thrust with a more critical stance; to ask questions regarding the way new technology is developed and used, and particularly to examine alternative forms of new technology and alternative ways of using it.

Indeed, the dominant response to the new industrial revolution has embraced the worst form of technological determinism since, in its blanket approval of the 'progressiveness' of new technology, there is a failure to examine taken-for-granted assumptions concerning either particular or general developments. In the name of 'progress' a futuristic fatalism is nurtured which generates an acceptance of the inevitability of technological developments and a reluctance to question the way it is used, even when this is consistently destructive of jobs and skills. In part, the problem stems from a tendency to treat new technology as a self-contained, uniform phenomenon, isolated from other societal and organisational influences and having an inexorable momentum of its own. Instead of aiding an understanding of technological developments, descriptive accounts conflated with utopian or 'gloom and doom' propaganda as simple and static snapshots, providing a multitude of conflicting views, contend with each other for media attention. A result has been that evidence can be cited to support virtually any position ranging from the view of microelectronics creating more 'open', prosperous, societies (Attenborough, 1984; Walton, 1982) to the opposite extreme where unemployment, poverty and a loss of freedom are seen as the inevitable outcome (Boyle *et al.,* 1980; Council for Science and Society, 1981).

If we are to break the 'grip' of this populist and often sensationalist literature, then what is needed are studies of new technology within the context of political, socio-cultural and organisational developments; its treatment not as an isolated or uniform phenomenon, but as something that varies depending on its particular form and on the nature of the organisation, industry and society in which it is developed and used; and finally, a view of new technology and the social organisation of production linked to historical change. This last consideration is especially important, since it is only through historical comparisons that a fuller understanding of the significance of contemporary developments in new technology may be gained.

Historical comparisons, and particularly the power that ownership of technology bestows, has been the concern of a number of writers. Marc Bloch (1985), for example, has explored how the development of the waterwheel in the Middle Ages enhanced the power of the feudal lord by increasing the dependence of his serfs on a highly productive capital resource which only the wealthy could purchase. Using the example of the textile industry during the Industrial Revolution, Rosenbrock (1981; 1982) has shown how inventions developed for their own use by self-employed weavers were designed to enhance skill as well as productivity. By contrast, those developed for use by employees under the factory system, whilst also designed to increase productivity, reduced the need for skill in order to cheapen labour and increase managerial control. Contemporary

observers in the eighteenth and nineteenth centuries, such as Smith
(1776), and Ure (1835), also saw technology as having this function,
as did Marx (1887) to whom we are indebted for the foundations of
labour process analysis. Babbage (1835, pp. 368–9) put the argument
most succinctly: 'when capital enlists science in her service, the re-
fractory hand of labour will always be taught docility' which represents a typical example of how power and knowledge have
combined throughout history to discipline and render subjects
docile (Foucault, 1979, p. 136). Yet 'where there is power, there is
resistance' (Foucault, 1979, p. 95) and the nineteenth century saw
many, sometimes bloody, attempts to challenge the combination of
science and capital (Berg, 1979; Pollard, 1965).

In the early part of this century Taylor's theory of Scientific
Management, became – and still to a large extent remains – a
dominant influence on managerial thinking and practice (Littler,
1978; Thompson, 1983) even though various revisions and
refinements of his have taken place since. The Human Relations
School which developed in the 1930's challenged many of the
assumptions of Scientific Management and continues to the present
day in various forms of managerial psychology (Herzberg, 1968;
McGregor, 1960; Likert, 1967). After the Second World War, Job
Redesign appeared (Davis and Canter, 1955, Trist *et al.,* 1963; Kelly
1982; Littler 1982; Knights *et al,* 1985) giving more emphasis to the
relationship between technology and labour. This relationship was
equally a focus of the technological determinists (Sayles, 1958;
Woodward, 1965; Woodward *et al.,* 1970) who established a number
of significant correlations between the type of technology/
production system and the structure of organisations including
certain behavioural responses of labour. The absence of a social
dimension to the analysis of technology and its impact on jobs
stimulated the development of socio-technical approaches (Trist and
Bamforth, 1951;) and eventually these diverse approaches began to
converge in an all-embracing systems theory (Emery, 1969; Miller
and Rice, 1970). A reaction against the assumptions of consensus
underlying systems theory, and the tendency for it to be imperialistic in
its domain, resulted in a more cautious approach to organisational
analysis. This caution was clearly evident in contingency theory
(Burns and Stalker, 1961; Lawrence and Lorsch, 1967, Hickson *et al.,*
1971) who regarded work organisation and control systems as
dependent or 'contingent' upon three main variables: environmental
uncertainty and dependence; organisation size; and technology.

However, in all these 'theories' technology tends to be viewed as a fixed and given entity which either determines the design of jobs or, at least, sets specific constraints on the choices available in the decision-making process. Even when managerial strategy is perceived as playing an important part in shaping the organisation of work (Child, 1985), new technology is still seen more as a constraint on, rather than as a sphere of, choice.

The more or less deterministic view of technology was also held by the main protagonists in the Automation Debate of the 1940s and 1950s (Bright, 1958; Diebold, 1952, Wiener, 1948). Rarely did discourse concern itself with the diversity of technological possibilities and uses. Its inevitability went unquestioned and, as in Bright's (1958) study of Automation, there was a tendency to simply demonstrate in great detail who the winners and losers were from the introduction of automation. At no time was there any question of whether or not it should be used or even how it could be used despite the fact that in some cases the economic argument for automation was quite weak. In this respect the Automation Debate, with its emphasis on the impact of the technology rather than alternatives, foreshadowed the way the New Technology debate has, in general, developed.

More recently, there has emerged an increasing criticism and questioning of the way that science and technology is developing and being used. Much of this has revolved around environmental, peace and civil liberties issues (Boyle *et al.*,1980; Dickson, 1974; Martin and Norman, 1973), but there is also a limited body of criticism of the way technology is developed for and used in the workplace. (Cooley, 1979; Noble, 1979; Mackenzie and Wajcman, 1985). Much of this has been inspired by Braverman's (1974) work on the Labour Process and therefore not surprisingly, the issues of management control, gender and skill, workers' resistance and the role of technology have become major areas of contention within the Labour Process Debate.

The specific value of a Labour Process focus is that it alerts us to ways in which (new) technology is developed and applied in the context of specific (i.e. capitalist) relations of production. That is, our attention is directed to the social processes whereby technology, in the form of information processing through the use of miniaturised electronic circuitry, is synthesised with the productive potential of human labour power. Precisely how this technology is developed and applied can be seen to reflect (and reproduce or transform) the institutional relations and strategies of power through which it is shaped and steered. As Wilkinson (1982, p. 20, emphasis added) has observed, 'the design and choice of technology may be seen as a result of *socially-derived* decisions, and the way in which technology is used can be explained in terms of... *political processes*'.

Fundamental to the structure of relations of production is an interdependence of capital and labour (Cressey and MacInnes, 1980) in which labour is placed in an institutionally subordinate situation. Occupying a dominant position, the agents of capital are able to impose a technological transformation of the workplace in pursuit of the extraction of surplus value from a workforce that has little or no power and knowledge to resist the unquestioned demand for 'technological progress'. From this perspective, the use and effects of new technology can be viewed in terms of an almost inevitable process of de-skilling, degradation, labour shedding, more insidious modes of control, etc., as labour fatalistically complies with capital's definition and selective promotion of its progressive demands. However, this is to emphasise only one side of Marx's labour process theory. Relative surplus value is secured through the private appropriation of socialised production and therefore depends as much upon the 'freely' given consent and co-operative interdependence, as on the direct control, of labour. In so far as the new technology extends the division of labour and specialisation, it becomes apparent that improved productivity will increasingly depend upon the strength and quality of labour's co-operation and interdependence. From this contrasting perspective, the design and application of new technologies in relation to the organisation and control of work is perceived as being mediated through the practical reasoning of both workers and managers. Each will develop their strategies in relation to how they interpret specific labour and product market conditions, corporate strength and union power, wage payment systems and the immediate quality of workplace relations. Quite clearly, strategic choices of capital and labour are not given. Rather, they have to be continuously defined and organised through the interdependent processes of conceptual and practical trial and error. Both workers and managers are 'knowledgeable and skilled' individuals (Giddens, 1979) capable of mobilising cultural and organisational resources (Offe and Weisenthal, 1980; Lash and Urry, 1984); they are not programmed automata or cultural dopes, and will tend to 'devise ways of avoiding being treated as such' (Giddens, 1982, p. 45).

However, while the determinism often associated with Braverman's formulation of labour process analysis must be rejected if adequate account is to be taken of the central and problematic nature of labour, an appreciation of the definition and mobilisation of interests in respect of, for example, the use of new technologies, must be informed by an understanding of the structure of product and labour markets, the organisation of production relations and the power-knowledge strategies that are their medium and outcome. So while the promotion and application of new technology is to be seen as a contested product of a political process of struggle which reflects the interdependency of capital and labour, it should also be recognised how the values which guide the 'strategic choices' of managers and workers are themselves shaped and constrained by a structure of relations that can pull capital and labour apart at the same time as it renders them more mutually dependent. It is the tension underlying the dual character of the relationship wherein a productive interdependence is framed within a structure of antagonism over power, knowledge and allocative resources that is often intensified by a change such as the introduction of new technology. Yet what might be classified as the second industrial revolution has not been accompanied by the kind of resistance usually associated with threats of standard (restrictive) practices in the workplace.

A number of explanations to account for labour's compliance with the demands of new technology are available some of which are discussed in the various papers. First, of course, the recession has quite clearly 'loosened' the labour market thus eroding one of the most significant sources of shopfloor power and resistance. Second, the twin-effects of commodification and individualisation renders labour more docile especially when job security is threatened. Third and finally, the ideological identification of new technology and 'progress' has discursively dominated the mass media, education and the workplace. When appropriating labour's co-operative and interdependent concerns with production, shopfloor acceptance of the new technology as a 'progressive' tool can almost be taken for granted. Moreover, most unions active in this field have not sought to 'block' developments; rather they have assumed its inevitability and simply set out with the 'positive' intention to establish 'new technology agreements'.

Given the context, and especially the fact that one of the most rapidly expanding spheres of the application of new technology is in information services where women predominate and unionisation is weak or non-existent, the effects on labour of the second industrial revolution is almost as oppressive as the first. Certainly, the emancipatory potential of new technology is of less concern than its power to improve market competitiveness, productivity and reduce labour costs. Docile labour forces and gendered segregation at work has facilitated this process (Knights and Sturdy, 1987)

As Aronowitz (1981) has commented, new technologies have been promoted and adopted primarily where they are shown or expected to 'reduce the amount of capital outlays required to produce means of production, reduce the size of variable capital, and thus recover the profit rate, at least temporarily'. Interestingly, this view is echoed by Child (1984) who, despite his well-known exposure of the role of strategic choice in the design of work organisation, has noted of employer policies on new technology that those which enhance rather than degrade or replace labour are the exception; and that where some enhancement does occur, it is mainly an unintended (and therefore especially vulnerable) consequence of a seach for increased flexibility and/or more economical manning.

Comprising papers selected from the 3rd and 4th annual Labour Process Conferences, the aim of this book is to develop the debate on the role of new technology through a critical examination of its application and adaptation. Generally the papers are dismissive of technological determinist views. Like Braverman, the authors believe that technology cannot be studied independently of the political economy of work in capitalist society. However, unlike Braverman, they see work organisation as a medium and outcome of conflicting and changing power relations. Management is viewed neither as homogeneous nor omnipotent; workers are considered to be active participants who can, sometimes, influence events; and it is suggested that technology is not always developed or used solely to enhance managerial power or to de-skill workers.

It is hoped, therefore, that the book will make a timely and useful contribution to the discussion of the role played by technology in the Labour Process, and, indeed, to the Labour Process debate in general. The papers are varied in the technologies studied and differ in emphasis and approaches adopted, but they are united by their efforts to combine theory with empirical evidence in order to deepen our understanding of, and clarify the issues involved in, the Labour Process.

In the first scene-setting chapter Wanda Orlikowski argues that the dominant view of Information Technology is one-dimensional, deterministic, largely ahistorical and non-dialectical, and that the relationship of technology to the economic and political context in which it is developed and used has typically been ignored, as have the social relations of production. These shortcomings are traced to the design of the studies that have been undertaken. Either they are based upon *post hoc* investigation of the impact of new technology using a balance sheet mentality; or they have adopted contingency approaches where various contextual conditions are seen as determining how new technology will be used within particular organisations. In contrast, Orlikowski is concerned to show that social relations in production, as well as technical relations, need to be considered seriously; that new technology should not therefore be treated as either universal or monolithic, even though there is a tendency in the development of computer systems, especially within large corporations, towards the creation of a new form of post-bureaucratic, administrative and control structure which links technocratic forms of organisation and neo-corporatist forms of political organisations. One of the characteristics of this new structure is the fusion of managerial and technical/professional roles which can lead to the downgrading and de-skilling of such jobs.

The author points out, however, that whilst these developments are facilitated by computerisation, they are not determined by it, and that other developments such as decentralisation, debureaucratisation, and enhanced skills could also take place. In conclusion, Orlikowski states that workers can influence technical change so as to create outcomes more favourable to themselves, and that such practices as participative design can provide the basis for questioning how technology is used, which in turn could create the conditions for the emergence of more democratic forms of work organisation.

The next three chapters by Hildebrandt, Wilson and Lee, all deal with the use of new technology in engineering companies. Hildebrandt begins by pointing out than an exchange of ideas between West German industrial sociologists and Anglo-American Labour Process theorists would be fruitful for both. This chapter, which is based on an examination of the introduction of Computer-Aided Production Planning and Management Systems (CAPPM) into 12 West German engineering companies, drawing, as it does, on material from both sources, illustrates that such an exchange is long overdue. Hildebrandt found that the companies introduced CAPPM in response to market changes which necessitated lower stock holdings and faster throughput times, which in turn required more up-to-date and better information regarding production activities. In the short-term, the introduction of CAPPM did not appear to change the existing balance of power between management and workers in these companies; however, the author argues, in the long-term it could undermine the basis of the trust which exists between them. These companies were all characterised by a high degree of trust between management and workers which was based on an implicit 'Productivity – Social Pact', whereby workers accepted their role in, and the goals of, the enterprise, and managers for their part were expected to act in the best interests of the organisation and its members. The basis of trust and thus of the Pact was an absence of secrecy between management and workers; however, changes in technology and markets had led to a breakdown in this transparency, and the introduction of CAPPM was a 'unilateral' attempt by management to overcome their lack of understanding of shopfloor activities.

The problem, as Hildebrandt perceives it, is that the new technology renders labour more visible to management but not vice versa. Such surveillance, it is argued, potentially undermines workers' trust of management thus weakening the Productivity–Social Pact. By drawing upon the industrial sociology and Labour Process literature, Hildebrandt presents a model of organisations as 'bounded space' where both managers and workers try to establish a balance, a consensus, regarding organisation aims and objectives. However, the use of new technology, especially when developed and introduced by outside consultants, has a tendency to upset this balance, the changes in technology lead to increased managerial power which undermines workers' trust in organisational aims and objectives, with the result than the changes in technology can lead to changes in the social relations of production.

The following chapter by Fiona Wilson critically examines the Braverman thesis that new technology will be used in a Tayloristic fashion to deskill workers, remove planning from the shopfloor and increase management control. She focuses on how the introduction of Computer Numerically Controlled machine tools (CNC) has affected the jobs of machinists in a large engineering company, concluding that the de-skilling thesis can both be supported yet also refuted by the evidence of her research.

On the one hand, the introduction of CNC has led to the separation of conception from execution because the CNC is controlled by a punched paper tape rather than manually by the machine operator. Thus the machine operator's decision-making capacity is reduced. For the same reason, the skill utilisation required of the operators is less, repetition is increased, and operators feel less involved in their work. On the other hand, the introduction of CNC has led to increased responsibility for operators and the need to learn, and use, new skills such as programming, the physical effort of machining has been reduced; the practice of part-machining a component on one machine and finishing it on another has been minimised, thus giving operators the opportunity to do a 'whole job'. These changes have led some workers to view their jobs as more interesting.

Therefore, Wilson argues, it is possible for the change to CNC to be seen as having both deskilled and reskilled machinists' jobs, demonstrating the fallacy of judging technical change to be all good or all bad. She also points out that, whilst managers wish to control workers, they also need their co-operation, and therefore, it is not always in management's interests to deskill workers. Nor is it the case that managers always have a clearly thought-out strategy for the implementation of new technology. Wilson concludes that the process of change is a political one whereby managers and workers, either consciously or unconsciously contest issues of control and skill, making the outcome more variable and unpredictable than Braverman assumed.

The third chapter in this group examines the influence of professional engineers on the introduction of new technology into engineering. Gloria Lee argues that new technology is not deterministic and that its impact will depend upon the context within which it is introduced, especially the relationship between management and workers. Professional engineers play a key role in the process of selecting and introducing new technology, yet, as Lee points out, they occupy an ambiguous position between management and labour. On the one hand, they are part of the managerial process, whilst on the other hand, they are subject to it. This leads some engineers to ally themselves firmly with management, whilst others, through trade union membership and activity, ally themselves with labour. She points out that their perception of their own alliances and interests affect their approach to the use of new technology. Those allying themselves with management are more likely to favour the introduction of new technology in ways that reduce jobs and skills, whilst those who ally themselves with labour may take the opposite stance. Lee concludes by arguing for professional engineers to adopt a more 'open' role in this process by drawing attention to the decisions that have to be made and their consequences. She believes that engineers, by going beyond technical rationality and adopting a humanist perspective, can help to create work structures and jobs which draw on and develop human potential rather than destroy it.

In the next two chapters, Dawson and Smith examine the introduction of new technology in British Rail and retail stores respectively. Dawson examines how the computerisation of British Rail's freight operations has affected the supervisory function in marshalling yards. He begins by reviewing the debate on management control systems and supervision; and by defining the role of supervisors, and how it could be changed by computerisation. He points out that there is an increasing tendency for the traditional labour control function of supervisors to become peripheral to production. This trend is being reinforced by the actions of senior management who introduce more sophisticated mechanisms of surveillance and control into the Labour Process that displace the requirement for direct supervision. This, Dawson argues, poses the question as to whether there is a role for the supervisor following the application of information technology. In order to answer this question the author proceeds to describe how the supervisory system at British Rail operated prior to computerisation, and the changes that its introduction brought. Dawson found that new technology allowed management to centralise the control of freight operations, but at the same time to devolve some additional elements of supervision to a local level. This resulted in increased technical control of freight operations, which in turn reduced the need for hierarchical structures of control and the reliance on individual experience built up over the years.

Therefore, although there was a distinct erosion of some supervisory functions and positions, this coincided with other supervisors securing additional responsibilities which had previously been carried out by more senior staff and divisional managers. From this, Dawson argues that what has taken place at British Rail is not the elimination of the supervisory role but a complex redefinition of it which can only be understood in the context of the activity as a whole, rather than by examining individual supervisory jobs.

Smith is concerned with the introduction of Electronic Point of Sale (EPOS) systems in the retail industry but he reverses the conventional focus by examining the 'impact of organisations on new technology' rather than the reverse. His central argument is that within retailing there are two extreme types of organisation. First, there is the large high volume, low value chain stores which conform to what can be described as a 'direct control' system of management. Second, the up-market quality stores are characterised by a craft-like 'responsible autonomy' which allows staff to use their discretion but demands that they give considerable emotional commitment to presenting the 'correct' store image or style.

Smith found that although EPOS systems had been introduced into both types of retail outlets, its potential as a control mechanism is not exploited to its full extent *even* in the mass retail stores where a strict and detailed Taylorian diversion of labour is in evidence. The main advantage of EPOS in all stores is the way in which it facilitates an efficient system of stock control and thereby enables the business to run on much smaller inventories than previously. But whereas the mass retailers expected the new technology to provide precisely such benefits, the craft retailers, having introduced EPOS intuitively as a kind of 'progressive' development, were pleasantly surprised to find that it improved information so much that stock inventories could be significantly reduced.

In mass retailing, one of the reasons why the new technology was not being used directly to measure, and thereby increase, productivity was the fear of resistance from staff at the checkout, where stores are particularly vulnerable to labour disruption. There were also very few redundancies; rather, any labour saving simply allowed for a redeployment of staff to the selling function. Furthermore, the speed and availability of data enabled stores to concentrate much more on their fastest selling lines thus vastly improving their sales turnover.

Although there were elements of de-skilling and reduced autonomy at the checkout within mass retailing, the impact on buyers and store managers was even greater. For the access to sales returns at head office facilitated an automatic buying system removing much of the remaining limited autonomy at the local level in the stores. In other words, the new technology was used to control management equally, if not more, than staff.

Within the craft retailers, EPOS was seen not as a replacement for, so much as an extension of, the art of retailing. Despite the increased quantity and availability of data provided by the new technology, it was not appropriated by national headquarters for purposes of central decision-making. Instead, responsible autonomy prevailed at the local level and this was reflected throughout the hierarchy within the stores. All staff had a measure of responsibility for sales and buying or, at least, overseeing these activities. Moreover, the less intensive division of labour also was accompanied by an apparent greater opportunity for women to secure positions higher in the hierarchy.

Smith's conclusion is that the type of market and organisation is the crucial determinant not of the decision to introduce a new technology like EPOS but on how it will ultimately be used or exploited. It could be that in time there will be a convergence towards the more intensive division of labour and centralisation of decision-making as self-service is seen to be equally as effective with up-market customers. On the other hand, as the technology releases labour time, mass retailers may see the potential of an increased quality of sales service on some of their more expensive or specialist lines. Because of the tendency for sales work to involve a 'commercialisation of self and emotion', Smith is sceptical that the development of such work in mass retailing is something to be applauded. Maybe, he argues, direct control is less alienating than responsible autonomy when the latter involves the emotional labour and commitment normally only expected of employers.

The next two chapters, by Giordano, and Beirne and Ramsay, address the relationship between new technology and Job Redesign/Quality of Working Life (QWL) issues. Giordano, writing from an American perspective, points out that the two major developments which are re-shaping organisations are new technology and QWL programmes. She argues that this is not a specifically new phenomenon, since organisations have always responded to major upheavals in their environment by changing both their technological and social structures in order to become more competitive. Giordano sees these twin developments as affecting the skill and autonomy of workers but, unlike Braverman, she does not believe that they will necessarily lead to the de-skilling and degrading of labour. Instead, she postulates that skill depends upon a range of factors such as the existing technological and social divisions of labour, the history of labour relations, market conditions and the competitive strength of individual organisations.

In some organisations, therefore, technological changes will result in enhanced skills. The author argues that this is especially likely when QWL programmes are adopted, for their objective is to improve organisational competitiveness by reducing the division of labour and enhancing skills in order to gain greater organisational flexibility. However, as Smith argues in his paper, a reduction in direct control does not necessarily imply a reduction in overall management control, particularly where, as Giordano demonstrates, it gives management greater scope to reorganise work at short notice with little or no union consultation. Giordano describes how, in America QWL programmes which provide management with this flexibility have undermined national agreements and threatened national and local union strength, because unions can no longer use the protection of national contracts to slow down, bargain over, and prevent unwelcome change. In concluding that new technology and QWL can have both positive and negative effects on workers, she supports the need for unions to develop new tactics and strategies if they are to defend their members against the threats implicit in technological change.

Beirne and Ramsay also take a sceptical view of the work reorganisation movement, which they consider to be a strategy by management to increase control over labour. In particular, they are concerned with the development of the participative design of computerised office systems. The authors point out that administrative functions now account for a major proportion of total labour costs, and that managers see the introduction of new technology in this area as potentially bringing significantly greater savings than on the shopfloor, where technological change has been reducing labour costs steadily since the nineteenth century. They point out also that Job Redesign schemes have been more successful in offices than on the shopfloor, where they have been met by resistance and suspicion. They attribute this partly to the high proportion of women in non-manual occupations, whose social position renders them less well organised to resist management reorganisation initiatives than male manual workers.

Therefore, for both economic and social reasons, Beirne and Ramsay consider it likely that there will be more schemes to re-design work around new technology in offices than on the shopfloor. These schemes are also more likely to be participative because of the growing realisation that the co-operation and knowledge of workers are of crucial importance in enabling management to reap the full benefits of the new systems. However, as Beirne and Ramsey argue, from a Labour Process perspective, there are strong grounds for being sceptical of user involvement and participation in design. They take the view that such exercises can lead to an intensification of work, job losses, health and safety problems, greater gender segregation, and less control over their work by workers. The authors do acknowledge that there can be benefits for staff in such schemes, and that management do not always set out with a conscious control strategy when embarking on the change process. Nevertheless, they do believe that scepticism is warranted, and point to the need for an independent, critical approach to the participative design of computer systems.

In the final chapter, Lothar Lappe's main concern is the need to understand the developmental nature of skills and qualifications in order to investigate how these are affected by technological change, and whether or not there is, as argued by Braverman, a long-run tendency towards deskilling.

Lappe, like Hildebrandt, writes from the perspective of German industrial sociology. He points out that there are difficulties in comparing Anglo-German experiences due to differences in work organisation, training, industrial relations and research strategies between the two countries.

With regard to the latter, Lappe argues that in Britain the tendency has been for industrial sociologists to orientate their work towards industrial conflict relating to the control of work and that there is also a strong tradition of using historical studies to strengthen current empirical research.

In West Germany industrial sociologists have only recently become interested in issues relating to the control of work. The tendency has been for researchers to concentrate on such issues as internal and external labour deployment. He points out that their strength is in the area of in-depth qualitative analysis of qualifications, stress and of aspects of jobs within occupational groups. In Lappe's view, this detailed approach to occupational structures has presented the consideration of the wider issues raised by Braverman. Braverman's de-skilling hypothesis is then examined in the light of German research on job qualifications and the development of technology. Lappe argues that the impact of technology is not uni-dimensional nor is the development of qualifications necessarily linear.

The studies of particular industries which are presented in the paper do not. in Lappe's view, confirm Braverman's hypothesis. On the other hand, neither do they support the opposite view that technology will increase skills.

He concludes by highlighting the developmental nature of technology and qualifications and pointing to the correlation, in his studies, between repetitive work and low mechanisation and vice versa.

This collection of papers explores a wide range of issues relating to the role of new technology within the Labour Process. They take the debate on new technology beyond just an empirical examination of its impact and towards a perception of organisations as dynamic and diverse complexes of social relations where change is both the condition and consequence of an unstable blend of technological, political, economic and social forces.

References

Attenborough, N. G. (1984) *Employment and Technical Change* (London: Department of Trade and Industry).

Aronowitz, S. (1981) *The Crisis in Historical Materialism* (New York: Praeger).

Babbage, C. (1835) *On the Economy of Machinery and Manufactures* (London: Knight).

Berg, M. (ed.) (1979) *Technology and Toil in Nineteenth Century Britain* (London: CSE Books).

Bloch, M. (1985) 'The Watermill and Feudal Authority', in D. Mackenzie and J. Wajcman, *The Social Shaping of Technology* (Milton Keynes: Open University Press).

Boyle, G., Elliott, D., Roy, R. (eds) (1980) *The Politics of Technology* (London: Longman).

Braverman, H. (1974) *Labor and Monopoly Capitalism* (New York: Monthly Review Press).

Bright, J. R. (1958) *Automation and Management* (Boston: Harvard University Press).

Burns, T and Stalker, G. M. (1961) *The Management of Innovation* (London: Tavistock).

Child, J. (1984) *Organisation* (Cambridge: Harper and Row).

Child, J. (1985) 'Management Strategies, New Technology and the Labour Process' in Knights, D. *et al.* (eds) *Job Redesign* (Aldershot: Gower).

Cooley, M. J. (1979) *Architect or Bee?* (Slough: Langley Technical Services).

Council for Science and Society (1981) *New Technology: Society, Employment and Skill* (London: CSS).

Cressey, P. and MacInnes, J. (1980) 'Voting for Ford: Industrial Democracy and the Control of Labour', *Capital and Class,* 11: 5–33.

Davis, Lee and Canter, R. R. (1955) 'Job Design', *Journal of Industrial Engineering,* 6, 1: 3.

Dickson, D. (1974) *Alternative Technology and the Politics of Technical Change* (London: Fontana).

Diebold, J. (1952) *Automation: The Advent of the Automatic Factory* (New York: Van Nostrand).

Emery, F. E. (ed.) (1969) *Systems Thinking* (Harmondsworth: Penguin).

Foucault, M. (1979) *The History of Sexuality Vol. 1* (Harmondsworth: Allen Lane).

Giddens, A. (1979) *Central Problems of Social Theory* (London: Macmillan).

Giddens, A. (1982) 'Power, the Dialectics of Control and Class Structuration' in A. Giddens and G. Mackenzie (eds) *Social Class and the Division of Labour* (Cambridge: Cambridge University Press).

Herzberg, F. (1968) 'One More Time: How Do You Motivate Employees?', *Harvard Business Review,* 46: 53–62.

Hickson, D. J., Hinings, C. R., Lee, C. A., Schneck, R. E., Denning, J. M., (1971) 'A Strategic Contingencies Theory of Intra-Organisational Power', *Administrative Science Quarterly,* 16: 216–29.

Kelly, J. (1982) *Scientific Management, Job Design and Work Performance* (London: Academic Press).

Knights, D., Wilmott, H. W. and Collinson, D., (eds) (1985) *Job Redesign* (Aldershot: Gower).

Knights, D. and Sturdy, A. (1987) 'Women's Work in Insurance: Information Technology and the Reproduction of Gendered Segregation' in M. Davidson and C. Cooper (eds) *Women and Information Technology* (London: Wiley).

Lash, S and Urry, J. (1984) 'The New Marxism of Collective Action; A Critical Analysis' *Sociology,* 18, 1: 33–50.

Lawrence, P. R. and Lorsch, J. W. (1967) *Organisation and Environment* (Cambridge, Mass.: Harvard Graduate School of Administration).

Likert, R. (1967) *The Human Organisation* (New York: McGraw-Hill).

Littler, C. R. (1978) 'Understanding Taylorism', *British Journal of Sociology,* 29, 2: 185–202.

Littler, C. R. (1982) *The Development of the Labour Process in Britain, Japan and the USA* (London: Heinemann).

Littler, C. R. and Salaman, G. (1982) 'Bravermania and Beyond: Recent Theories of the Labour Process', *Sociology,* 16, 2: 251–69.

McGregor, D. (1960) *The Human Side of Enterprise* (New York: McGraw Hill).

Mackenzie, D. and Wajcman, J. (eds) (1985) *The Social Shaping of Technology* (Milton Keynes: Open University Press).

Martin, J. and Norman, A. R. D. (1973) *The Computerised Society* (Harmondsworth: Allen Lane).

Marx, K. (1887) *Capital, Vol. 1* (London: Lawrence and Wishant).

Miller, E. J. and Rice, A. K. (1967) *Systems of Organisation* (London: Tavistock).

Noble, D. (1979) 'Social Choice in Machine Design: The Case of Automatically Controlled Machine Tools', in A. Zimbalist (ed.) *Case Studies in the Labor Process* (New York: Monthly Review Press).

Nora, S. and Minc, A. (1980) *The Computerisation of Society: A Report to the President of France* (Cambridge, Mass.: MIT Press).

Offe, C. and Wiesenthal, H. (1980) 'Two Logics of Collective Action: Theoretical Notes on Social Class and Organisational Form', *Political Power and Social Theory*, 1: 67–115.

Pollard, S. (1965) *The Genesis of Modern Management* (Harmondsworth: Allen Love).

Rathenau Commission (1980) *Societal Consequences of Microelectronics* (The Hague: State Publishing House).

Rosenbrock, H. H. (1981) *Engineers and the Work People Do* (London: Work Research Unit).

Rosenbrock, H. H. (1982) 'Unmanned Engineering'. Report No. 12 to the FMS Steering Committee, Manchester: UMIST.

Sayles, L. (1958) *Behaviour of Industrial Work Groups* (Chichester: Wiley).

Smith, A. (1776) *The Wealth of Nations* (London: Methuen).

Thompson, P. (1983) *The Nature of Work* (London: Macmillan).

Trist, E. L. and Bamforth, K. W. (1951) 'Some Social and Psychological Consequences of the Longwall Method of Coal-Getting' *Human Relation*, Vol. 4.

Trist, E. L., Higgin, G. W., Murray, H., Pollock, A. B., (1963) *Organisational Choice* (London: Tavistock).

Ure, A. (1835) *The Philosophy of Manufactures* (London: Frank Cass).

Wakeham, P. and Beresford-Knox, J. E. (1980) *Microelectronics and the Future* (London: IMS).

Walton, R. E. (1982) 'New Perspectives on the World of Work: Social Choice in the Development of Advance Information Technology' *Human Relations*, 35, 12:1073–84.

Wiener, N. (1948) *Cybernetics* (New York: The Technology Press).

Wilkinson, B. (1982) *The Shopfloor Politics of New Technology* (London: Heinemann).

Woodward, J. (1965) *Industrial Organisation: Theory and Practice* (London: Oxford University Press).

Woodward, J. (ed.) (1970) *Industrial Organisation: Behaviour and Control* (London: Oxford University).

2 Computer Technology in Organisations: Some Critical Notes*

Wanda J. Orlikowski

INTRODUCTION

In this paper I wish to address the issue of computer technology, in particular information systems technology, and its implementation within organisations and interpenetration of the workplace. I want to suggest that the current dominant conceptualisation of information technology is one-dimensional, deterministic and linear. Partly as a result of this poor concepualisation and understanding of the phenomenon, studies of the implementation of computer technology within organisations are reduced to either (a) *post hoc* studies of the 'impacts' of computer technology on workers and jobs (i.e. on unemployment, de-skilling, re-skilling, job enrichment, productivity, satisfaction), that invokes a balance sheet mentality (do the benefits outweigh the costs? – Attewell and Rule, 1984; Buchanan and Boddy, 1983; Shepard, 1977); or (b) a contingency approach of specifying the contextual conditions within organisations when various types of computer-based managerial strategies will be introduced (Child, 1985; Olson, 1982, 1984). Research vacillates between technological neutrality (Olson, 1982, 1984) or technological complicity (Dickson, 1974a, 1974b; Marcuse, 1964) as well as between technological determinism (Winner, 1977), technological choice (Mumford, 1981, 1985; Pava, 1983; Trist, 1981), or class determinism (technology as a hegemonic tool in the hands of capitalist managers – Braverman, 1974; Cooley, 1980; Kraft, 1977; Rosen and Baroudi, 1985).

It needs to be recognised that information technology has many dimensions and many moments, and to treat it as universally monolithic is misleading. It is also necessary to realise the significance and

*I am grateful for the helpful comments of Wolf Heydebrand, Michael Rosen and Jack Baroudi (all of New York University) on an earlier draft of this paper.

implications of the changing nature and application of this technology over its exponential development. While the deployment and exploitation of computer technology within organisations is purposive and intentional, many changes instituted are in fact driven by the dramatic technological changes that have been erupting from this billion dollar industry (boosted heavily by aggressive corporate innovation and massive military funding of research and development). I am not proposing technological determinism as an explanation but rather suggesting, as does Burawoy (1985, pp. 51–2) that we recognise both *technical* and social relations in production. These technical relations constrain as well as provide an impetus to managers for technological deployment, and such factors cannot be disregarded.

Characterising information technology cannot be simply done. It appears on many levels, in many forms and has many repercussions. On the one hand technology degrades the jobs and skills of certain levels of employees while on the other hand it enhances those of employees at different levels. On the one hand it provides more and more innovative and convenient services to the public while it also increases the risks of privacy invasion, stereotyping and pre-defined options. While we have dramatic technological development that substantially decreases the cost performance ratio of machines allowing more and more complex computerisation, we also have increased automation, rationalisation and depoliticisation. While micro-technology has become available to many smaller enterprises, schools and individuals, it has fostered even greater dependence on technology, technical rationality, instrumental action and greater emphasis on competition, efficiency, innovation, new products and services, to the neglect of moral, cultural, political and social issues.

The treatment of information technology in social research to date, has been largely ahistorical and non-dialectical. The relationship of the technology to the economic and political context typically has been ignored. Technological 'effects' have been portrayed dichotomously: either as good or bad. There is no allowance for or explanation of contradictions and inherent tensions. The role of technology in the production, reproduction and possible transformation of social relations is not considered. Technology, as portrayed in the research literature, is either (a) facilitating the linear progression towards some better society (Huber, 1984); or (b) essentially neutral and hence infinitely malleable to the designers' will; or

(c) immanently related to the domination of nature and man, and hence solely harnessed to the purposes of the ruling interests (the de-skilling thesis). The last proposition posits technology as submerging contradictions in the workplace and installing uncontestable hegemonic rule (Braverman, 1974; Cooley, 1980; Rosen and Baroudi, 1985). But all of the above positions are one-dimensional and ignore the dialectical tension that exists between the technological forces of production and the social relations of production (Mishra, 1979, p. 135). For technology, far from bringing about a utopian society, or reducing contradictions, is in fact playing an increasingly contradictory role, where the 'contradictions arise from the very features that render this form of mental labour desirable to capital in the first place' (Goldhaber, 1980, p. 10).

INFORMATION TECHNOLOGY: A REASSESSMENT

There is considerable ambiguity about the definition of computer technology. I take as my orientation the notion of technology expressed by Penn (cited in Storey, 1985, p. 198): 'Technology does not simply mean machinery around which there is a given "logic" of working or paratechnical relations; it involves negotiated structures of production.' Technology can be conceived as an emergent social institution (Dickson, 1974b, p. 29) that changes and shapes both social relations and human consciousness, while at the same time being shaped by social relations and human agency. It is thus not treated as an independent variable, fixed and reified (Woodward, 1965), nor is it seen as merely a tool of economic or political domination (Braverman, 1974; Cooley, 1980; Marcuse, 1964) and neither is it relegated to the status of a neutral, intervening conduit by which managerial strategies are implemented (Child, 1985; Olson, 1984). Thus technology is viewed as both a productive force (via technological innovations) while also constituting and reinforcing the social relations of production (via the established technological processes).

It will be the thrust of this paper to suggest that not only does technology reinforce social relations, but that it also undermines them. The technological focus here is on any computer-based information system that is employed within firms, with the imputed intent of achieving organisational goals, either in the direct form of production of goods and delivery of services for markets, or in the indirect form of facilitation and support of internal administrative functions of the firm. 'Information systems' is the typical term used to characterise any hardware/software capability employed within organisations to do some task.

Heydebrand (1985) suggests that the new organisational forms and control structures making their appearances on our societal horizon are sufficiently deviant from the traditional bureaucratic and professional forms of control and organisation that they are best understood by a new concept, that of technarchy. Technarchy is an administration and control structure that encompasses technocratic forms of organisation (Heydebrand, 1983) linked to neo-corporatist forms of political organisation (Clegg and Dunkerley, 1980, pp. 551–3; Schmitter, 1983). The important features of technarchy include: a fusion of managerial and professional/technical roles; the extensive use of systems analysis, social engineering and planning oriented towards crisis prevention and management; increased rationalisation and automation of substantial decision-making procedures, and the primacy of technical rationality over democratic and social values (Heydebrand, 1985, p. 71).

Heydebrand (1983, 1985) argues that large-scale organisations are adopting increasingly technarchic control structures and strategies in order to meet the exigencies and turbulence of their environments, in which professional and bureaucratic modes of control are proving ineffectual. Within such organisations, a number of diverse control practices can simultaneously be discerned. Akin to Storey's (1985) non-monistic levels and circuits of control, technarchic control practices embrace new technology, job restructuring, work humanisation, redundancy, labour intensification, deprofessionalisation and de-skilling, loose coupling and welfarism. Multiple strategies are being adopted to cope with crises, structural contradictions, conflicts and numerous pressures for efficiency, productivity, responsiveness and control, not only from technical experts and managers, but also from politicians, clients, environmentalists, unions and other varied interest groups. The premise of technarchic control structures is that the *system* is pre-eminent; a premise that necessarily incorporates and transcends both bureaucratic as well as professional authority, i.e. all are 'subordinated to the imperatives of "the system" and the common or "public interest" ' (Heydebrand, 1983, p. 104).

The concept of technarchy provides a valuable framework within which we can begin to understand and study the nature of advanced computer technology and the relationship of this to the labour process. Rosen and Baroudi (1985, p. 2) argue similarly that 'computer and communications technologies are important mechanisms for achieving a new form of post-bureaucratic organizational control'. They, as well as Dickson (1974a, 1974b) underscore the material and symbolic forms of control and legitimation that technology imparts to the workplace. While such insights are valuable, the analysis is limiting for the technology is treated as one-dimensional and monistic. It does not make provision for contradictions, countervailing tendencies, resistance, and even transcendence. Such an approach neglects the role of workers as 'knowledgeable, capable agents' (Giddens, 1983, p. 199) as it is premised on managerial determinism, on the belief 'that capital must and can devise coherent systems of control to ensure the structurally necessary extraction of surplus value' (Storey 1985, p. 194). As the utilisation of computer technology escalates it becomes imperative that we understand its real limitations and possibilities. Zuboff suggests that it is insufficient 'to view information technology as just another step in a long line of innovations in the workplace' (1982b, p. 53). Treating information technology as a monolithic, relatively immutable extension of the typewriter or telephone ignores its nature as a social product and the significant potential available for its shaping, by workers, through their interaction with its construction and use.

I wish to suggest that information technology is both a symptom as well as a cause of technarchic structures, i.e. both sustaining, as well as being sustained by, these strategies. It is within the context of such a proposition that the dimensions, changes and contradictions of current information technology can be usefully analysed. Heydebrand notes (1985, p. 91) 'that technarchy is as much a type of social structure as it is a technically shaped control system'. It is this technical shaping of the control structures where information technology assumes a pivotal and constitutive role. In the following sections I examine the many ways in which information technology has facilitated the implementation of various technarchic strategies, and then in the final section I examine how information technology itself can be a substantive force in undermining the very control structures and strategies it serves.

SYSTEMS THEORY

One of the theoretical underpinnings of technarchic strategies is general systems theory and systems concepts (Boguslaw, 1982, pp. 8–23; Churchman, 1968; Scott, 1981). The intellectual development of the systems approach shares with computer technology a genesis in the massive military research efforts of the Second World War. In the aftermath of the war, the operations research, systems analysis and management science – spawned by engineering and the physical sciences and used to formulate war strategies – emerged within public and private bodies as central and dominant methodologies for social planning and engineering (Boguslaw, 1982, pp. 13–14). And a significant means of realising these intellectual forays into peacetime social management, was the computer. The diffusion of computer technology within organisations proceeded slowly at first (in the 1940s and 1950s), but since the 1960s its growth has become exponential. The introduction of computer technology and the concomitant implementation of information systems signifies a commitment (conscious or otherwise) to 'systems thinking', for the entire study of information technology is premised on the adoption of a systems perspective, and its attendant terminology (riddled with references to systems concepts) is indicative of the inherent predilection. The information technology installed in organisations takes the form of computer-based information systems: purposive systems whose intent it is to reduce complexity, unpredictability, inconsistency and information overload by formalisation, standardisation, rationalisation and routinisation. Franz and Robey (1984, p. 1203) indicate that 'The computer and computer processed information, in fact, have become icons of rationality in cultures committed to the idea of intelligent choice.' Rosen and Baroudi (1985, p. 9) note that as computer technologies spread throughout organisations, technocratic rationality becomes institutionalised to the extent that this one form of reason *per se*, so totally dominates consciousness that it appears as the only form of reason, the only arbiter of rationality. ... [it] thus functions as a network of shared meanings for understanding or interpreting social processes within and without work'.

Habermas (1971, p. 105) has explored the technocracy thesis and how 'with the institutionalization of scientific-technical progress, the potential of the productive forces has assumed a form owing to which men lose consciousness of the dualism of work and inter-action.' Technocracy comes to serve as a new ideology which attains a legitimating power within society. This new ideology is less obviously ideological than previous ideologies, yet more invidious and less vulnerable to detection, reflection and resistance. Technoc-racy wrenches from social life, understanding of symbolic inter-action, cultural meaning and communicative action, installing in its place the 'self-reification of men under categories of purposive-rational action and adaptive behavior' (1971, p. 106). Technocratic consciousness comes to dominate socio-cultural life; scientific rationality gains objective power, where technically exploitable knowledge compels 'a reconstruction of traditional world inter-pretations along the lines of scientific standards' (1971, p. 114). However Habermas (1973) indicates that cultural and communica-tive systems of meaning remain resistant to technocratic domina-tion, and that their manipulation and distortion engender a crisis of legitimation, through unintended effects of repoliticisation and the development of models of participation and alternative forms of life and work (see later for examples of these in the present context).

Information systems are typically installed by analysing the current manual situation (obtaining information through technical experts' observation and interview of workers) and then implemen-ted via custom-built software programs that operate on general-purpose hardware. The particular manner of this system development clearly objectifies the subjective knowledge had by the workers and institutionalises it into the system's software procedures. Not only have the workers suffered information loss, but they are now forced to interact with an external, artificial facticity that circumscribes their actions, manner of work and access of information into standardised and coercive patterns. 'Computer-based systems struc-ture the dialogue and type of interaction one has with the system and thus with one's task' (Rosen and Baroudi, 1985, p. 4). Technology 'abstracts most of the work it reorganizes. . . . the electronic symbols, the language of the computer, mediate between the workers and the work they once performed directly' Zuboff (1982b, p. 54). This reification of human knowledge and toil is one of the more perni-cious and least acknowledged consequences of information technology use.

Zuboff (1982a, 1982b) suggests that information systems have embedded within them managerial philosophies and management styles. She indicates how computerised work becomes intangible and its control invisible, subject to surveillance and timing. The meaning of work becomes 'thinned out' and less accessible, while the 'immediacy of access to information and consequent increase in the volume of transactions or operations that can take place also has the effect of compressing time and altering the rhythm of work' (1982a, p. 57). Social relationships are disrupted or eliminated and system failure or slow response time raise anxiety and stress levels. Crozier (1983, p. 92) shows how information systems, by making the procedures and actions transparent can disturb sensitive issues and disrupt the operation of the social system (e.g. loss of supervisor status and power, dissolution of work groups, inability to cover up for and help colleagues). The concerns expressed about mechanisation of the factory floor apply for information technology as well. Evidence indicates that in some organisations workers who interact with computers full-time have been isolated, subjected to losses in mobility, constant monitoring and machine pacing (Howard, 1985; Newman, 1982; Zuboff, 1982b).

The systems described above are examples of what are known as procedural or transaction processing systems: software procedures that automate fairly routine, typically low-level clerical functions, and that tend to reduce the discretion of, and increase control over workers. The purpose of the system design procedures is to 'find *efficient solutions* to administrative or control tasks, involving the lowest possible usage of resources' (Borum, 1980, p. 291, emphases in original). As Borum (1980, pp. 292–3) shows, the system developers characterise system users as 'standard individuals' and thus design standard, formalised methods of interaction with the system, and isolated, individual modes of operation rather than systems designed for group use. There are other major types of systems that are being developed in organisations. These are management information systems that attempt to assist the functions of managers via systems for project management, exception reporting, decision support and financial planning. Some of these systems are less atomistic and make provision for group interaction and collaboration. Most of them embody only particular (highly quantified and rational) models of reality, but they also provide the ability for dynamic modification of the models under diverse conditions. This whole endeavour creates the appearance of competence and control, and promotes an ideolgy of mastery over external and internal exigencies. Such systems are premised on the ability of the models to accurately capture and simulate reality, on the sufficiency of quantifiable and objective measure to reflect the complexity of situations, and on the ability of the system designers to appropriately anticipate future conditions. All are highly tenable assumptions, and yet none of them are made explicit.

On the one hand, such use of objective models may be a deliberate attempt to obscure and obtain consent for the imposition of some undemocratic social policy (Dickson, 1974b, p. 41); while on the other hand many systems' users may employ such models uncritically and with an unwitting acquiescence to their built-in assumptions. Zuboff (1982b, p. 53) notes '[W]hen senior managers work with computer-based models of economic activity without having full access to the theoretical biases built into the program, forecasts based on such complex planning models can become self-fulfilling prophecies, dictating actions in response to rational assessments of how a diverse set of variables should interact. . . . a reliance on such models can limit the type of information that managers seek.' The consequences are not trivial: the utilisation of such systems tends to propogate and reinforce a 'reality' that is rooted in the myopia of past errors and formalisable data, and that may bear little relation to the concrete, complex and ambiguous circumstances that managers are attempting to understand. An illusion is created, that via their flexibility and open-endedness the systems are capable of handling the crises of tomorrow. Rosen and Baroudi (1985, p. 10) suggest that under such an ideology, 'substantive questions concerning the social ramifications of increased technology in the workplace are culturally suppressed to the degree that they appear "unrealistic", or more correctly, irrational given the need for effectiveness and efficiency'. However they neglect to show how such an ideology breeds a dependence on and commitment to the models, that may constrain the future responsiveness and legitimacy of the organisations, and lead to decreased efficacy. Crozier (1983, p. 88) observes 'Although computers can indeed provide some much needed technocratic help with the quantitative problems associated with the decision-making process, they are less able to solve qualitative problems.' He notes (1983, p. 94) thus, that a real danger of information systems is their potential for 'being irrelevant to the real needs of the organization'.

TECHNOLOGICAL INNOVATIONS

The use of computer technology today pervades not only society but also organisations. It is found on the factory floor where computers are directly involved in the production process via robots, numerical control systems, or flexible manufacturing systems (Cooley, 1980; Hirschhorn, 1984; Noble, 1977; Shaiken, 1984), on the shop floor where computers are directly involved in the delivery of services (systems for electronic funds transfer, airline reservation, library catalogue searching, medical diagnosis), and in the offices where computer technology is intimately involved in storing, processing and reporting the information that controls the firm. Computer systems are employed in the public sector, e.g. in the legal and criminal justice system (Laudon, 1984), in the maintenance of massive personal data banks, in the determination of welfare eligibilty, in the military establishments, and within the decision-making processes of governments. Håmålåinen (1985) reports the use of a highly quantified, analytic computerised decision-making aid by the Finnish parliament in their determination of a national energy policy and plan. But lest we become infatuated with all this technology, and its apparent inexorable, independent, natural and rational development, we need to underline the cultural, social and political nature of information technology.

Heydebrand (1985, p. 89) notes that 'technological innovations are an integral part of the social relations of work and of the social structure of production and service delivery.' Not only do information systems increase productivity and efficiency, they also increase control and rationalisation. Worse, they increase invidious control by the controlling of available choices and the reduction of discretion (under the guise of increased discretion through self-selection facilities and preplanned menus). Such technology requires predefined and standardised responses, where 'much of the variance in possible outcomes will already have been eliminated' (Pfeffer, quoted in Heydebrand 1985, p. 106). Reality is obscured by the imposition of a particular type of reality, and a 'false praxis' is generated (in J. Benson's (1983, p. 39) understanding of praxis as a process through which humans shape the social world). Rosen and Baroudi (1985) show how such technology is ideally suited to instituting hegemonic domination, where consent to the relations of production is obtained by embedding control within the system and internalising it within the workers. Dickson (1974b, p. 36) suggests that the essence of technological domination is its nature as a political process and its institutionalisation via governmental, academic and industrial linkages that ensure the economic growth and political stability of society.

Heydebrand (1985, p. 90) posits technical rationality as being inherently contradictory, and we can see some ways that the increased reliance on information technology may engender such tension. Firstly, managers and technical experts often create their own obsolescence. A clear example of this can be found among data processing workers, where their efforts to develop sophisticated user-accessible software and program generating packages, may well induce a significant reduction in, or even elimination of, the need for computer programmers (Martin, 1982; Mclean, 1979; Wasserman and Gutz, 1982). A second example comes from the XCON expert system developed by Digital Equipment Corp., that configures computer systems for its customers (Winston, 1984, pp. 174–5). Understanding the properties of several hundred VAX computer component types, the XCON system expertly prepares an appropriate configuration plan and specification tailored to meet customers' unique needs. The system was developed on the basis of the knowledge of many customer support managers, who have now been rendered redundant by the system.

Secondly, the internal labour force gets segmented and stratified into those who are de-professionalised and de-skilled, and those who appropriate new skills and status. Hence competition between workers in the internal labour market is encouraged (Herman, 1982, p. 15). In particular the use of information technology can divide a labour force where data processing workers side with management to control a recalcitrant work force. Sterling (1984) describes how the American FAA (Federal Aviation Administration) was able to maintain 80 per cent normal commercial aviation when 11 000 Air Traffic Controllers went on strike in 1981. By using sophisticated information systems designed and operated by non-union data processing workers, the FAA successfully managed to withstand the strike action. As Kling (1984, p. 130) notes 'When there are sharp conflicts of interest, CBP [computer based packages] may be turned into instruments of conflict.' But what needs to be explored is the potential for data processing personnel to wield substantial power

within organisations. In those sectors and countries where data processing workers are unionised in significant numbers, their role in
labour-management conflicts may be decisive. A recent survey
(Friedman *et al.*, 1984) found that in the USA 2 per cent of private
sector data processing workers are unionised, as opposed to 82 per
cent in the public sector, while in Europe union participation rates
among data processing workers are on average 53 per cent, and
much higher for the Scandinavian countries. From these few
examples it is clear that information technology cannot be assumed
to be linear or monolithic; it is borne out of contradictions while also
generating others. Critical analyses of information technology
cannot ignore these tendencies.

DE-BUREAUCRATISATION AND NEW ORGANISATIONAL ARRANGEMENTS

Heydebrand (1983, p. 105) suggests that de-bureaucratisation is
associated with dissolution of various bureaucratic elements such as
fixed divisions of labour, rigid hierarchies or creating a larger, systematic control structure via matrix formations, loose coupling and
linking or boundary-spanning roles. The introduction of information technology has been associated with a number of hierarchical
changes within organisations (Galbraith, 1973; Robey, 1981). Kling
(1984, p. 224) notes 'New office information systems frequently cut
across the boundaries of organizational units that are relatively
autonomous.' It appears that the implementation of information
technology provides a useful pretext within which managers can
make certain structural adjustments. There is ambiguity about the
implications of these modifications, but many have tended to be in
the directions of decentralisation, loose coupling of functional units
(Olson and Turner, 1985, p. 26), extension of lateral communication
and creation of matrix-styled task forces and multidisciplinary
teams (Hirschhorn, 1984, p. 162).

Buchanan and Boddy (1983, p. 244) found significant structural
changes in all of the organisations they studied, as a result of
implementing computer systems. Most of the changes created new
specialist positions and structural ramifications. Olson reports that
information technology can reduce horizontal and vertical
specialisation via the installation of 'intelligent workstations' and

distributed work locations (1985, p. 29). King (1983) in reviewing issues around the decentralisation/centralisation of information technology suggests that decentralisation has associated with it many hidden costs (for managers) such as the dispersal of information, the loss of functional integration, the inability to control users' development of systems, and the unmanageability of computer networks. Hirschhorn (1984, p. 150) suggests that sociotechnically designed organisations will transcend the centralisation/decentralisation dichotomy via the use of autonomous teams and the dismantling of hierarchy. His technocratic solution to the demands of 'post-industrial conditions' relieves workers from operating machine controls. Instead they 'control the controls', which (1984, p. 98) he idealistically suggests arouses consciousness as 'the worker beomes more aware of his work environment, but he also begins to reflect self-consciously on his own actions and becomes aware of how he learns and develops'. The introduction of production and inventory control systems as well as office automation potentially reduce the number of supervisors required and hence the number of hierarchical levels (Crozier, 1983, p. 90). This need not decrease control, indeed it may even increase actual as well as perceived control, for now the control is embedded in rigid, unsympathetic, aparently omnipresent and omniscient hardware and software procedures. The move to more flexible work arrangements may be merely cosmetic. 'Thus, what appears to be greater decentralization may simply entail the delegation of more routine decisions whose outcomes are more closely controlled' (Robey, 1981, p. 681). We are reminded that centralisation and decentralisation 'are no longer opposites or alternatives, but they are mutually dependent and operate simultaneously' (Heydebrand, 1985, p. 105).

Pessimism and cynicism notwithstanding, there are cases where information technology has indeed fostered increased autonomy among, and distributed control to, the trenches. Crozier (1983, p. 90) shows how computer systems can substantially reduce or even replace the tasks of supervisors and lower-level managers. Armed with portable terminals, salesmen are less dependent on their home office for data entry, query processing and report production. End-user computing, the recent technological phenomemon (D. Benson, 1983; McLean, 1979; Rockart and Flannery, 1983) puts sophisticated computer capability directly in the hands of workers, allowing them to develop and operate their own information systems. Intra-organisational computer networks allow the spontaneous and rapid transfer of data and communications (via electronic mail and facsimile transmission). These and teleconferencing facilities allow collaboration among dispersed workers, removing the constraint for the co-location of workers involved on the same project (Hiltz and Turoff, 1978). Remote workstations and ability to work from home (Olson, 1983) can increase independence of distributed workers, able to flexibly choose their hours and often the manner of work. However each of these has a potential exploitive dimension, and in each case the very means that facilitate decoupling and de-emphasis of formal structural arrangements, may be used to impose increased conformance and control. Child (1985, p. 127) suggests that the 'new technology can substitute supervision at a distance for supervision in the workplace'. Telecommuting, as this trend has also been called, reduces costs of operating by shifting the costs of physical space and facilities onto the employees. Further, electronic mail can be monitored, filtered and even modified (Huber, 1984, p. 945), workstations at remote sites and homes can serve to dismantle worker solidarity, dissolve shared work experiences and engender both isolationism and individualism. Increased reliance on electronic communications also has psychological costs that are typically ignored, i.e. the loss of dynamic personal information, the focus on the medium to the neglect of the subjectivity of the human communicator, decreased sense of empathy and accountability, and a greater sense of anonymity (Kiesler, 1986, p. 48). Work-at-home arrangements may reduce pay, decrease responsibility, reduce visibility, stunt careers, increase formal supervision, and impose a reliance on measurable outputs (Olson, 1982, pp. 89–90).

Client orientation has become a major priority for many organisations, and information technology is being used to facilitate the tailoring of products and services to individual requirements (provided these correspond to the designers' *a priori* anticipation of demands). Hirschhorn (1984, p. 108) suggests that as the demands of clients for quality and relevance increase, managers redesign jobs and create flexible work settings so as to reflect the changes in priorities In contradistinction to the systems that attempt to internalise external complexity, some systems rationalise the delegation of responsibility for such complexity to their environment. There has been a shift of responsibility for data entry to clients in the provision of services to them (Olson, 1985, p. 21). Clients at automated tellers now enter their own information and invoke their desired function. Services are available for home banking, shopping and airline ticket reservation. While this use of information technology has allowed for increased client participation, this is of a circumscribed and predetermined form. It also signifies a shift in responsibility, data-entry costs and time to clients who may or may not welcome it. Concomitant with the delegation of certain tasks to clients, is a significant displacement of data entry and lower-level employees. For example, the provision of computer-based voice synthesisers in American Telephone and Telegraph services replaced hundreds of telephone operators.

The growth of computer and microelectronic technology in the last decade has spawned hundreds of small electronics firms and software development 'houses'. In this sector at least, as Goldhaber (1980, p. 16) indicates 'the trend observed by Marx for competition to lead to monopoly is countered by another trend – monopolistic firms, through their research policies, inadvertently create competition. . . . Since the industry is a glamor investment and entry costs are relatively low, it will likely remain very competititive.' The 'high tech' industry has created not only corporate giants but has also spawned self-employment among amateur and professional software package writers, contract analysts and programmers, data processing consultants and training instructors (Olson, 1985, p. 27). Child (1980, pp. 122–5) shows how increased reliance on computer technology has led managers to draw heavily on the 'putting-out' option, and how many individuals now make their living via such 'freelancing'. Rosen (1986) however, suggests that this competitive trend in both hardare and software markets is short-lived, and that the tide has already turned towards increasingly monopolistic conditions that will attenuate the opportunities for a computer 'cottage industry'.

Accompanying the growth of the data processing function within firms, has been a growth in its importance, centrality and elitism (Danziger, 1979). Today significant numbers of large organisations have data processing personnel bearing titles such as 'corporate information planner', 'business analyst', 'information resource manager'. Their task is essentially to employ systems techniques in order to devise long-term information technology strategies, to prepare corporate information systems plans (King, 1978; McFarlan and McKenney, 1983; McLean and Soden, 1977) and to advise and consult senior managers on potential ways to secure competitive advantage via information technology (Lucas and Turner, 1982; McFarlan *et al.*, 1983; Parsons, 1984; Porter, 1985). In the execution of such consultancy services a new development within the deployment arsenal of information technicians is the use of information technology to develop innovative products/services in order to gain competitive advantages, market share and to forge significant inter-organisational relationships (Barrett & Konsynski, 1982; Benjamin *et al.*, 1984; Ives and Learmonth, 1984; Parsons, 1984; Porter, 1985). This trend has been referred to as a repositioning of information technology that entails the transition from supporting the business to being the business (Kanter, 1985, p. 15). The McKesson Pharmaceutical and American Hospital Supply companies have established round-the-clock, order-entry systems with terminals at their customers' sites allowing direct input into the companies' computers. Order-entry is now done by the customers, and order-entry clerks at the supply companies have become obsolete. Such systems illustrate the use of information technology to link organisations and to establish relationships of mutual advantage and collaboration among them. The creation of such apparently voluntary associations of power and dependence raises many questions about the alleged neutrality of technological developments, which can be better understood within the neo-corporatist mode of a technarchic framework of analysis.

DE-PROFESSIONALISATION

Haug (1973, 1977) has explicitly suggested the possibility that computer technology will downgrade professional work. She suggests (1977, p. 215) that professional autonomy and authority will be eroded by the computer and its storage and handling of knowledge that was previously the preserve of professionals. Freidson (1984, p. 8) in countering her argument suggests that professionals will still be needed to 'determine what is to be stored and how it is to be done, and . . . to interpret and employ what is retrieved effectively'. Both arguments however, go too far and yet not far enough. Haug overestimates the power and capabilities of computers and underestimates their limitations. She writes 'almost by definition *academic* knowledge, upon which the diploma credentials validating professional's expertise are largely based, is codifiable and therefore amenable to computer input' (1973, p. 201, emphasis in original). This is a contestable assertion. While much of the formal knowledge of professional work can be so codified, this is by no means all (and I would suggest not even the most important) knowledge required by professional practice. Also significant is the array of tacit, intuitive and judgemental knowledge acquired through case experience and informal interaction with clients and colleagues. Not only is most of this knowledge difficult to codify, it is usually impossible for professionals to articulate. One of the most persistent problems to date in the field of knowledge engineering (that branch of artificial intelligence research that is concerned with the building of 'expert systems') is the codification and representation of commonsensical knowledge. Deprived of such basic skills, the expert systems can only be highly specialised, formalised and rather weak approximations to the 'real thing'.

Freidson's suggestion that professionals control the content and conduct of computerisation is insensitive to the nature of the systems development effort. The current mode of creating an expert system within a discipline, say the medical diagnosis of cardiovascular diseases, involves a number of computer scientists observing and interviewing one or two noted specialists in that field. Based on their data collection and their understanding of the patterns and rules of association and causation, the computer scientists codify the knowledge and establish the software logic that links the knowledge in meaningful ways. While the input of the professional at the analysis stage is large, the ultimate creation of the 'intelligence' of the system lies solely in the hands of the technically initiated. Not only do the professionals involved in the project have little ability or opportunity to control it, but the rest of their profession has no possibility of contributing to this endeavour. So the system, at best accurately reflects the specific, codifiable idiosyncracies and cognitive schemas of one or two professionals. To be sure, this is not the only way to develop systems that enhance human intelligence, but the current practice tends to emphasise the disempowering of professionals, even as cheaper, less-skilled workers, who have access to the expert systems are empowered (Rosen and Baroudi, 1985, p. 22).

Freidson suggests that professionals will be needed to interpret the data that is stored. This is not strictly true, for technicians and para-professionals can be trained to understand the formalised responses of the system. Whether or not society is prepared to delegate responsibility for such interpretation to non-professionals is a different matter. To date the few medical diagnosis systems in existence are being used by technicians as supplements to the personal diagnoses of practitioners. This is not to say that things may not change, and indeed tendencies in other disciplines suggest that not all areas of human expertise are sacrosanct. An expert system being developed for a large New York insurance firm is intended to replace many of the functions of highly experienced and expensive professional actuaries. Both Freidson and Haug however, do not go far enough, in that their arguments omit the social and political shift in priorities that is behind the ascendancy of professional computerisation. It is not just the technological imperative that is spawning such expert systems, nor the desire by capitalists to de-skill and control professional work that is at issue here, but that organisations and managers today are willing to countenance, support and rely on necessarily incomplete, rationalised, narrow and rigid models of human expertise, often to the exclusion of human judgement.

Herman (1982, p. 21) citing Derber, suggests two ways of proletarianising professionals either via technical or via ideological proletarianisation. In the latter case, professionals, while still possessing technical authority and a specialised set of skills, lose control over the *ends* of their work, i.e. they lose control over the determination and disposition of goods and services and the purposes of their work organisation. Technical proletarianisation occurs when professionals lose control over their *means* of work, i.e. their technical authority is diminished through task fragmentation, de-skilling and increased rationalisation. The rise of para-professionals and semi-professionals attests to the increasing viability of technical proletarianisation via the employment of cheaper and less-skilled workers to accomplish previously 'professional labour'. Typically these strategies are aided and abetted by the use of sophisticated technology. As an example, engineering and architectural offices are beginning to assimilate computer-aided design equipment, and hiring non-professional workers to operate the machines, and to perform design work previously done by professionals. The rationale behind the implementation of this technology is that it relieves the professionals from routine, manual draughting work, allowing them the opportunity for client liaison, problem analysis and concept development. This ideology however, obscures the reality that in many large architectural and engineering firms most professionals already do specialised, fragmented draughting work (the client contact and creative tasks being reserved for the elite). Within such a context, the use of computer technology will remove more responsibilities and further downgrade the already tenuous skills of these professionals. The attempts by professionals to protect what they see as encroachments on their turf, curbs on their autonomy and increased effort to measure their work, is likely to lead to more conflict and resistance to the introduction of computer technology (Heydebrand, 1979; Zuboff, 1982a, 1982b).

SYNTHESIS OF ROLES

Emerging out of the ashes, as it were, of the traditional bureaucratic and professionalised workers comes a new speciality, that forged by converging professional and administrative functions. Here technical experts manage, as well as perform substantive work. Such new 'professionals' while having significant technical expertise have concurrently risen to powerful levels within policy-making boards and management steering committees. Prime examples are senior data processing specialists who typically have strategic input into corporate decision-making, and who may even assume executive positions (Kanter, 1985, p. 14). Within many organisations, internal and external (independent and computer vendor related) data processing consultants are attaining roles of significant influence (Ferreira and Harris, 1985). Montagna (1973) describes the growth and importance within public accounting firms of the management consultancy specialisation (referred to as Management Advisory Services). Many of these management consultants are trained in data processing and are essentially involved in helping senior managers create long-term information technology strategies, constructing business plans, designing/installing information systems and training potential users. The resources and priorities assigned to such work suggests the increasing spread of technarchic power and the undermining of prior, more established professional and bureaucratic authority. Within such an orientation the technical-rational considerations assume a priority and indeed dominate over social or political concerns, i.e. there is 'an implicit appeal to a univocal notion of rationality, embodied in scientific and technical expertise, ... [which is] inseparable from the *depoliticization* of social and economic issues' (Larson, 1973, p. 5, emphasis in original). As a consequence social and political activity is evaluated primarily in instrumental terms.

CRISIS MANAGEMENT

Technarchic strategies are exacerbated by accelerated turbulence in the environment and by what is perceived as continual crises situations. The problems of complexity, instability, unpredictability, productivity and efficiency decline are interpreted within a particular systemic schema, that imputes universal, abstracted and ahistorical causes to the perceived problems. Consequently, the interventions proposed and implemented are increasingly technical-rational and increasingly encapsulated within automated and computerised 'solutions'. These responses are couched in neutral and system logical language, yet they constitute ideological, politicised and reactionary modes of action. Dickson (1974b, p. 39) suggests that 'the myth of the neutrality of technology legitimates the contemporary social function of technology by attempting to take it out of the realm of political debate'. This myth constituted of a general mechanistic and functionalist ideology, legitimates the continued pursuit of economic growth and is reinforced by an ideology of scientism that sustains the belief that 'an apparently "scientific" approach to any problem or situation is both necessary and significant to indicate how its objective politically-neutral resolution can be achieved' (Dickson, 1974b, p. 40).

'Whether we like it or not, the design of machines reflects social values as well as technical needs' (Shaiken, 1984, p. 278). The misconception that technology is a neutral, passive and natural tool that can be used under varying situations, neglects the social and political nature of the technological development and deployment processes. Information systems are commissioned, designed and implemented by individuals and groups with certain parochial interests, predilections, resources and goals (explicit and implicit). These prior biases are reflected in the exercise of discriminatory attention to details and features that guide the production of the information system and its related data contents. By their very nature, computer-based information systems cannot be neutral. They are human artefacts, constructed essentially and entirely by the interaction and action of individuals. Much like writing a book, writing software bears the indelible stamp of the authors' intentions and/or their mandate. Once developed, the information systems are then maintained over their lifetimes and the frequency, manner and

nature of such activity (or its lack thereof) too reflects current exigencies and political agendas.

There is a presumption about all such systems that the data collected and stored is accurate, up-to-date and adequately reflects the
appropriate characteristics of individuals, events, etc. There is
however no evidence to guarantee this condition. No database can
ever capture all data, so what is stored is always a highly selected
categorical subset of information as well as being of a particular
form: typically abbreviated, coded and monotonic. Once captured,
the data is not only vulnerable to intrusion, manipulation and destruction (as manifest by recent data security encroachments in the
USA), but also subject to quality violations in the form of incorrect,
incomplete, ambiguous and out-of-date records. Laudon (1986)
reports the results of a six-year assessment of the quality of data
stored in the computerised files of the American criminal justice
system. He found (by comparing the computerised information
against hard-copy, original documents of known veracity) that the
number of computerised criminal history records that are incomplete, inaccurate and ambiguous varies from 51 per cent to 88 per
cent for the individual states, and from 55 per cent to 75 per cent for
the FBI.

One consequence of the depoliticised language used to handle
crises, is that the technology itself is often made a convenient
scapegoat; appeals to the mystique and immutability of computer
technology obscure the social and political agendas behind its
implementation. Further, and paradoxically, such language also
engenders a mentality of 'technological-fix', Dickson's (1974b, p. 49)
term for a claim that 'the social problems apparently created by
technology can be solved by the application of yet more
technology'.

TECHNOLOGY UNDERMINING TECHNARCHY

Heydebrand (1979, 1983, 1985) suggests that technarchy is a tran-
sitional phase. Technarchic strategies are but *ad hoc* responses to
crises that merely ameliorate symptoms without attacking the
causes, which are left to fester, grow and exacerbate the tension and
trauma. Storey notes 'Control structures and strategies typically
contain their own inherent *contradictions*. These undermine any
ultimate or absolute logic in the means of control' (1985, p. 197,

emphasis in original). Information technology in particular, can be seen to cause instability and tension. Hirschhorn (1984, p. 73) notes that automation is always technically incomplete, flawed and prone to breakdown. Cooley (1980, p. 530) suggests that the emphasis in computer systems on quantitative information to the neglect of qualitative data is short-sighted, inevitably distortive and destructive of design quality. Insofar as managers rely uncritically on their information systems and computer-based models, they will be working with abstracted, incomplete, and possibly misleading models of reality. Not that current manual models are not also constrained, but in this case there is at least a recognition of the models' potential weaknesses and biases. In the case of the former models there is little awareness of the inherent limitations and premises of the systems, and the infatuation with, and dependence on, technical-rationality to the exclusion of other values and issues, will necessarily constrain the managers' response repertoires. Crozier (1983, p. 99) notes that as computer-based systems make procedures more transparent and information more accessible, the legitimacy of public institutions will be threatened, for 'The political system cannot accept an overdose of rationality . . . [and hence, it] makes it impossible to achieve the necessary deals that relieve the political pressure, and rely on secret negotiations, both at top and local levels.'

The discussion of information technology above, may have suggested a certain inevitability about the direction and implementation of information systems. This is not at all the case. While some jobs are de-skilled or eliminated, new ones are created (albeit, to date, a smaller number have been created than lost, and these have tended to be of a highly technical nature) and others can become more integrated (Goldhaber, 1980, p. 23; Herman, 1982, p. 14). Also, workers actively strive to make meaning in their work. Workers can and do act against what they perceive as unfair and undesirable technological innovations, as in attempting to prevent its implementation via strike action (Newman, 1982) and bargaining (not of great significance in the USA), or attempting to disrupt the systems' operations by entering incorrect data, withholding knowledge, refusing to co-operate with the implementation, choosing not to use the system (where use is voluntary), playing games (informal use of the electronic mail) and by resorting to outright sabotage (destruction or loss of hardware, software and data). As society becomes more dependent on ideas and knowledge, certain workers can gain more leverage. They can exchange information or they can quit their jobs, taking their ideas and skills with them, in effect 'destroying one form of capital' (Goldhaber, 1980, p. 25). However it is not clear that this is a significant option, within the computer industry, given that computer knowledge and skills are diffusing rapidly, and that data processing skills may no longer be so scarce or valued in the future. Algera and Koopman (1984, p. 1039) suggest that an increasing population of computer-literate users will cause a decrease and eventual decline in specialised computer and data processing personnel.

The development of the technology, in attempting to meet the demands of organisations operating in volatile, complex and interdependent markets, is also developing in ways that could be used to undermine the very strategies they are meant to foster. King (1983 p. 331) notes that as information systems grow more complex, they cause greater disruptions during implementation, as they require more preparation, training, time and money. Furthermore 'complex systems are more likely to malfunction and more difficult to fix because of their interdependency in operation'. He adds that 'Most fixes are like "patches" sewn in on the fabric of the system. Often, they do not solve the problem, but "work around" it.' Organisations are facing difficulties controlling the data accessed and used by their employees. A major feature of systemic solutions is their flexibility, for which easy, rapid and *ad hoc* access to a vast array of data is a prime requirement. Microelectronics and software that is accessible to users, has diffused computers to homes and offices and encourages the independent generation and access of information, as well as its proliferation through national and international computer networks, electronic bulletin boards, etc. A number of extensive on-line databases have been established and many are available for public consumption. The amount of resources and effort that would be needed to control, monitor and secure all data paths and communication channels is prohibitive. A tension develops between the need to facilitate fast determination of and response to changing conditions, and the need to discipline information transfer.

In the development of information systems, user involvement is becoming an important factor in obtaining co-operation and commitment, and in forming appropriate expectations as well as adding user knowledge to the design of the procedures (Bjørn-Anderson and Hedberg, 1977). Some systems implementation strategies now rely heavily on user participation at all stages of systems development. Many of these are modelled on socio-technical interventions

(Hirschhorn, 1984; Mumford and Sackman, 1975; Mumford and Weir, 1979; Mumford, 1981, 1985; Pava, 1983; Trist, 1981). Many of these attempt to produce passivity, consent and commitment, as well as being hegemonic and rooted in managerial ideology. The practice of such social interventions 'for the benefit of workers' amounts to what Kelly (1985, p. 1081) describes as 'a false praxis, that is, as social action subordinated to an imposed economic rationality'. But this is not to imply that all user interaction and participation is inevitably so limited, for these concessions to nonrationality are contradictory to the dominant ideology and hence worthy of serious attention. While humanisation of work, from a critical perspective, has been welcomed by some (Wrenn, 1982; Zimbalist, 1975) and condemned by others (Braverman, 1974; Ramsay, 1985; Rosen, 1985), I would suggest that its influence is ambiguous enough to raise questions about its 'liberative potentials'. Herman (1982, p. 17) notes that 'Worker participation *cum* hegemony is effective only to the extent that it allows genuine autonomy and control over the labour process circumscribed though this autonomy may be.' Thus he suggests (1982, p. 19) that 'exploiting the space available for questioning the relations in production can establish a platform for challenging the relations of production'. Worker involvement in the design of the technology that they are to use can have a number of unintended consequences.

End-use computing and the direct involvement of workers in the creation of their own software routines, and independent control over modelling, data access, information formating and nature and timing of computer use, has implications for the discretionary aspects of work and the sense of autonomy and responsibility that individuals can derive from their jobs. This in itself is not remarkable but it can create conflict in the workplace through raised expectations, loss of centralised control through distribution of technological capability (King, 1983) and via undermining the legitimacy of scientific-technical rationality. Kiesler (1986, p. 53) suggests that distributed networks and electronic communication may lead to increased sharing of information, decreased importance of status differentials via the loosening of cultural constraints and possible organisational instability. Rockart and Flannery (1983) indicate that end-user computing is growing at a rate of approximately 50–90 per cent per annum, while Benjamin (1982) predicts that by 1990 this capability will account for 75 per cent of the corporate computer resource. This trend may not be reversible and its consequences may not be controllable. The technology has already outgrown the regulative capacity of managers and organisations, and it almost appears to have attained a dynamic of its own (King, 1983). As automation becomes cheaper, more powerful and more widespread in its use, firms may have to automate to survive. Goldhaber (1980, p. 22) suggests that such automation, bringing 'radically increased and altered productivity... coupled with the obsolescence of many other forms of labour, would be the basis of a moral and social crises as well'. We cannot of course discount the possibility of technarchic strategies being replaced by more authoritarian ones. However much we may wish it to be, democracy is not inevitable, and in a manner reminiscent of Orwell's 1984, the computer know-how is definitely available for a technological despotism. Storey (1985, pp. 206–7) suggests that information technology can and does tend to create intensified and integrated means of control, i.e. the fully-integrated control system. However as he observes (1985, p. 208) 'the logic of the dialectical analysis suggests that even a development such as this seems unlikely to usher in unproblemmatical monistic means of managerial control'. It does not seem possible that the energy and rationalisation necessary to sustain such totalitarian control can be achieved, given the widespread proliferation of technological expertise, networks and facilities that exist already. And as technology assists in the production and reproduction of social relations, the contradictions and conflicts that arise may begin to challenge and undermine existing patterns of domination and even transform those social relations into more democratic forms. Heydebrand (1979, p. 55) reminds us that 'like the sorcerer's apprentice, the spirits they summoned became demons who began to assume control in their own right'.

CONCLUSION

In this paper I have tried to show that it is inadequate to treat information technology as one-dimensional, neutral, universal and either over-determined or totally autonomous. Technology needs to be assessed within the structure of a dialectical relationship between social relations of production and the forces of production. The multiple and unprecedented changes being wrought by advanced computer and information technology today, cannot be understood within the frameworks of a neo-Weberian approach (positing interaction between various factors without situating them within a social and political structure that limits such interaction – Mishra, 1979, p. 156) nor within the framework of a deterministic de-skilling analysis. It was suggested that a useful context within which we can attempt to understand and explain the deployment of information and computer technology in organisations, is that of technarchic control structures and strategies.

References

Algera, Jen A., Koopman, Paul L. (1984) 'Automation: Design Process and Implementation', in Drenth, P. J. D. *et al.* (ed.) *Handbook of Work and Organizational Psychology* (John Wiley, 1037–66).

Attewell, Paul, Rule, James (Dec. 1984) 'Computing and Organizations: What we know and what we don't know', *Comm. of the ACM*, vol. 27: no. 12, 1184–91.

Barrett, Stephanie, Konsynski, Benn (1982) 'Inter-Organization Information Sharing Systems', *MIS Quarterly*, 93–105.

Benjamin, Robert I. *et al.* (Spring 1984) 'Information Technology: A Strategic Opportunity', *Sloan Management Review*, 49–58.

Benson, David H. (Dec. 1983) 'A Field Study of End User Computing: Findings and Issues', *MIS Quarterly*, 35–45.

Benson, J. Kenneth (1983) 'Paradigm and Praxis in Organizational Analysis', *Research in Organizational Behavior.* vol. 5: 33–56.

Bjørn-Andersen, Niels Hedberg, Bo L. T. (1977) 'Designing Information Systems in an Organizational Perspective', *TIMS Studies in Management Sciences*, vol. 5: 125–42.

Boguslaw, Robert (1982) *Systems Analysis and Social Planning: Human Problems of Post-Industrial Society* (Irvington Publishers, New York).

Borum, Finn (1980) Systems Design and Scientific Management', *Acta Sociologica*, vol. 23: no. 4, 287–97.

Braverman, Harry (1974) '*Labor and Monopoly Capital: The Degradation of Work in the Twentieth Century*' (Monthly Review Press, New York).

Buchanan, David A., Boddy, David (1983) *Organizations in the Computer Age: Technological Imperatives and Strategic Choice* (Gower, Aldershot).

Burawoy, Michael (1985) *The Politics of Production: Factory Regimes Under Capitalism and Socialism* (Verso, London).

Child, John (1985) 'Managerial Strategies, New Technology and the Labour Process' in Knights, David (ed.) *Job Redesign: Critical Perspectives on the Labour Process* (Gower, Aldershot) 107–41.

Churchman, C. West (1968) *The Systems Approach* (Laurel Books, New York).

Clegg, Stewart, Dunkerley, David (1980) *Organization, Class and Control* (Routledge & Kegan Paul, London).

Cooley, Mike (1980) 'Computerization: Taylor's Latest Disguise' *Economic and Industrial Democracy*, vol. 1: 523–39.

46   *Computer Technology in Organisations*

Crozier, Michel (1983) 'Implications for the Organization' in Otway, Harry J., Peltu, Malcolm (eds) *New Office Technology* (Ablex, London) 86 – 101.
Danziger, James N. (May 1979) 'The "Skill Bureaucracy" and Intraorganizational Control', *Sociology of Work and Occupations*, vol. 6: no. 2, 204–26.
Dickson, David (1974a) *The Politics of Alternative Technology* (Universe Books, New York).
Dickson, David (Jan. 1974b) 'Technology and the Construction of Social Reality', *Radical Science Journal*. vol. 1: 29–50.
Ferreira, Joseph, Harris, Philip R. (Autumn 1985) 'The Changing Roles of IRM Professionals', *Information Strategy*, 18–22.
Franz, Charles R., Robey, Daniel (Dec. 1984) 'An Investigation of User-Led System Design: Rational and Political Perspectives', *Comm. of the ACM*, vol. 27: no. 12.
Freidson, Eliot (1984) 'The Changing Nature of Professional Control', *Annual Review of Sociology*, vol. 10: 1–20.
Friedman, Andrew *et al.* (Sep. 1984) 'The Challenge of Users and Unions', *Datamation*, 93–100
Galbraith, Jay R. (1973) *Designing Complex Organizations* (Addison-Wesley, Reading, MA).
Giddens, Anthony (1983) *Profiles and Critiques in Social Theory* (University of California Press, Berkeley, CA).
Goldhaber, Michael (1980) 'Politics and Technology: Microprocessors and the Prospect of a New Industrial Revolution', *Socialist Review*, vol. 10: no. 4, 9–32.
Habermas, Jürgen (1971) *Toward a Rational Society* (Heinemann Educational Books, London).
Habermas, Jürgen (1973) 'What Does a Crisis Mean Today? Legitimation Problems in Late Capitalism', *Social Research*, vol. 40: no. 4, 643 –67.
Håmåläinen, Raimo P. *et al.* (1985) 'A Microcomputer-Based Decision Support Tool and its Application to a Complex Energy Decision Problem', Helsinki University of Technology, Espoo, Finland.
Haug, M. R. (Dec. 1973) 'Deprofessionalization, and Alternate Hypothesis for the Future', *Sociological Review*, 195–211.
Haug, Marie (1977) 'Computer Technology and the Obsolescence of the Concept of Profession' in Haug, Marie R., Dofny, Jaques (eds) *Work and Technology*, (SAGE Publications, Beverly Hills, CA) 215–28.
Herman, Andrew (1982) 'Conceptualizing Control: Domination and Hegemony in the Capitalist Labor Process', *The Insurgent Sociologist*, vol. 11: no. 3, 7–22.
Heydebrand, Wolf V. (1985) 'Technarchy and Neo-Corporatism: Toward a Theory of Organizational Change under Advanced Capitalism and Early State Socialism', *Current Perspectives in Social Theory*, vol. 6: 71–128.
Heydebrand, Wolf (1979)) 'The Technocratic Administration of Justice', *Research in Law and Sociology*, 29–69.
Heydebrand, Wolf V. (1983) 'Technocratic Corporatism: Toward a Theory of Occupational and Organizational Transformation' in Hall, Richard H., Quinn, Robert E. (eds) *Organizational Theory and Public Policy* (SAGE Publishers, Beverly Hills, CA) 93–113.

Hiltz, S. R., Turoff M. (1978) *The Network Nation*: *Human Communication via Computers* (Addison-Wesly, Reading, MA).

Hirschhorn, Larry (1984) *Beyond Mechanization*: *Work and Technology in a Postindustrial Age* (The MIT Press, London).

Howard, Robert (1985) *Brave New Workplace* (Viking Penguin, New York).

Huber, George P. (1984) The Nature and Design of Post-Industrial Organizations', *Management Science*, vol. 30: no. 8, 928–951.

Ives, Blake, Learmonth, Gerard P. (1984) 'The Information System as a Competitive Weapon', *Comm of the ACM*, vol. 27: no. 12, 1193–201.

Kanter, Jerome (Autumn 1985) 'Ten Information Systems Megatrends', *Information Strategy*, 13–17.

Kelly, John (1985) 'Management's Redesign of Work: Labour Process, Labour Markets and Product Markets' in Knights, David *et al.* (ed.) *Job Redesign*: *Critical Perspectives on the Labour Process* (Gower, Aldershot), 30–51.

Kiesler, Sara (Jan.–Feb.1986) 'The Hidden Messages in Computer Networks', *Harvard Business Review*, 46–59.

King, John Leslie (1983) 'Centralized versus Decentralized Computing: Organizational Considerations and Management Options', *Computing Surveys*, vol. 15: no. 4, 319–49.

King, William R. (1978) 'Strategic Planning for Management Information Systems', *MIS Quarterly*, vol. 2: no. 1, 27–37.

Kling, Rob (1984) *Assimilating Social Values in Computer-Based Technologies* (Butterworth & Co., London) 127–47.

Kraft, Philip (1979) *Programmers and Managers: The Routinization of Computer Programming in the United States* (Springer-Verlag, New York).

Larson, Magali Sarfatti (1972–3) 'Notes on Technocracy: Some Problems of Theory, Ideology and Power', *Berkeley Journal of Sociology*, 1–34.

Laudon, Kenneth C. (1986) 'Data Quality and Due Process in Large Interorganizational Record Systems', *Comm of the ACM*, vol. 29. no. 1, 4–11.

Lucas, Henry C., Turner, Jon A. (Spring 1982) 'A Corporate Strategy for the Control of Information Processing', *Sloan Management Review*, 25–36.

Marcuse, Herbert (1964) *One-Dimensional Man* (Routledge & Kegan Paul, London).

Martin, James (1982) *Application Development Without Programmers* (Prentice-Hall, Englewood Cliffs, NJ).

McFarlan, F. Warren *et al.* (Jan.–Feb. 1983) 'The Information Archipelago-Plotting a Course', *Harvard Business Review*, 145–56.

McFarlan, F. W., McKenney, J. L. (1983) *Corporate Information Systems Management*: *The Issues Facing Senior Executives* (R. D. Irwin, Homewood, IL).

McLean, E., Soden, J (1977) *Strategic Planning for MIS* (Wiley, New York).

McLean, E. R. (Dec. 1979) 'End Users as Application Developers', *MIS Quarterly*, 37–46.

Mishra, Ramesh (1979) Technology and Social Structure in Marx's Theory: An Exploratory Analysis', *Science of Society*, vol. 43. no. 2, 132 –57.

Montagna, Paul D. (1973) 'The Public Accounting Profession' in Freidson, Eliot (ed.) *The Professions and their Prospects*, 2nd edn (SAGE Publications, Beverly Hills, CA) 135–51.

Mumford, Enid (1985) 'From Bank Teller to Office Worker: The Pursuit of Systems Designed for People in Practice and Research', *Proceedings of the Sixth International Conference on Information Systems*, Indianapolis, Indiana, 249–58.

Mumford, Enid (1981) 'Participative Systems Design: Structure and Method', *Systems, Objectives, Solutions*, vol. 1: 5–19.

Mumford, Enid, Sackman, Harold (eds) (1975) *Human Choice and Computers* (North-Holland Publishing Co., New York).

Mumford, Enid, Weir, Mary (1979) *Computer Systems in Work Design: the ETHICS method* (Halsted Press, New York).

Newman, David (Winter 1982) 'Work & Technology in Telephone', *Dissent*, 59 ff.

Noble, David F. (1977) *America by Design: Science, Technology, and the Rise of Corporate Capitalism*, Alfred A. Knopf, New York.

Olson, Margrethe H. (1984) ' "1984" and After: The Societal Challenge of Information Technologies', *Procs. Conf. of the German Government and the OECD, on the Impact of Information Technology on Work Organization*, Federal Republic of Germany.

Olson, Margrethe H. (1982) 'New Information Technology and Organizational Culture', *Technology and Organizational Culture*, 71–92.

Olson, Margrethe H. (1983) 'Remote Office Work: Changing Work Patterns in Space and Time', *Comm of the ACM.* vol. 26: no. 3, 182–7.

Olson, Margrethe H., Turner, Jon A. Rethinking Office Automation *Proceedings of the Sixth International Conference on Information Systems*, Indianapolis, Indiana, December 1985.

Parsons, Gregory L. (Autumn 1983) 'Information Technology: A New Competitive Weapon', *Sloan Management Review*, 3–14.

Pava, H. P. Calvin (1983) *Managing New Office Technology: An Organizational Strategy* (The Free Press, New York).

Porter, Michael E. (1983) *Competitive Advantage: Creating and Sustaining Superior Performance* (The Free Press, London).

Ramsay, Harvie (1985) 'What is Participation For? A Critical Evaluation of "Labour Process" Analyses of Job Reform' in Knights, David *et al.* (ed.) *Job Redesign: Critical Perspectives on the Labour Process* (Gower, Aldershot) 52–80.

Robey, Daniel (1981) 'Computer Information Systems and Organization Structure', *Comm of the ACM*, vol. 24: no. 10, 679–87.

Rockart, J. F., Flannery, L. S. (1983) 'The Management of End-User Computing', *Comm. of the ACM*, vol. 26: no. 10, 776–84.

Rosen, Michael, private communication, New York, January 1986.

Rosen, Michael (Sep. 1985) 'Organizational Praxis: Topography and Critique' in *Procs. Conference on Critical Perspectives in Organizational Analysis*, New York.

Rosen, Michael, Baroudi, Jack (1985) Telematics, Technocracy, and Hegemonic Control Graduate School of Business Administration, New York University, New York, May 1985.

Schmitter, Philippe C. (1983) 'Democratic Theory and Neocorporatist Practice', *Social Research*. vol. 50: no. 4, 885–928.
Scott, W. Richard (1981) *Organizations: Rational, Natural and Open Systems* (Prentice-Hall, Englewood Cliffs, NJ).
Shaiken, Harley (1984) *Automation & Labor in the Computer Age* (Holt, Rinehart & Winston, New York).
Shepard, Jon (1977) 'Technology, Alienation, and Job Satisfaction', *Annual Review of Sociology*, vol. 3: 1–21.
Sterling, Theodore D. (Feb. 1984) 'The Emerging Key Role of White-Collar Computer Workers vis-à-vis Organized Labor', *Office: Technology and People*, 155–65.
Storey, John (1985) 'The Means of Management Control', *Sociology*, vol. 19: no. 2, 193–211.
Trist, Eric L. (1981) 'The Sociotechnical Perspective' in Van de Ven, Andrew H., Joyce, William F. (eds) *Perspectives on Organization Design and Behavior* (John Wiley, New York), 19–75.
Wasserman, Anthony I. & Gutz, Steven (1982) 'The Future of Programming', *Comm of the ACM*, vol. 25: no. 3, 196–206.
Winner, L. (1977) *Autonomous Technology* (MIT Press, Cambridge Mass.).
Winston, Patrick H. (1984) *Artificial Intelligence*, (Addison-Wesley, Reading MA).
Woodward, Joan (1965) *Industrial Organization: Theory and Practice* (Oxford University Press, London).
Wrenn, Robert (1982) 'Management and Work Humanization', *The Insurgent Sociologist*, vol. 11: no. 3, 23–38.
Zimbalist, Andrew (1975) 'The Limits of Work Humanization'. *Review of Radical Political Economics*, vol. 7: no. 2, 50–59.
Zuboff, Shoshanah (Sep.–Oct. 1982a) 'New Worlds of Computer-Mediated Work', *Harvard Business Review*, 142–52.
Zuboff, Shoshanah (Winter 1982b) 'Problems of Symbolic Toil: How People Fare with Computer-Mediated Work', *Dissent*, 51–61.

3 Work, Participation and Co-Determination in Computer-Based Manufacturing

Eckart Hildebrandt

I. INTRODUCTION

Up to now, there has been a minimal exchange of ideas between West German industrial sociology research and the Anglo-American 'labour process' debate. For this reason we invited two representatives of the trend towards a greater exchange, Craig Littler and Paul Thompson, to our semi-annual conference last year.

In the following, I will give a brief report on a theoretical and empirical research project that has received considerable stimulus from the labour process debate. The project is entitled 'Politics and Control in Computer-Aided Production Planning and Management'. It is conducted by the Wissenschaftszentrum in Berlin. The introduction of computer-aided production planning and management systems (CAPPM systems) was studied in twelve medium-sized machine tool companies. In addition, interviews were carried out at the leading consulting firms in this area.

II. INITIAL FORMULATION OF QUESTIONS FOR THE PROJECT

The project's starting point is to be found in the West German discussion of the varying of the *organisation* of work during the introduction of new technology in a company as well as in the

---

*The contents of the paper are derived from the research I conducted together with Dr. Rüdiger Seltz during the last year. It was translated by David Paskin.

limitedness, up to now, of theoretical description of the work process with regard to the aspects of skill and workload. First of all, what was lacking were variables to enable the comprehension of the changed co-operation relationships, horizontal and vertical, as well as of individual and collective possibilities for action. In this point we had been inspired by the control notion of Braverman, Edwards and Friedman. Secondly, a concept was lacking that would question the approaches of 'rational choice' in management decisions, of a deterministic top-down emplacing of new production technologies in the company, and of a narrow technical-organisational adjustment at the level of the work place. For us the discussion of management strategies and the concept of 'Politics in Production' by Burawoy were helpful here.

With this background, we posed the four groups of questions that follow for our study of the companies. As was frequently emphasised in the ensuing debates, these questions themselves meant that the concept of control was barred from operationalisation for the empirical investigation.

1. Who gives the impetus to the planning and production of a new CAPPM system? What are their conceptions of the goals of such? Does the management have clear ideas of the productive effectiveness of the system, of the internal company conditions surrounding its introduction, and of the far-reaching, particularly social, consequences of its introduction? Moreover, what importance is attached to this new potential of control over the performance and behaviour of workers?
2. How does the process of introduction proceed? Which departments and groups of employees participate? What are their orientations as they set about the task? How does the decision-making process develop? To what extent and in what ways is the initial CAPPM-concept modified by the foregoing?
3. What are the effects at the level of the work place? Are co-operation and relationships of authority changing? Is there an alteration in the type of control towards 'systemic control'? Is control further intensified? Is there a new combination of skill standards, responsibility, and control? Finally, does the introduction of CAPPM produce conflicts over control on the shop floor?
4. What is the role of the workers representatives during the introduction? What points of view are of special importance for them? How do they deal with the issue of control?

III. SOME EMPIRICAL FINDINGS

As has already become clear, it was central for us to start with management's control over work. This was not, however, seen as a relation between internal company groups and/or individuals, but rather as a conscious exercise of power on the part of management. We intended to examine the centrality and rationality of the control motive and of the increase in control through information technology. The change, in the form of control and the difference, due to 'politics in production', between the potential of the information technology for control and the realization of that potential was the initial focus of investigation. We selected medium-sized machine tool companies for this purpose because a proportionally higher percentage of skilled workers is employed in such firms because processes of improvisation and co-ordination commonly occur there, and because the workers' representation is traditionally strong.

The following results are understood by us to be limited to this type of company. We have not yet conceptualized the applicability of our work to other company sizes and branches of industry, nor have we yet related our work directly to a phase model of capitalist development and its connection to the organization of work, as some labour process analysts have.

An explicit and common control strategy on the part of management was not discernible
The firms which produce highly customer-determined and market-dependent individual installations and/or short production run series react to intensified market conditions. The following objectives are strongly determined by the market and basically represent survival conditions which cannot be influenced by the firm:
- the offering of customer-specific products and services
- the maintenance of rigid deadlines
- the desire for high product quality
- the necessity of cost optimalization

Thus, these firms attempt to offset such external demands through internal flexibility. This 'organisation of chaos' is not a new situation for them. What is, however, new is the attempt to manage it by replacing a largely personnel-based organisation and improvisation capacity with information technology. In most machine tool companies, management's knowledge about information technology and conceptions of integrated planning and management processes for such a purpose is quite limited. The same goes for practical knowledge of the complex co-ordination processes which take place on the shop floor. During the acquisition of CAPPM systems, the management acts almost exclusively out of a 'market' mentality, that is, with a concern for the shifting demands inside the company in regard to certain managed variables, such as flow-through time, stocks of intermediate and finished goods, and quality control. At the same time, the management is aware that the reorganisation of the work process that is bound up with the introduction of CAPPM does the following:

- It changes the previously evolved social organisation (for example thought-domains and communication among the personnel).
- It changes the status and the work situations of important occupations close to the production process (for example, those involving work preparation and those of the shop masters).
- It requires a change in the understanding of one's roles and of the conduct of one's work for those affected because of the integrating of various functions which were formerly relatively autonomous.
- It leaves, however, as before, production management dependent on experience and knowledge stemming from the shop floor.

The knowledge about these social conditions of the productive introduction of new technology is of a general sort, diffuse, and little thematised. Technical-economic object-orientated notions, which are subject to the making of mathematical calculations, dominate the statements of the managers. The social dimension is given voice by way of general statements, such as 'the human being is the centre of our attentions' or occasionally through 'philosophies of new production concepts', which however fail to find expression beyond the general planning phase of the system. As a rule direct control ambitions on the part of the employees are plausibly rejected.

In our experience, the question 'What is being controlled?' has up to now received too little attention. Management, in accordance with a concept of control that is more oriented toward information technology, and specifically, that is connected with CAPPM systems, has its own set of explicit managerial ambitions. In particular, they are connected with:

- the current state of the working up of the product, that is, the task-flow and the concrete processing status,
- the productive capacity and effectiveness of the departments.

(NOTE: The attentions of management have always been directed towards the effectiveness of the shop. This is the traditional focal point of rationalisation in the firm. With CAPPM, what occurs is that preproduction departments, such as design and production planning, are subsumed to an ever greater extent under the purview of rationalisation.)

Viewed separately, and as a rule, not enclosed in stronger control ambitions of management is
– control over the performance and behaviour of the individual employees.

This state of affairs is based on, among other things, the fact that particularly the production domain already possesses traditional instruments of control that are regarded as sufficient to the task and that control directed at individuals is an issue recognised as sensitive and conflict-laden. The extent to which the separation in an analysis between departmental, task-related, process, and personnel control holds up requires further clarification.

It remains to be emphasised in this section, that the determination by technical-economic framework data is divergent from the internal indeterminateness and openness of the social formation. The organising of the system in the social sense is relegated to a process in which consultants and functional groups within the company participate to varying degrees.

The organisation of a process of participation, by means of which a strategy for introduction is developed, is substituted for a management designed strategy

In the vast majority of the firms that were questioned and intensively studied, the process of adaptation of the CAPPM system into the company structure is worked out by a project team, which frequently has several sub-teams.

The teams are composed of representatives of the various affected departments. Team members are, on the one hand, advocates within the team of interests and of ways of looking at things specific to their own departments, and on the other hand, are advocates of team decisions, normally made on a consensus basis, back in the departments. Appointment to membership on the team is regarded as an honour and is generally associated with the prospect of a responsible position in the future planning and management organisation. Department heads are appointed reluctantly because of their tendency towards distinctly department-orientated thinking.

Thus, with the project teams arises a new intermediate field of politics between upper management and departmental management. The necessity for the establishing of such teams has its roots in the integrative, network-forming character of the new information technology, which produces greater circulation of functions among departments due to its specific technological nature. Equally important is the fact that the machine tool industry traditionally has not had organisational entities at its disposal, that is, project and information management groups, that would have been capable of conceptualising and putting in place such systems. At present, there is justification in the suspicion that major effects on the social relations within the company arise directly and indirectly from this reorganisation, the effects of which can neither be assessed beforehand nor centrally guided.

The teams differ in at least two ways from the previous system existing in the industry of frequent 'co-ordinating' meetings. For example, formerly there might have been conferences between sales, production management, and production twice a week. Whereas in the old system the needs and current state of the work were simply given to an open clarification, in the new system inter-departmental and strategic thinking towards the goal of a common solution becomes necessary. This first significant difference – the demand for a change in traditional thought and behaviour patterns – should not be underestimated. It means the transition from a departmentally-bound and narrow functionally-bound thinking to an integrative type that is appropriate to an overlapping of functions. It means as well the transition from an implementation-oriented thinking to a type suited to strategic planning. This is concurrent with the acquisition of the latest technological knowledge.

The second difference is that the teams now form a new element in the social infrastructure of the company, through the commonality of meeting, training, reviewing, making test-runs, etc. Because they overtake parts of the traditional areas of competence of management, they constitute a new power factor within the firm as well. The power of the team is indeed decisively shaped by the fact that top management stands behind it. But while on the one hand, the latter must give its seal of approval step-by-step to the decisions of the former, on the other hand management becomes dependent on the team for strategy development.

The development of strategy in teams raises once again the question of interests in various regards. Here, however, not the unambiguous interests of management become manifest but the interests of employees, from various departments, having differing positions within the hierarchy, with respect to function, status and to the work itself. These team members represent group interests that are not straight-forwardly discussed as such. The interests are usually expressed indirectly as aspects of the technical organisation of work and of productivity, in accordance with the subject at hand. In short, clear, assignable interests related to life and work situations are rarely identifiable. This is also valid as regards the issue of control, even though the team members are indeed those directly affected by the system changeover. More striking still was the impression received that there was a general consensus as to the lightening of the work load and the functional effectiveness of the new system. It is not the case that social points of view do not play a role in team negotiations. I would attempt the following provisional formulation: Social points of view are directly represented by team members, but are predominantly put forth in a hidden manner, that is, in the form of object-related argumentation, through cajoling, by definite avoidance of thematising, etc.

Thus the teams already constitute a new forum for the bringing about of a consensus over technical-functional and social issues, as for example, how the new technology is to be adapted in various ways into the evolved company structure. Simultaneously, a new system for the negotiating among interests is thereby constituted, that settles itself functionally somewhere between the tasks of the system designers, for whom CAPPM conceptualisation appears as job categories, and that of the previously institutionalised workers' representatives, where conceptualisation manifests itself as co-determination. The taking on of this latter function by the teams represents a questioning of the, up to now, only legitimate body for the negotiating among interests, that is, the works council.

These research findings raise the question of the stability of this new locus of authority, the project team. Moreover, there is suggested a topic for future investigation: To what extent do these teams represent prefigurings of a new organisation of work, that is, to what extent do they already embody the characteristics of new processes of co-operation? Some of the reorganisation concepts in the corporate domain which have been our concern, for example, 'group technology' and 'edp-delegates', are of interest in this regard.

The role of the shop in the process of rationalisation through CAPPM is small

Not a single case out of the above studies of organisation involved the inclusion of the shop, that is, of the parts production and assembly departments, in either the strategy development or in its particular adaptation into the company. All relevant parties previously mentioned, that is, management, department representatives, and works councils regarded the effects of CAPPM at the level of the machine operators to be very minor. This includes as well the control aspect. It is important to note here, that the main effects of rationalisation by means of CAPPM, such as, economising of work places, changes of work processes, and control, fall on the work preparation departments, in other words, on the technical employees. Changes in the shop floor can be perceived only in the broader perspective, as for example, through the introduction of semi-automatic and semi-integrated transport and processing technology, through the reorganisation of the production floor, or through the increase in subcontractor provision of component parts. In this context, a tendency has been observed towards a contraction of production departments into centralised operations, used as much as possible at full capacity. This in turn means a tendency towards the development of engineering and service companies. Noteworthy in regard to the shop employees is the erosion of the formerly central role of the supervisors (*meister*). The development of skill requirements will, however, not be discussed here.

Apprentices, trained in some enterprises to be the 'new speciality worker', take on increasingly greater importance. They perceive the propagation of information technology positively as making an interesting and future-oriented demand on them. A dividing line develops between them and the older workers, who do not generally either feel themselves equal to the task of being retrained for the new technology or, as the case may be, are simply looking towards their own retirement. These older workers, whose contribution is subject to widely varying estimations, are not laid off, rather, they are able to be retained until retirement due to the delays in the changeover process and to the simple continued existence of traditional functions. Adaptation then of personnel to the new system proceeds not from a 'hire and fire' policy but rather through a change of generations.

The imposition of new control methods on the shop floor that we observed, seemed to markedly contradict our expectations for such events. We found neither massive fear of the new controls nor conflict over them. This discovery is, for us, momentous. The following four possible interpretations could be followed up in greater detail to arrive at a satisfactory explanation:

- The majority of the problems having to do with the controls are defused before they reach the shop floor by the project teams.
- Indirect controls that systematically regulate the processing of work, which are not aimed directly at personnel, are not perceived by the workers as control *per se.*
- The mechanisms of control in the shop have already developed to such an extent, as for example, inspections by the shop masters, wage accords, and group norms, that CAPPM is not felt as an additional intensification. (The parallel occurring abrogation of accords must however be considered here.)
- The changes due to CAPPM on the shop floor are so negleglible as to be irrelevant.

In favour of the last idea is that, in the majority of the cases studied, the separation between production data and personnel data was maintained, or if necessary, carried out at the very beginning, either by the team or by the shop council. This indicates both the awareness of the importance of such a separation on the part of the employees and a concentration on the protection of personnel data.

IV. CONTROL AND TRUST, A SOCIAL MODEL OF THE COMPANY

The take-off point for control can be seen in the following problem: How can it be guaranteed, within the company on an everyday basis, that the product emerges on time, with the desired quality, and is efficiently produced? Control, moreover, is seen to be grounded in the fundamental assumption, that a universal distrust exists on the part of capital for labour, a distrust which arises due to the difference of interest between the two parties. This, in turn, demands for capital to apply comprehensive controls.

We have indeed perceived the tendency towards expansion of controls on the part of management as an element of the process of corporate regulation. But, there was also another opposing element to be found, and one with only a limited possibility of being reconciled with personnel control, that is: Trust. Trust in a mutual readiness to perform for a common company goal was named by all groups of employees as the fundamental principle of their attitude towards the work. Correspondingly, breaches of trust were decisive experiences for them and were seen as threats. This trust must be distinguished from an adaptive compliant behaviour that is based on the acceptance of the unalterable asymmetry of power that permeates every company process. Burawoy has termed positively the source of the trust to be 'manufacturing consent'.

In order to be able to properly classify the various aspects of control, we have been led by our findings to look in the direction of the form and content of the company consensus-forming process. By doing this however, especially in Germany, one rapidly gets caught in various historical and ideological traps. The fundamental trade-unionist, as well as Marxist understanding is that what takes place in a business is structured by the exploitation relation. Any notion of a common interest among all company groups is quickly identified with the ideology of the employers and thus made taboo, as for example, by viewing a company as a 'family' or a 'partnership'. Burawoy has stated this contradiction succinctly:

> So we face a paradox: At the same time that the factory is regarded as the crucible of class consciousness and collective resistance, it is presented as an arena of undisputed domination, of fragmentation, degradation, and mystification. (M. Burawoy, 'The Contours of Production Politics', IIVG/pre854–206, p.5)

The taboo notwithstanding, we have developed, with resort to the concept of the 'high trust organisation' of A. Fox, a hypothetical model, which will be outlined below. With its help, the introduction of CAPPM, with particular regard to its control aspects, can be analysed as violations of a basic consensus. The ultimate soundness and range of applicability of this hypothesis has not yet been clarified. The formulation is as follows.

The High Trust Organisation is founded on a pact of reciprocity between company management and employees. This is the 'Productivity-Social Pact'. It contains two components:
- The 'Productivity Pact' is a mutual agreement that states that every member of the organisation works for the common goals of the enterprise, each in his or her particular functional capacity. This means for the employees the application of their abilities and skills in a motivated and co-operative production fashion. Management is bound by the pact to take the requisite leadership initiatives to secure the company's position in the market, and in addition, to care for the social assets of the workforce.

- Directly linked to the Productivity Pact is a company 'Social Pact'. This contains in principle a recognition of the relationships within the company as to the giving and carrying out of directives and as to the proportional distribution of the returns. In regard to this latter, the pact involves acknowledgment of the necessity of profits for the enterprise which derive from current investments in new technology and product development. Another part of the distribution is agreed to be invested for the protection of the life and work standards of the employees. This is to produce stable employment, assured and growing incomes, appropriate levels of qualification and intensity of work, protection from occupational hazards, etc.

The Productivity-Social Pact can be seen as a framework that enables management to adapt to market variations in both product and labour markets. In addition, it is of assistance in organising the day-to-day production process. Simultaneously, it stands as the framework for social integration of the employees into the organisation.

The validity of such a pact reveals the *de facto* acceptance, within a given company, of norms and of regulation by consensus, both of which would have had up to that point a variety of origins and formal characteristics. The pact is either adhered to or called into question by everyday company practice. The existence of a pact means that certain matters central to the operation of the business are regulated and that certain oppositions of interest are subject, at least potentially, to being balanced out.

The Productivity Pact requires, in order to become effective and continually reaffirmed, the following two conditions:
- a mutual exchange of information and a transparent openness of company functioning,
- the mutual assistance of both parties during the performing of the work tasks *per se*.

With these two prerequisites in mind, the introduction of new information technology can now be regarded as being caused by a reaction to a changed situation inside the company, thus making it a starting point for reorganisation. In this event, both management and the workers in the shop agree that the mutual transparency has diminished. Management complains that the shop represents a 'black box', and that problems arising in this area, for example, extensions of deadlines and mechanical disruptions, are wrought with uncertainties, expensive, and not readily subject to being remedied. The causes are, for management, difficult to discern. Correspondingly, the shop complains that directives from above, as to time and 'material' matters, are frequently imprecise and incomplete, that transparency with regard to work lying ahead has been lost, and that directives as to cost-economies only throw the shop into confusion.

The introduction of CAPPM system is the unilateral attempt on the part of the management to make up for the mutual loss of transparency and assistance. Through CAPPM, a one-sided transparency is re-established that enables management, at the very least, to view the progress of the work. In addition, possibilities are created for direct intervention on the shop floor, as for example, through the newfound abilities to change task and capacity arrangements. Finally, the unmediated control of the productivity of specific functions in the shop becomes feasible.

The High Trust Organisation model assumes that a certain allocation of information inside the shop concerning the current status of the work, of quality, of performance, and of the causes of disruptions is a basic requirement under a Productivity Pact. It is therefore undisputed. The allocation only becomes an issue when a new form of control, that is, 'systemic control', makes its appearance. With this, sensitive information begins to leave the shop floor. How it will then be used becomes obscure to those in the shop and no longer open to discussion. Moreover, boundaries delineating the pre-existing scope of individual freedom are likely to be violated by the new data acquisition.

It has been discussed above, in what ways machine tool companies, with respect to their social organisation, can be described as 'high trust organisations'. The framework of consensus involved in Productivity-Social Pacts forms the foundation for the establishment of a complex social infrastructure in the companies, over which in the concrete everyday, production plays itself out.

This infrastructure is made up of a multitude of modes of regulations, co-operation relationships, and institutions, the exact combination of which is specific to each firm. A typical example of such a 'mode of regulation' is the daily round made by the production manager through the shop, a tradition in medium-sized machine tool companies. Here, the conventional functions are: the personal visual observation of the state of the shop, the inspection of the activities of the workers, and possible direct involvement with particular problems and/or especially urgent work. The face-to-face interaction between a representative of management and individual workers gives daily, reciprocal expression to a Productivity Pact.

With the introduction of CAPPM, this ritual would appear to have become obsolete for technical reasons: These systems are designed to provide management with information more rapidly and more systematically than would have ever been possible under the daily round system. Our company studies bear this out. In general, the round has either been thinned out or totally eliminated. Where neither of these has been the case, its preservation was interpreted as a policy relic still maintained by an older generation of managers.

Surprisingly, given the above, we often encountered the opinion that the abolition of daily rounds had led to some sort of deficiency. Management then made compensatory efforts to, once again, strengthen its personal presence in the shop. Thus occurred the curious resumption of the use of a personnel-based ritual, thought to be anachronistic, right in the midst of a period of increasing introduction of CAPPM systems. This phenomenon is explanable by our High Trust Organisation model. Indicated here in general is how little thought is given during modernisation of production systems to an appropriate reorganisation of social relations. The daily round of our example appears to be an essential building block of these relations because, while it does perform production functions, it also carries on quite directly personal functions such as social bonding, affirmation, and representation of interests. In fact, in the new situation the latter are particularly emphasised because the CAPPM systems contain no substitutes. This demonstrates in an exemplary fashion that with this technology the social functions become increasingly independent of technical functions within the organisation.

Major significance must be attributed to information and communication related to and conveyed by individuals when considering processes of consensus and negotiation. A comprehensively formulated model of the social relations in a given company must not only incorporate aspects of control, such as modes of regulation, structure of the hierarchy, and schedules of wages, but must also bring to bear socio-cultural understandings of behaviour.

The above example shows that it may well be the case that some norms and controls only became visible after a violation of them has occurred. This in turn is because, rather than existing in the form of written regulations, these norms and controls are more the stuff of custom, apparent only in daily practice. Thus is suggested an intrinsic limit to both the pacts per se and to social models of them that restricts the absolute calculability of proposed social changes.

We did not find any machine tool companies that, with the introduction of CAPPM, consciously attempted to convert to 'low trust' organisations. However, the accompanying revisions of the relations between responsibility, co-operation, and control affecting various functional groups within the company implies that a rearrangement in what is now considered to be a 'high trust' situation is necessary. In so far, the analysis of the introduction of CAPPM systems demonstrates the variability of such high trust type as well as its permanent and essential instability.

V. TWO ADDITIONAL TENDENCIES THAT ENDANGER THE ESTABLISHMENT OF NEW BALANCES IN THE COMPANY WITH RESPECT TO BOTH THE ORGANISATION OF PRODUCTION AND SOCIAL RELATIONS

1. The type of model that has been discussed regards the firm as a bounded 'space' inside of which it is attempted, by means of company politics, to produce the new balances. However, it is an integral property of the new information technology that it has the potential, so to speak, to break out of this company space. A problem that was touched on once before in the above arises here as well, that is: It is the state of affairs with companies of the size under consideration that they usually do not possess beforehand the expertise required to effectively adopt the new systems on their own. More and more such companies are constrained therefore to resort to external consultants, the latter implying externally predetermined notions of how the new controls are to be put into operation.

Another factor of external dependence is the growing interdependence between companies by means of edp-networks – for example the edp-connections between installation producer and customer. This factor and other similar ones taken together, the space within the company for matching the reorganisation of production and social relations is decreasing. The final result is frequently that a situation of excessive stress arises on the social relations, this being further enhanced in its effects by a shifting of the burden of adjustment from the technical to the social realm.

2. Up to this point the description of models of the social relations has not emphasised the role of the workers' representatives in the

companies. Historically the introduction of Productivity-Social Pacts is, however, closely related to the institutionalisation of works councils as well as to the general consolidation of the power of trade unions. In Germany, a two-fold structure of interest representation has come into being. On the one hand, there is the system of the shop councils, which are constrained in their concerns to matters within an individual company. On the other hand, there are the politics of unionism that obviously go beyond such a limitation, being oriented towards legislation and governmental regulation.

In this connection, we offer two theses. The first states that either the separation between interest representation inside the company and that which is external is increased with the High Trust Organisation or, that the Productivity-Social Pact is founded on such a separation, to begin with. One of the most important observations we made in the machine tool companies studied was that inclusion of the works councils in the introduction process of new information technology was deliberately aimed at precluding external union involvement. Indeed, the exclusion of the unions 'from outside' was in many cases a stipulated condition for the participation of the councils. The success of a pact thus meant for the company an increment in its autonomy as against external politics. In 'high trust' companies, the results of the regional or national contracts between trade unions and employers' associations are further 'translated' in each individual firm. This can mean that such results become essentially superfluous because their analogue has long since already been generated by internal politics. If this extreme development has not occurred, then these results are often at least modified by means of internal consensus or sometimes simply evaded. The economic situation of recent years has indeed provided a pressure in this regard, complementary to that of the new information technology.

The second thesis has to do with the relation between work *per se* and the activity of representing interests. The historical development of the shop council marks a separation between activities of production and those of political co-determination. Co-determination became, with the appearance of the councils, a function separated in space and time from the productive work, performed by delegated individuals, and carried on in regulated proceedings around standardised themes. This type of institutionalised co-determination deals with working arrangements only indirectly, that is, by means of regulations, for example, as to skill requirements, co-operation structures and authorisation procedures for decision-making. Rationalisation through information technology has the following effects that are relevant here: It changes the configuration of working arrangements and, as has been discussed above, it requires the selective participation of employees for its introduction. This latter further involves, case-by-case, a tapping of human resources in ways previously not agreed upon. This initiative on the part of management cuts across established domains of responsibility and patterns of regulation, ones that management had indeed itself helped to set up in the first place. Traditional institutionalised forms of co-determination are subverted or even annulled.

One of the most important questions for the future is: Whether, and if so in what form, a new balance will be struck among strategies for participation, new forms of work, and institutionalised co-determination.

4 Computer Numerical Control and Constraint

Fiona Wilson

In Braverman's (1974) classic work, *Labor and Monopoly Capital,* the case of the development and use of numerically controlled (NC) machines helps describe the evolutionary tendency of human work towards a simultaneous decrease in level of skill in production tasks, and an increase in managerial control. Braverman (1974, p. 197) claims that it is worth considering the application of numerical control (NC) machine tools to small batch production to demonstrate the effect on the labour process and the worker. According to Braverman, craft knowledge is destroyed, labour functions are cheapened and fragmented, and the task skills of execution are separated from those of conception, effectively reducing the knowledge of any of these new occupations.

In support of this view, Braverman describes the content of the new tasks involved in machining by NC on the basis of engineering literature, principally Leone (1967), and his own experience. He describes the job of 'part-programming', the conversion of the machining instructions from drawings into instructions for a computer, as limiting the technical knowledge required and stripping machining tasks of their former skill content. Braverman concedes that there is nothing in NC technology to preclude for example, 'the unity of this process in the hands of the skilled machinist . . . since the knowledge of metal-cutting practices which is required for programming is already mastered by the machinist' (1974, p. 199). This does not happen because the capitalist mode of production fragments and cheapens jobs.

Braverman's essential thesis is that there is a general and progressive de-skilling of jobs in the twentieth century, that there is a long-term trend for jobs to be increasingly devoid of intrinsic content, routinised and mechanical. The basis of Braverman's argument is that work is geared to the creation of profit rather than the satisfaction of worker's needs. This creates a fundamental conflict of interests between workers and capitalists, and in order that capital can realise the full potential of the labour employed, control is necessary. Workers cannot be expected to work in the best interests of capital in a context of antagonistic relations.

Taylor was, according to Braverman, the first management theorist to recognise the importance of managerial control. The essence of Taylor's scientific management, Braverman stresses is its divorce of conception from execution, such that management is totally responsible for the planning and design of work tasks and workers are restricted to simple manual operation. This is the de-skilling to which Braverman refers; work is progressively degraded, as all elements of knowledge, responsibility and judgement are taken from the worker and his tasks beome totally programmed.

Braverman's work is valuable because it attempts to understand the basic principles underlying the design of work under capitalism; it relates these to the nature of society from which they occur and looks behind the ideological assurances of neutrality and inevitability of current work forms uncovering the interests and powers that inform these practices. This is an essential consideration for any empirical study of skill; it is important to understand the perspectives which place work activity within the total system of production. However, Braverman is not without his critics. The critiques of Braverman are now well rehearsed, but a selective view of these criticisms helps point towards a more constructive basis for any examination of the changing nature of skill.

Braverman's argument closely follows that of Marx. Marx set out to study the objective development of nineteenth-century capitalism, and an equally objective ideology of capitalist society. Braverman takes a self-professed Marxist standpoint and develops a highly abstract conception of class. He says that he is concerned with the 'objective' nature of class and not with the subjective will (Braverman, 1974, p. 27). The result is, as Giddens (1982, p. 207) notes, that he drastically underestimates the knowledgeability and the capability of workers faced with a range of management imperatives. However, contrary to Braverman's claims, the subjective will of management, as expressed in Taylorist strategies of control, is more than adequately represented in the book. What is lacking is a parallel discussion of the reactions of workers, as themselves knowledgeable and capable agents to the technical division of labour and Taylorism. Braverman does not talk of specific trade unions or shop floor resistance to the labour process.

Braverman also ignores the variability of worker resistance, the fact that some changes are resisted more than others, some groups resist more than others, some groups achieve a negoiated order while some groups become a privileged elite (Littler and Salaman, 1982). Worker resistance can, and does, prevent the development of any straight-forward relationship between employer's production methods and the skill structure of the labour force.

The technological changes taking place in capitalist economies are more complicated in their effects on the labour process than Braverman describes. Certainly old craft skills are, for the most part disappearing, but new types of skilled activity albeit different in character, are being created. What counts as 'skill' is a complicated matter, as this chapter will show. Workers can, if necessary sustain a definition of themselves as 'skilled' in spite of changes in the nature of the labour task.

Braverman's argument exaggerates the coincidence of Taylorism with capitalism. A great deal of Braverman's account of the changing nature of work is based on Taylor's prescriptions and their implementation. He thus treats as unproblematic, both historically and theoretically, the implementation of Taylorism. Capitalists and their agents are seen to be fully conscious of their economic interests which they organise and conspire to realise. There is an assumption that managements always get their own way. Braverman portrays management as omniscient and employees as infinitely malleable. His conception of Taylorism as the 'explicit verbalisation of the capitalist mode of production' is too simplistic. Taylorism does not dominate the world of production but coexists with a variety of non-Taylorist practices, for example the granting of work discretion to generate commitment and trust.

In reality, managers conduct a rather less sophisticated strategy than that with which they are often credited. A survey by Lockyer *et al*. (1981) found that British managers often ignore available production techniques. Despite all the discussion of Taylorism amongst sociologists, over a third of the respondents used no work study at all.

Managerial strategies concerned with new technology must, then, be explored. Specific managerial strategies have been explored by Child (1972) and Buchanan (1983). They believe that the choices which they form in decision making over technical change, concerning why and how the technology is to be used, determine the outcomes of technological change. The technological imperatives are weak, the strategic choices are crucial. A further point to note is that the notion of skill may refer either to the requirements of the job or to the capabilities of the worker. Failure to indicate precisely which sense of the word is intended in a given context will cause confusion. Braverman writes as if 'the degradation of labour' and the 'de-skilling of workers' are interchangable terms but thay are not (Lee, 1981). Thompson (1983, p. 92) points out that the concept of skill can have three dimensions: knowledge, unity of conception and execution and discretion.

This chapter aims to examine:
1. how the managerial objectives in terms of skill levels are formulated and defined by managers in order to understand their intentions and whether or not these are easily or readily articulated. If strategies have been formulated with the aim of lowering skill levels of jobs, have these strategies been successfully implemented?
2. how workers' interests are affected by managerial strategy and whether or not they have attempted to resist any negative consequences for skill levels.
3. whether or not the skills of the job or the skills of the individual (or both), are subjectively perceived as affected by technical change.

Marx, Weber and Braverman have all, in one way or another addressed the rationalisation of the labour process under capitalism, but they have not always addressed its contradictions. This chapter will look at empirical evidence from the engineering industry, to see whether or not the data from one company leads us to support or refute a deskilling hypothesis. Before looking at the data, the technology, the company and the research method will be briefly described.

THE TECHNOLOGY

A CNC machine is used to cut away surplus material from a piece of metal in order to provide a component of the desired shape, size and finish. The machine may be a horizontal or vertical boring machine, a flame-cutting machine, a lathe or a machining centre that is flexible and can perform a number of different operations on the same component, minimising the need for lifts and changes to other machines.

CNC's advantage over traditional forms of automation is that it is far more flexible. Traditional automated machines can only carry out a limited range of functions and need large batches of components to be economic. Smaller batches of more complex components are usually produced on general purpose machines which are operated manually. These often need expensive jigs and fixtures to allow complex components to be manufactured.

CNC offers the advantage of automation with the flexibility of general purpose machines. It allows small batches of complex components to be machined faster and, generally more accurately than could be done by any other method. In addition it allows shapes to be machined which previously would not have been possible or practical.

CNC refers to the control of a machine tool by a computer which is built into a machine. The computer is programmed, usually with information fed in on a punched paper tape, to carry out a particular sequence of operations. Alternatively the machine can be programmed through Manual Data Input, (MDI) which can be done by the operator on the machine's console. In this company machines were programmed by programmers, away from the shop floor. However operators are allowed to change and edit tapes and have been trained to programme the machines.

THE COMPANY

The company is a large engineering company, manufacturing turbine generators for the electricity supply industry. The company is a member of a group of companies; the group, a product of the merger boom in the late 1960s, is a large private sector employer, employing approximately 8500 people. This research was restricted to one company site where there are 1500 employees.

Large steam turbines are one-off products. The typical turbine has 6500 to 7000 parts which make up 350 sub assemblies. Final assembly takes place on the customer's site. This degree of complexity of the manufacturing process is reflected in the work allocated to the different machines in the company. In the heavy machine shop, where the bulk of the work is carried out, the batch sizes are very small; in the light machine shop, batch sizes are between one and two hundred.

The company has invested over £3 000 000 in new machine tools. It was hoped that the new technology would help reduce cycle time and so cost, and would help ensure product quality. There are ten CNC machines in light and heavy machine shops. There is also a CNC lathe in the toolroom and a CNC flame profiling machine in fabrication.

Approximately 38 per cent of the workforce are manual workers. Of those, 24 per cent are skilled, 13 per cent semi-skilled and 1 per cent unskilled. The manual workers are all members of unions, mainly the Amalgamated Union of Engineering Workers (AUEW). The union has negotiated that only skilled men can operate the CNC machines. To this the management had agreed. All CNC operators are, then apprentice-trained craftsmen and have all, at some stage, operated conventional machines. Operators have also been sent on training courses so they can operate and progamme the machines. CNC workers are paid a special machine rate for operating the CNC machines.

THE RESEARCH METHOD

The research method used to collect this data was as unstructured as possible. This data, and much more besides, was collected while talking to operatives as they worked, and observing what they were doing, or in interviews with managers responsible for the new technology. Thirty one CNC operators, and their managers, were interviewed in this plant which shall be called 'Odessy Engineering'.

Operators were told, at the beginning of the interview, that the researcher was interested to find out how they thought the new technology had affected their jobs, particularly their job content. They were asked two specific questions: 'What was your job like before the introduction of the new technology?' and 'What is it like now?' They were left to talk at length about the two jobs and the differences. Only qualifying questions were asked after the initial intoduction, for example, 'What do you mean by . . . ?' The aim was to allow operators to speak for themselves, and not to impose issues, for example how job satisfaction had been affected, by using a questionnaire or some other very structured method. Interview length varied dramatically between individuals and was dependent on how much the operator wanted to talk or how much pressure he was under to produce the job he was working on. Interviews lasted from half an hour to approximately four hours.

While the operator was talking, the researcher was making notes on what he said. He was able to read those notes if he wished. The researcher was particularly listening for, and recording, the words and expressions the operators used to describe how their jobs had been affected by technical change.

FINDINGS FROM INTERVIEWS IN ODESSY ENGINEERING

The division of labour necessitated by the introduction of the technology creates 'a separation of conception from execution'. The number of decisions operators make about how to do the jobs allocated have been reduced. The tape instructs the machine on where and how to cut, and determines the machine's speed and feed rate. It also includes the number of checks the operator will make on the work in progress as the machine will stop when the operator is required to make a check. Thus the number of decisions an operator makes are reduced, as the decisions over how to do the job have been made by the programmer.

The reduction in decision making was associated with skill as the following quotes demonstrate:

> It's taking away a considerable amount of skill. Everything is done for you. To work to a tape, you've got to do the job as the tape says. When I was on a conventional machine I could choose how to do a job. If I want the tape changed, I have to go and inform the programmer which is time consuming and infuriating sometimes. You are more or less told what to do; you don't have the freedom to do it your own way. Take one job; four different people would probably do it four different ways.

> It takes the skill out of the job because you are not doing anything by hand. If your program is right, you don't have to do anything. You do certain things, but the job is done by the programmer.

This idea of 'not doing anything by hand' occured many times but was usually expressed as a 'physical' or 'manual' aspect of work which is lost. New jobs were, in contrast, described as 'less physical' and 'more mental'.

Operators no longer grind their own tools. Tooling used on the new machines is often pre-set. Operators no longer decide which tooling to use; that decision has already been determined and the information on tooling will be on the printed programme. This responsibility no longer lies with the operator.

Nine operators complained that their variety of work had been reduced. This factor is dependent on the work allocated to the machine by the foreman and the planning department, and the number of tapes that have been prepared for the machine. Concern for variety and decision making is highlighted in the following quote:

> With this particular machine, you get quantities. You get a bit tired producing the same job over and over again. It's a bit depressing. You come in one morning and you can do the same job all day, producing the same thing. In one way it relieves all the pressure, but it can get depressing so you have to have a few minutes rest time to recuperate... There was more variety of work, more skills and that *producing* a component... I had to make decisions, different decisions, because there was a bigger range of jobs... The jobs on this machine are dead easy, there is less skill.

Here the operator is associating the use of skill with variety and decision-making.

An operator on a machine which produced mainly batch work complained about the lack of variety in the job he was given to do. 'The job is repetitive, there's no two ways about it. There is a lot more work that could be done on these CNCs.' He was particularly disappointed about the lack of variety because, when the machine was first introduced, he had specifically asked if he would be doing repetitive work, and had been assured that he would not.

As some jobs have been reduced in variety and decision-making content, operators feel less involved in their jobs.

> Jobs on here are more monotonous than on a conventional machine. Once you are set up, the machine will do it all for you from start to finish. You put the tape in and then it's all the same. You just stand back and watch it. You watch it to see if the tool wears out. You are less involved than you were on a conventional machine. You don't have to stop and think what you are doing on

a CNC but on a conventional machine you did. There is no involvement after the first one.

This man went on to complain that he was given drilling jobs to do, 'but this is a *milling* machine ... It's the quality of work we are looking for but they don't bother; it's just what they want to put on the machine ... These people don't know anything about milling. On the computer it is a drilling machine.' There is a danger then that this particular man's job is being de-skilled because of the work he is given to do. As a result his interest and motivation are reduced by working on CNC.

> It takes away interest. There is more to actually remember to operate the machine but less to know about the product. The only one who knows how to turn a job is probably the computer programmer. The interest in the job was in the actual *physical* production of a job. It makes you lazy. You do a short burst to set up a job, feed the tape in and so on and then you watch it ... I used to like coming to work, but CNC has killed it for me.

Job satisfaction is reduced because operators feel they no longer produce the work. The technology is seen to produce the work and is in control This affects job satisfaction.

> You have more job satisfaction on a conventional machine because you are doing the job yourself, aren't you. On here you are a human robot, to be perfectly honest. Your only skill on here is to get the job going ... All you are doing is lifting the job in, and lifting the job out and maintaining sizes ... The only way you can have job satisfaction is if you are doing a complete job yourself ... No one on CNC likes their job and no one finds it satisfying.

Operators also report that they feel their sense of control has been reduced by the machine. The CNC miller spoke of how this sense of loss of control could lead to stress. He gave the example of how, if a programmer had made an error, the tool could smash. 'It's because *you've* got no *control*. To a certain degree you don't know what is going to happen next.' He told the story of how, one day, the programmer had made a mistake. The machine had rammed into a vice and "another part had ended up embedded in the wall." The operator involved had, apparently, experienced nightmares as a result.

Using the new technology can also lead to a sense of isolation; some mentioned that they felt like 'social outcasts'. The operators in heavy machine shops felt particularly isolated as they worked a 3-shift system, rather than a 2-shift system as the other operators in the plant worked. They also had very large areas cordoned off for the machines and so were more physically isolated. Operators there have less opportunity to discuss grievances and exchange views on, for example, pay and conditions. It is interesting to note that heavy machine shop operators had less to say in response to questions and interviews were shorter in this shop.

The pressure of work isolates workers. There is no doubt that CNC operators are under more pressure to produce work faster. Added to this is the fact that CNC machines are given priority for inspection, cranes and maintenance, which increases the pace of work. The managers and foremen closely supervise the CNC technology. The machines are treated as 'showcases' and potential customers and other visitors are brought to see the machinery. Operators feel they have to 'perform'.

Operators were aware of how the technology could mean a loss of ultimate control over jobs by skilled men. 'I could get one of the proved tapes and give it to a kid out of school and have him producing components. If they were all the same components, he would easily do the job.'

Managers provide data which supports a de-skilling hypotheses. Not only did they recognise that work could be de-skilled, they also found that the workforce could be reduced. They found that if they could produce more accurate work, the number of fitters employed could be reduced. 'The machine also takes some of the responsibility for accuracy away from the operator. They used to make jigs and fixtures to determine where, for example, the holes were to be bored. Now this information is in the memory of the machine. Minimal Manual Intervention is the aim. Skill is taken away be telling the man what to do.' Managers are then actively encouraging operators to minimise the utilisation of skill.

The other advantages are clearly articulated. 'The machining centres will automatically select the correct tool as this information is in the tape. This can be advantageous as it is time saving. The tools on all the machines are better as they are more flexible, more universal.'

While describing how the technology had changed the operator's job, this manager added,

> Don't get me wrong, I mean you couldn't put an idiot on there, it needs some common sense. I'm just taking it very clean, telling you what used to happen and what happens now to try to give you some idea how the job's been de-skilled.
>
> We have chosen people for CNC who have proved capable on manual machines, and also those who are younger and will accept the new technology. We train apprentices to use both manual and CNC machines. The ideal situation would be where you had a man on a traditional machine for three or four years, then switch him to a CNC machine. Young people pick up CNC quicker. They understand the language. Operators will edit programs. It is feasible, if you've got the confidence to put a program in. But on the big machines it's a bit more complicated; it's quite expensive machinery and they're expensive holes. I would think they don't do it, [program the machines] because they lack confidence. They don't lack the confidence of being manual machinists but lack confidence understanding the software. That's purely my opinion. We should be aiming to get operators to program their own machines. We'd be silly not to do that and we keep aiming to get them to do it and I think we are getting more to do it. On the small lathes we are moving quickly; on the big machines, it's a bit slow.
>
> We are aiming for combining the job of operator and programmer as the ultimate reward of technology. But we need to maximise the use of spindle cutting time so we have a progammer writing a program while the operator is making sure the spindle is cutting. We stress to both the operator and the foreman to maximise cutting time and save time. Minimal Manual Intervention is what we want.

There are then two competing and contradictory strategies for the utilisation of CNC. This manager would like to see the job of programmer and operator combined which would increase the utilisation of skill on the shop floor. On the other hand, the reality, at the moment is that he believes the operator's job has been de-skilled as some decision making has been removed from the operator. However, one could argue that they have also been re-skilled as they have been trained to use the new technology, and to programme and adjust the machine. The strategy adopted, where the programmer plans how, where and when the machine should cut, and the operator only feeds in the instructions to the machine, takes advantage of the fact that cutting time can be maximised. The first strategy could lead to the loss of programmers' jobs; the second strategy could lead to further degradation of work.

So far, we can see that the job of CNC operator has been de-skilled because operators no longer plan how they do a job. The programmed tape determines many of the decisions which, as a conventional operator, he would have made. The potential exists for managment to fully control work organisation, taking all responsibility and control from the shop-floor by encouraging Minimal Manual Intervention. If all the work planned for CNC machines used proved tapes, this aim could easily be realised. But this does not seem, at the moment, to be reality.

A discourse which argues solely that de-skilling takes place is incomplete. Counter arguments can be found in the interviews which contradict each element of decreased control and skill as discussed. Not all operators argue that technology degrades work. Whether they do or not is dependent, in part, on the machines they operate. If operators work on a milling machine or on a lathe producing multiples or a limited number of different components, they will be more likely to argue that work has been degraded. In demonstrating how jobs have been degraded, only a part of the data from initial interviews has been used.

Despite the fact that managers believed that CNC de-skills jobs, they are actually dependent on the use of operator's traditional and CNC skills. As has already been noted, the operators in Odessy Engineering have the training, knowledge and experience associated with conventional machining plus that associated with CNC. Management's main problem is uncertainty. Uncertainty is created by the fact that tapes and machines cannot always be relied on to function as they should or could and so the machines have to be carefully monitored while in operation. This problem is compounded by the fact that, particularly in the heavy machine shops, the components on machines are very expensive and have had value added to them at each stage of the production process. Any mistake could be an expensive mistake. Also because new work often comes on to the machines, many of the tapes are first issue tapes and so experimental. Further, management have recognised the need to develop operator's skill; these skills help provide flexibility, for example, the operator does not need to wait for a programmer to change or alter a tape. Management are, then, dependent on the use of craftmen's skill to reduce this uncertainty. They are dependent on CNC operators:

1. for proving new tapes;
2. for coping with the variety of new work that comes on to the machine;
3. so they can use part programme, i.e. adapt parts of proved programmes for new work;
4. to check work in progress;
5. to write parts of programme omitted, either consciously or in error by the programmers;
6. to adjust machine speeds and feeds if quality of work is going to be affected by programmed speeds and feeds;
7. to understand the machine's controls and capabilities sufficiently to operate it;
8. to prevent smash ups if the machine goes wrong;
9. to know when to change tool tips in order to produce 'quality' work. (It is actually possible to include, in the programme, information which will tell the operator when to change a tool tip. This information will appear on the screen at the appropriate time in the programme. But this control mechanism has been abandoned and the decision when to change the tool tip is left to the operator. As the superintendent said, 'All that technology will do is stop the machine when the tip is gone; it doesn't change the tip for you.') As a result, operators argue that there has been an increase in the use of their skill and responsibility and so job interest has increased. For some variety of work is increased. A turner links skill with responsibility in the next quote:

> Since they have put me on this machine I feel more responsible. I think that it's brightened my working future up. What brightens me up is the computer, it's like having a new toy. It's a new skill and it makes your working day brighter because it gives you more responsibility.

For another operator, the 'extra responsibility is looking after the machine. Everything works so fast that it makes it easy to crash. It is easy to put the wrong information in and smash the job up.' The same operator argued that setting up was harder on CNC. The job was made more difficult because before CNC jobs were marked out.

You just had to drill to marking out. On NC you are more responsible for making things come in the right place. The tape has all
the coordinates for the hole but you have to set the drill in the
right place. When it's marked out, you can see if it's right or wrong.
On NC you always have this doubt in your mind . . . People tend
to look on CNC as a god; the machine can't be wrong. But I can be
wrong and will get severely bounced around the shop for
it . . . anyone can press buttons, but you have to think to
press buttons.

This particular operator was, at the time of the interview, using MDI
as there was no tape available. 'There have been jobs left for 6 weeks
and no tape prepared. The programmers are not always notified of
the jobs to be done.' One operator described how he felt. He was now
'more than a borer' because he had learned to use CNC and also his
job was interesting and varied. The technology made his job easier.
He said, 'Once the machine is set up you only have to watch the job.
You have to have the confidence to let the machine do what it is pro-
gammed to do.' But then he said, 'You always have to change the
program. The machine will only produce accurate scrap. It is always
the programmer or the operator who have made an error, never the
machine. While there are these machines, the welders will always
have a job.' Management are thus dependent on the operators' use of
skill to ensure that scrap is not produced and quality is
maintained.

NC has brought interest into my life because it's new technology
to the likes of me as my previous experience is on older
machinery, very old. Suddenly you are given a brand new toy. It
gives me more responsibility. It might have saved my job. It's hard
to tell whether or not I have more job security.

For some, variety of work was increased. Operators enjoyed the
variety of work on the machines. 'Lots of different jobs come on to
the machine. They are all turning jobs but there are different metals
to work on, different radius's and the different jobs present different
problems.' The operator on the next machine agreed with his
neighbour's view. 'Work on here is more interesting, you are learning
new jobs, new techniques, how to read a program better. On here you
get a variety of jobs. On a conventional machine, not so much
important work came on. It is more interesting on here although the
machine can do the same work.' An operator on a different machine

said that he would not like to return to a conventional machine because he had more variety of work, as such small numbers of each component were allocated to his machine. 'I like the fact that it is only one's and two's off,' he said.

By this stage, it should be clear that there are no unilinear arguments to be found in the accounts which describe either degrading or regrading. While operators feel their jobs have been degraded, they are also seen as regraded or unchanged. The argument is, in part dependent on the work allocated to the particular machine, but even then the argument is not simplistic or unilinear. In the following account, you begin to realise the complexity of the arguments.

> If you've done one job and the tape is right, the jobs are all the same after that. It makes life easy. That is when I become a button pusher. That is a sign of the times. But very rarely do we have a proved tape. You need the basic skills of a borer, miller and driller to work one of these CNC machines. On top of that you need the capability to take in the knowledge of CNC and the controls. The old hands can't grasp the new jobs to do themselves. It is in your interest to work CNC because there is going to be a time when there are no conventional machines left.

Nowhere was the fact that jobs can be seen as simultaneously degraded and regraded so clearly demonstrated than in this account:

> You need an added skill to work on here, for working the computer itself. Down there you've got the skill, whereas when they put you on one of these, the actual skill has gone, the actual feel. You work in a thousandth of an inch. On a conventional machine you are putting that on by hand, whereas on here the computer puts that on. Saying that, I've got to feed the information into the computer and alter it through the computer. At the end of the day, that's all stored in the computer memory. Once this lot has been fed in, you can do a number of components with that memory. This can store my skill really, can't it? My skill is producing a component through that computer. On a conventional lathe, my skill produced a job. The computer down there was you. I stored that information for doing that job; that's where skill is. Now I've come up here, I can make a job and store it with the memory here and then make another one exactly the same by using a few switches and buttons.

He then spoke of how he felt he used more skill to produce the same component on a conventionl machine.

> In one way they are taking it [skill] off you, and then they are giving it you back, on this machine ... I never believed that they could make machines to do what I did down there. Now I've seen it for myself. I'm actually working it. At the end of the day, I'm really worn out and tired, (even more than on a conventional machine), even though I'm not physically making the component.

He still feels that he controls the machine. But the computer is seen as an intermediary between the use of the man's skill and the production of a component. Here the notion of re-skilling and de-skilling are represented in a complex form. Skill is acquired through training and resides in the person.

> This is an added skill because they had to retrain me. I reckon the skill I had won't be in practice all the time. I will always have the skill, but the future generation, they won't have the skill I had. Say, in few years' time, they had all CNCs and CNC operators, they will be working the computers to produce those components but they won't be producing that with their hands like the old conventional turners. Our skill will disappear.

The value of being trained under an apprenticeship, coupled with the experience of work on a conventional machine are seen to be invaluable training. Future generations will not be given the same training and the 'old' skills will be lost. 'It might be easier for the future kids to work on CNCs but when the problems arise, they won't know what to do.' Thus jobs will, in the future, be de-skilled.

The new CNC machine operators are, in the older operators' view, less skilled as they have been through a new, slightly shorter apprentice training programme and have not been allocated to a conventional machine before working on the CNC machines. In the older CNC operators' view jobs are being de-skilled but it would be difficult to argue this point objectively as the quality of the apprenticeship is the same and the apprentices are trained to use conventional machines. Over time, however, as there are fewer and fewer conventional machines, they may only be trained to use CNC machines and proved tapes and the new apprentices may be less skilled. Meanwhile, this is a social construction of skill where skill is seen to be greater for those older, more experienced CNC operatives, and there is a fear that this skill could be lost. They are using this social construction of skill to protect their jobs and enhance their status.

The new technology is accepted positively by some despite the degradation it can cause. Operators realise the necessity of the introduction of the technology to ensure the company's future. Using that technology can also help preserve their own future both in the company and in the labour market. The increased skill can be seen to give the operators an increased sense of their bargaining power. The added knowledge of CNC increases the value of their skills to be bought and sold in the labour market.

> CNC makes the job quicker. That's an advantage for the company. It's technology, something you have to do. Management did have to bring the technology in, and someone had to learn to use it. I was pleased to use it. I'd rather work on here than on a conventional machine. I have to think of my future.

Management appear to have been reasonably successful in making operators internalise the information they have given about the company's aims. The operators, while understanding these aims, also realise that they are not necessarily commensurate with their own interests and aims.

The CNC operators in the toolroom were particularly aware that the machine they operated might be better utilised in the production areas. The existence of the toolroom was under threat, they believed, because the Works Manager wanted to eliminate the need for a toolroom. While understanding this aim, and the advantages of CNC they could not, of course, agree with the proposal for their own redundancy, and they also wanted to protect others' jobs.

> CNC cuts the hours down on a job so it's got to be an advantage on cost. But you lose 5 skilled men for one machine. This machine will be the first to go if the redundancies go ahead because it would be better for production work. This machine does the job quicker and more accurately. There are loads of things the machine can do that management don't know about. We don't want people to go down the road. We don't just want to maintain our own position; we have to watch for others' jobs as well.

Management are telling you that you have to speed up production. But there is not enough work so what's the point of speeding
jobs up? We get bitter because the machines are not used properly
and the way we are treated as fodder. There will probably be a day
when I just watch 5 jobs on 5 machines; we'll just have routine
mundane jobs. If you take away people's usefulness, they
become apathetic.

Where operators have perceived and describe the negative effects of
the technological change on their jobs, they can be found to make
comment such as this. They perceive the inequality; they are on the
receiving end of the negative as well as the positive aspects of not
only technological change, but the employment relationship.

We have seen how the words 'manual' and 'physical' are often
used while describing that change. The words are often used to
describe men's, rather than women's work; it has gender connotations. But the word 'manual' takes on a different meaning in the
following context: 'We get the impression that we are the *low* ones,
being the *manual* workers. If we make a suggestion, it is not always
followed through. You ask anyone this, and they will tell you the
same.' This time the word is associated with status and recognition
and the new technology does not always enhance this despite the
fact that it could be argued that the skill that resides in the person
has been increased.

Where operators express dissatisfaction with management, they
can also be found to be resisting managerial control, particularly
when operators are being asked to use their new skills to enhance the
efficiency of the technology. There are a number of examples of
this.

If an error is found, by the operator, in the programme, he ought to
telephone the programmer from the foreman's office. They will then
go through the tape together and rectify the problem. The same will
happen if the operator disagrees with the stipulated speeds and
feeds. If the programmer is on holiday or if the operator is on a night
shift when there is no programmer available, he is allowed to alter
the programme without consultation. Sometimes the operator will
just alter the tape and tell the programmer when he sees him, even if
he was available. Sometimes they will just refuse to alter a tape until
a programmer appears. 'If there is a mistake [in the programme] it is
a matter of waiting an hour or so for the programmer to sort it out.'

This operator was asked if he could sort out the problem. 'I could, but we are not paid to do it, so we don't. If we did sort it out and made a bit of a goolie of it, we'd get dragged into the office for it.' The operators also realise the strength of their position in the employment relationship, in this particular company, and will wield this power to resist management's control.

If operators programmed their own machines, skill status would be enhanced further. At the moment, this does not seem likely to happen. One operator was interviewed while he was waiting for a programmer. 'Management want us to write our own programs eventually. We think we should get more money for it, but they don't. If they paid us extra money, I would do it.'

Operators are often found to have apprentices 'standing by'. The operators are supposed to train the apprentices to use the new technology. One operator spoke of how his apprentice had been standing by for 3 years. 'I wouldn't let him loose on it. The only way to learn is to use the machine.'

The new technology, to be used to its full capacity, requires some flexibility on the part of operators. If a CNC operator is off sick or on holiday, another CNC operator is needed to run the machine. As control panels differ from machine to machine, flexibility is reduced. Operators are very reluctant to learn how to use different control panels.

Operators are required to consent to managers' needs for high efficiency by not leaving their machines for any reason, apart from an official one, for example, going to collect tools. Tea breaks are unofficial. Operators resent this. Foremen allow some slack in order to allow for tea breaks. They also may tell the operator to 'go and hide somewhere' if their machine is down. Normally, if a machine is down the operator is required to 'look busy'. The official rules are not broken but bent in order to reduce the operators' frustration with the rules.

The frustration remains, reduced. As a result operators refuse to work overtime, for example weekends. One operator, having just complained about his lack of official tea break, said, 'I just want to get home and put my feet up. I can manage without the money.'

It must be noted that no one operator can be found to be presenting a one-sided case. No-one is arguing that the new technology has only served to degrade their job or re-skill it. A full analysis of all the data collected on how operators perceive the changes demonstrates evidence of both de-skilling and re-skilling. How then do we account for the fact that operators will systematically describe de-skilling with re-skilling or no change in skill in their accounts? The following is one explanation.

While operators understand and share management's interests in the employment relationship, they also realise that management interests should not be blindly accepted. A sharing, and therefore consent to managerial aims helps secure their future as employees of the company. They will argue the case for the acceptance and compliance of the new work organisation because the new skills associated with the new technology are highly valued skills both in the company and in the labour market. Management are, for the moment' dependent on the use of both traditional and CNC skills to produce the product faster and more accurately. Having operators with both sets of skills helps alleviate the problems that are encountered when first issue tapes are being used; when operators are required to work on different types of metals, to steady vibration, produce very small numbers of components of many different types high skill levels are required. Having, and utilising, these skills increases the status of the skills. CNC operators are raised above the level of the traditional operator. The older CNC operatives consider their skills to be superior to those of the younger CNC operatives. However the new CNC operatives are seen to be a threat.

On the other hand they will argue that CNC has degrading effects because they see the strength of their position in the employment relationship as threatened by the new technology and associated work organisation, as can be seen in the accounts of the degradation of work. Work has been de-skilled if that means, by definition, that the skills of the employee are carried into the machine, rendering one operator's work indistinguishable from the next. Potentially, control and responsibility for the work process schedules and standards can be removed and lodged in the programmed machine. The operators' position and strength in the employment relationship has been, and could be, further eroded. Employees do not always like or accept the way they are treated in that employment relationship and so they complain and resist various aspects of managerial needs for flexibility and increased performance.

The negative effects of the degradation have to be camouflaged to strengthen their position. Skill, its utilisation and skill levels have important implications for, not only status, but rewards, pay and employment opportunity.

Another, simpler explanation is that there are always two sides to every argument and the operators are just articulating both sides of the argument. The research method allowed for this; a more structured method may not have revealed such dualism in operators' accounts.

SUMMARY AND CONCLUSIONS

There is in the data some support for Braverman's de-skilling hypothesis. Work has been degraded as the task skills of execution are separated from those of conception; work has been divided between the operator and the programmer. Further, management's need for greater efficiency and productivity has meant that, for some, the variety of work has been reduced and a miller has found that he is now required to do what he, and other skilled men, regard as semi-skilled work, that of drilling. Some complain that decision-making, control over the machine and how the job is done, and variety of work has been reduced and so less skill is required. As a result some feel that there is less job interest, involvement and satisfaction. Some workers also experience a feeling of isolation.

Managers encourage Minimal Manual Intervention and have reduced the number of fitters employed. The potential exists for management to de-skill jobs further. If there were a larger catalogue of 'proved tapes', if the work allocated to machines could be further reduced in variety and if uncertainty could be eliminatd from the production process, craftmen's use of knowledge, responsibility and judgement could be reduced over time.

However, the trade union has negotiated that only skilled men operate CNC machines. This particular group of CNC operatives are relatively priveleged as they have secured higher earnings through their 'special machine rate' and may have a more secure position both in the company and the labour market. Their skill status has been enhanced due to the training given which enables them to operate and programme the machines. These skills are utilised to help reduce uncertainty in production. Managers are still dependent on the use of a craftman's skill.

Management's strategy concerning the organisation of work around CNC is not a coherent strategy; it contains contradictions.

These contradictions will remain unless management can reduce uncertainty in the production process and gain greater control.

It would appear to be imperative to distinguish between the degradation of work and the de-skilling of workers. As Burawoy (1979) notes, Braverman assumes that if management investigate and acquire knowledge of a production process, the workers are supposed to lose this knowledge and be incapable of regaining it. This is clearly not the case in this study. Job knowledge has both remained the same and been increased. The findings are consistent with those of Wilkinson (1983) where operators utilising the CNC were skilled men. The findings support Buchanan's (1985) hypotheses that skill and discretion will be retained where:

a) novel variations arise which planning and equipment alone cannot deal with;

b) technical designs assume the importance of skilled and motivated intervention to guarantee safe and effective performance;

c) the product range is broad, rapidly changing, novel, complex, of high value, high quality, produced in small batches, delivered to tight schedules, threatened by competitors.

Child (1984a) similarly argues that frequent batch changes, a high incidence of new work, and variability in materials and physical conditions, demand flexibility of response in production that requires human initiative, skill and competence.

How consistently and for how long operators can argue that jobs have been re-graded and re-skilled is dependent, in part, on the ability of the CNC operators to maintain or extend their status as skilled men in the face of technological change. Child *et al.* (1983) and Child (1984b) argue that the ability of occupational groups to maintain or extend their status in this situation depends on their 'strategic position' in the organisation which is dependent on the nature of the task they perform, ideological claims and their labour market position. In this company, as was the case in the company cited by Buchanan (1985), the task is, for most, complex and the cost of errors is high. Operators and their trade union representatives were able to argue that new jobs should rate highly in job evaluation. Management's reliance on the skills acquired in traditional craft training make it very difficult for them to use semi-skilled men to operate the machines.

The position adopted in this chapter is that ideological and political factors have affected the influence of technological change on skill, but that skill status is, however, under serious threat. That threat has become evident in operators' accounts of de-skilling and re-skilling. It is also evident in operators' accounts of how, while they understand management's aims and interests in introducing the technology, they also perceive a need to contest managerial interests in order to protect and strengthen their own. Managers need to harness the co-operation of the workforce and ensure that jobs are not threatened any further.

This chapter has reported the findings from one engineering company at one particular point in time. The findings on work organisation, for example, whether or not operators are allowed to change and edit tapes will differ from one company to another. In Wilkinson's (1983) study, operators had no programming training but of the eight operators, three were doing some programming and another four were tape editing. Jones (1982) found that, in four of his five companies, machine controls were locked. In some plants in Noble's (1979) study operators were not allowed to make their own tapes or edit tapes. This was also the case in the company which was chosen as a contrast for further research; semi-skilled men are used to operating CNC machines and jobs are extremely repetitive and monotonous. The work is simple. The operators use few of the craftman type skills. The job uses little job knowledge and allows virtually no autonomy. Operators are required to run two or more machines at a time. The job consists of loading the machine with a component, closing the machine's door, (unless the machine is automatically loaded), pressing a start button, then, when the machine's cycle finishes, unloading the component and beginning the cycle again. Operators also monitor machine tool tip wear and put 'off-sets' in the machine (alter the machine's co-ordinates), to allow for tool tip wear. When the tool tip is thoroughly worn, they change tool tips. Operators have had to agree to 'flexible' working which means there has to be no demarcation and they must perform 'unskilled' tasks, for example, clean around their machines at the end of the shift. This situation arose because managers found themselves in a position where they were able to make these demands as conditions of employment. They actively sought to de-skill jobs and the nature of the product allowed this to happen. (For a fuller description, see Wilson, 1987.)

Managers have choices concerning how the work should be organised around new technology. A key structural element of management is control but a pursuit of control objectives will, in some instances, conflict with strategic and operational objectives. This was the case in Odessy Engineering.

Workers' interests are also threatened and the workforce, if in a strategically strong position, will resist that control. Control strategies contain contradicitons. The structures and means of control are socially produced (Storey, 1985) and there is variegation in the means of this control to be found in the engineering industry. These contradictions and various strategies, in turn, are reflected in the way in which work is organised, which is then reflected in workers' responses to that work organisation. The whole process of experienced change has hinged on how it was decided and agreed to employ the new technology. The accounts of experienced change also contain contradictions. In the case of Odessy Engineering, jobs were experienced as both de-skilled and re-skilled. Whether or not this will be an enduring experience will depend on the future strategy adopted by management and the union's ability to modify or resist that strategy.

References

Braverman, H. (1974) *Labor and Monopoly Capital: The degradation of work in the twentieth century* (Monthly Review Press, New York).

Buchanan, D. A. (1983) 'Using the new technology: management objectives and organisational choices', European Management Journal, vol. 1, no. 2. pp. 70–79.

Buchanan, D. A. (1985) 'Canned Cycles and Dancing Tools: who's really in control of computer aided machinery?' Paper presented to the 3rd Annual Labour Process Conference.

Burawoy, M. (1979) *Manufacturing Consent* (University of Chicago Press, Chicago).

Child, J. (1972) 'Organisation structure, environment and performance: the role of strategic choice', *Sociology*, vol. 6, no. 1, pp. 1–22.

Child, J. (1984a) *Organisation: A Guide to Problems and Practice* (Harper and Row, London).

Child, J. (1984b) 'New technology and developments in management organisation', *Omega*, vol. 12, no. 3, pp. 211–33.

Child, J., Loveridge, R., Harvey, J., Spencer, A. (1983) 'Microelectronics and the quality of employment in service industries'. Paper presented to the British Association for the Advancement of Science Conference, Section X, August.

Giddens, A. (1982) 'Power, The Dialectic of Control and Class Structuration' in A. Giddens and G. McKenzie, (eds) *Social Class and the Division of Labour* (Cambridge University Press).

Jones, B. (1982) 'Destruction or Redistribution of Skills? The case of numerical control' in S. Wood *The Degradation of Work?* (Hutchinson, London).

Lee, D. J. (1981) 'Skill, craft and class: a theoretical critique and a critical case', *Sociology*, vol. 15, no. 1, pp. 56–78.

Leone, W. C. (1967) *Production Automation and Numerical Control*, Wiley, New York.

Littler, C. R., Salaman, G. (1982) 'Bravermania and beyond: recent theories of the labour process', *Sociology*, vol. 16, no. 2, pp. 251–69.

Lockyer, K. G., Oakland, J. S., Duprey, C. H. (1983) 'Work study techniques in U.K. industry', *Omega*, vol. 11, no. 3, pp. 293–302.

Noble, D. F. (1979) 'Social Choice in Machine Design: The case of automatically controlled machine tools', in Andrew Zimbalist (ed.), *Case Studies in the labour Process* (Monthly Review Press, London).

Storey, J. (1985) 'The means of management control', *Sociology*, vol. 19, no. 2, pp. 193–212.

Thompson, P. (1983) *The Nature of Work* (Macmillan, London).

Wilkinson, B. (1983) *The Shopfloor Politics of New Technology* (Heinemann Educational, London).

Wilson, F. M. (1987) 'Deskilling of Work?: The Case of Computer Numerical Control in the Engineering Industry'. To be published in J. McGoldrick (ed.) *Business Case File in Behavioural Science* (Van Nostrand Reinhold).

5 Managerial Strategies, Information Technology and Engineers

Gloria L. Lee

The engineering industry was one of the earliest users of computer based systems in the field of design, but during the 1960s these were mainly 'in house' systems developed by large organisations in the aerospace, automotive and shipbuilding industries. During the last decade with the microprocessor breakthrough, computer applications in design and manufacture have become commercially available and the development of 'turn-key' systems has significantly widened the potential user population.

Computer-based systems in engineering impact upon design, manufacture and scheduling and the relationship between these areas of work. Computer Aided Design (CAD) systems can transform the utilisation of skills and the structuring of work within the design function. The advent of Computer Numerical Control (CNC) and Direct Numerical Control (DNC) machines has created Computer Aided Manufacture (CAM), which is further advanced with the use of Robotics, Automatically Guided Vehicles (AGVs) and other types of computer controlled handling equipment which can be linked into Flexible Manufacturing Systems (FMS) to change radically the production environment. Computer linking across design and manufacturing systems is now taking place, variously called Computer Integrated Manufacturing (CIM) and Computer Integrated Engineering (CIE). These latest developments, cutting across traditional functional boundaries, have still further implications for the organisation of work and control of the labour process.

From the labour process perspective, implementation of information technology (IT) can affect the balance of control between capital and labour. Here managerial strategies for adoption, the response of labour faced with working with new technologies and the impact upon work in engineering are examined, focusing in particular upon the design function.

This chapter opens with an overview of the pressure upon capital in Britain to recognise IT as the key to regaining competitive advantage in world markets, and sets out the issues surrounding its adoption as a context in which to explore the interface between strategy and occupation. The significance of early experiences for managerial strategies are considered, including assumptions about worker resistance. The push towards more rapid technological change is related to some of the social science critiques of managerial strategies on work organisation, pointing to the danger that the human consequences of these changes can be submerged by the technological imperative. Engineers are identified as key providers of knowledge on which to base strategies and it is argued that they therefore need to be aware of the potential for a human-centred rather than simply a machine-centred approach.

PRESSURE FOR THE ADOPTION OF IT

Although there has been a rapid rise in the implementation of computer-based technologies during the 1980s, the level of usage in this country is still seen by many to be leaving Britain lagging behind her European neighbours in terms of competitive advantage. Harrison and Dunn, commenting on the National Economic Development Office's (NEDO) advanced manufacturing technology (AMT) study group report suggests that making a start on introducing AMT in a British batch production engineering firm can mean:

> no more than installing computerised inventory control.
> To its West German, Japanese or American competitor it might mean the implementation of a full-blown CADCAM system. (Harrison and Dunn 1986, p. 22)

Concern over the consequences of what is seen as the reluctance of British industry to invest is also, for instance, spelled out in the ACARD Report (1983) arguing that:

> too many companies had not yet applied AMT to their manufacturing process. These companies will become progressively less competitive and many will not survive the next ten years. (ACARD, 1983, p. 7).

Pronouncements of this sort are intended to spur management into rethinking its approach to work organisation. In doing so the pro-IT lobby extols its potential, laments the cautionary approach of British management, and emphasises the successful lead taken by those who do innovate.

The NEDO Report (1985) on AMT exemplifies the encouraging message to British engineering industry. The aim is to persuade British engineering manufacturing firms to move into AMT by citing case studies of the experiences of 40 firms who have adopted AMT. By implication job losses and de-skilling are not the issues, as it is claimed that the majority of these firms brought about the changes by retraining their existing employees, who were said to have welcomed the opportunity to learn new skills.

This hopeful message has been taken up by government, who have used this and other reports as the basis for a new drive to encourage investment in CADCAM, robotics and computer numerical controlled machine tools.

There are indications that the message is getting through, although not quickly enough from a competitiveness standpoint. For instance the Policy Studies Institute Report on micro-electronics uptake, which is a follow-up to a similar survey carried out by them two years before, shows that product applications of microelectronics have risen by almost 25 per cent, and their use in processes 'has soared by two-thirds'. Nevertheless the report also shows that the user rate for foreign-owned companies was well above that of British companies, a half of whom were not using microelectronics in their products or processes, and had no such plans to do so (Northcott and Rogers, 1984).

Commenting on this report, *The Engineer* added their own anecdotal evidence which confirms 'that ignorance of new technology is much more widespread than the hopeful pronouncements of government ministers would have us believe'. They explain:

We have, for example, been writing about flexible manufacturing systems for years. We have talked of computer numerical control and computer aided design and manufacture for the best part of a decade. Yet still when we mention fms or cadcam or cnc, we get phone calls from people who say they don't understand. (*The Engineer*, 8 March 1984, p. 5)

This comes as a very clear indictment of management and professional engineers from a leading journal for engineering management.

At the regional level the West Midlands County Council in a survey of AMT usage in the area also found that outside mechanical and electrical engineering, there was a considerable lack of awareness of AMT throughout the rest of West Midlands industry, with only the larger firms making installations (*The Engineer*, 7 August 1985).

If the prospects opened up by AMT are so promising, why then has British management apparently been slow to innovate? A number of reasons have been put forward for this apparent reluctance. The ACARD Report (1983), for instance, ascribes it to a lack of conviction amongst such firms of the vital importance of doing so. Another Policy Studies Report argues that although there is general awareness of the power of the silicon chip:

> many of those who take the management decisions in industry, commerce and other services appear to be still unaware of the scope for applications in their particular kind of activity. (Northcott, Fogarty and Trevor, 1985, p. 89)

Other explanations, however, suggest that management has been put off by early experiences which have not matched expectations and this is due to managerial as well as technical failures.

Voss discussing the 'failure' of new manufacturing technologies to realise full benefits, cites factors like the inappropriateness of traditional management approaches, failure to manage the learning process and inadequate management of the workforce. He argues that most organisations consider that implementation has been successful if the technical 'bugs' have been ironed out, the system is working reliably and there is high utilisation but this alone does not ensure realisation of the full potential of the technology. He calls for capacity and resources to be set aside to support the learning process for management and workers. He also argues that traditional mechanistic approaches to the management of the workforce based on Taylorism are inappropriate for new technologies which are characterised by uncertainty, low task definition and change (Voss, 1984, pp. 41-46).

Other factors associated with the gap between experience and expectations with AMT have been summarised by Johns (1985) as the lack

of technical knowledge and understanding amongst top management, a piecemeal approach, which sees the investment in isolation,
without appreciating the impact upon the rest of the organisation,
the failure to identify and evaluate alternative and cheaper courses
of action and ill-conceived systems that simply do not work. All the
above factors were identified within the NEDO Report (1985) on
advanced manufacturing technology which also stressed the in-
adequacy of training in unsuccessful ventures and the importance of
trade union support and co-operation.

It has also been argued that British reliance upon clear functional
specialisation provides an organisational environment which can
hinder successful innovation. In a review of the relationship between
organisational design and new manufacturing technologies, Child
points to the highly departmentalised functional structure of British
industry as inhibiting the full realisation of the potential of new
manufacturing technologies. He argues that to be consistent with
CADCAM's integrative capabilities there is a need for cross
functional teams with clear objectives and targets. His view is
optimistic, seeing new manufacturing technology (NMT) as offering
certain freedoms for organisation and task design, which could meet
the needs of people. He cautions that this takes time, as a wide
understanding of the nature of changing strategic contingencies and
their possibilities has to be created, through participation in
discussions concerning organisational changes. He also suggests
that an incremental approach with pilot projects would facilitate the
learning process (Child, 1987).

Expectations concerning likely reactions from organised labour
also influence managerial strategy for IT-based innovation.
Northcott. Fogarty and Trevor, reviewing trends in management
thinking and practice since the 1960s, argue that it rests on the
rationale that 'even in a time of recession unions and work forces
still have considerable power to obstruct change' (1985, p. 37).
Despite these concerns and various instances of organised opposition, they conclude that on the whole the industrial relations
situation has been 'a positive factor in the acceptance of new
technology at the workplace in Britain'. (1985, p. 66). Nevertheless
they caution that a greater impact upon work and employment,
which would accompany more widespread and advanced forms of
implementation, could lead to an upsurge in resistance.

The importance of consultation and information disclosure to
the workforce cited in the Northcott study is widely stressed in the

literature. For instance the Electronics EDC's Employment and Technology Task Force Report (NEDO 1983) on the introduction of new technology, which surveyed procedures used to introduce new technology, concluded that where consultation and information disclosure occurred early in the process of change, this was associated with improved industrial relations and co-operation for change.

A cautionary note of a different kind is contained in the Ingersol Engineers Report (1985) which warned that information technology is not the solution to everything for everyone. According to this account, Computer Integrated Manufacture and Flexible Manufacturing Systems are more a vision than a reality. The report also makes the point that the latest computerware is too often being used by British industry to solve problems which are the result of outdated manufacturing and business practices and this aggravates rather than resolves these problems.

Whilst strategic considerations of the impact of IT encompass a range of contingency aspects – the nature of the market and market share, product demand, investment considerations and the wider economic context – the focus here is upon the implications for work organisation, job and task design in engineering, as part of a broader perspective on innovation.

Whereas the political 'pro-IT' lobby in its enthusiasm to regenerate British industry stresses the technological imperative and plays down the negative social implications which can be associated with such changes, social science research provides some alternative perspectives.

Early forms of automation in manufacturing based upon the managerial and technicist principles of Scientific Management were challenged by the behavioural approach of the Human Relations School and its later developments, including the Quality of Working Life movement. These perspectives based upon theories of individual motivation and the need for self actualisation within work led to managerial prescriptions for new methods of work organisation including job rotation, job enlargement, job enrichment and more recently quality circles and autonomous work groups. Whilst these approaches drew attention to the human consequences of different forms of work organisation, as an interventionist strategy they have not had a widespread effect. As Kelly points out:

Judged by its scale, by the numbers of jobs 'enriched' in advanced capitalist countries in the post-war period, job redesign is not a particularly significant movement, as compared with say the spread of assembly lines and work study in the 1920s and 1930s. (Kelly, 1985, p. 30)

In the more recent social science critique of automation which has developed around the Labour Process Debate, some writers have focused on de-skilling and the intensification of work with the introduction of various forms of IT in engineering, as a new dimension to control of the labour process (e.g. Jones 1983; Wilkinson, 1983; Baldry and Connolly, 1984; Smith, 1984; Winch, 1984; Buchanan, 1985; F. Wilson, 1985).

As indicated in some of the earlier discussion of managerial strategy and IT, there have also been a range of recent studies relating to the engineering industry, the impact of IT and change, which focus on the strategy and technology rather than labour process issues (Arnold and Senker, 1982a & b; Northcott and Rogers, 1982, 1984; Incomes Data Services, 1983; R. A. Wilson 1984; Voss 1984; Arnold, 1984; Ingersol Engineers, 1985; NEDO, 1983, 1985; Technical Change Centre, 1986).

A number of commentaries also address questions of skills, deployment and the future of engineering work under technical change in the context of international comparisons. (Sorge *et al.*, 1983; Warner, 1984; Northcott and Rogers 1984; Northcott *et al.*, 1985; Streek and Hoff, 1983; Streek, 1985). This chapter draws on the different perspectives in an analysis of some of the changes which are taking place within the engineering industry, to draw out some of the human consequences of this type of technological innovation. This requires a recognition of the complexities of the relationship between strategy, occupation, technology and outcome.

ENGINEERS AND IT

Professional engineers have been at the forefront of the development of microelectronics on which information technology is based and they play a key role in both product and process innovations based upon these technologies. Whilst some engineers are involved in strategy formulation and implementation others within the technical skills hierarchy are experiencing these changes as the end user. Thus from different standpoints engineering occupations have a pivotal position within the process of technological change.

For instance, engineers as a broad occupational group provide a number of bridges between capital and labour. Technical occupations at craft, technician and professional engineering levels offer limited opportunities for advancement within their own skills category. Also, due to the differences in early training and entry points there is little movement upwards from craftsman or technician to that of professional engineer. Traditionally there have been separate apprenticeship schemes for craftsmen and technicians at the age of sixteen, whilst professional engineers have increasingly become a graduate occupation.

In contrast, in manufacturing industry management offers a number of career entry points, with prerequisites for entry based more upon experience than formal qualifications. Hence for engineers at different levels in the technical skills hierarchy there are opportunities for advancement through management. For instance craftsmen and to a lesser extent technicians have the opportunity to move into first line supervision positions and in the past in particular have then been promoted to management positions within the production function. In the case of professional engineers technical hierarchies are generally very limited and hence they too move into appropriate levels of management to gain career advancement.

Thus within management there are those at different levels who have been drawn from manual and technical-professional work, often bringing with them experiences as organised labour. The introduction of computer-based control systems are a costly and technically complex innovation for management and engineers are key providers of knowledge on which to base managerial strategies. The ways in which engineers and those drawn into management from this background perceive their relationship with capital will influence their role in strategy formulation, how they as work organisers use information technology and the impact that this will have upon the work of others, including engineers below them in the technical hierarchy.

SKILLS, TASK AND ORGANISATION

Technological change threatens the boundaries of role, task and skill and potentially their place within the division of labour. Skills, which are acquired through education, training and/or experience become the property of the holder and are the basis on which individuals sell their labour. Within the organisation, through the division of labour, skills are located within tasks, which are incorporated into the role structure of the organisation.

In the case of engineering, CAD for instance provides the engineering designer with a new tool which speeds up the design process and removes tedious operations. However, the innovation has consequences beyond the substitution of an electronic workstation for a drawing board. CAD influences the skill components of the work, the design task, the division of labour within design and with CIE/CIM the boundaries between design and production.

Cockburn (1985) examining the nature of skill amongst printers suggests that there are three aspects of skill, the personal, the technical and the political. Developing this distinction in relation to the impact of IT in engineering, aspects of skill which reside within the person, built up through training and experience, may become redundant with the introduction of new technology, as in the case of the draughtsperson's ability to produce immaculate drawings or the machinist's ability to work to close tolerances. Not only will the skill element within the task have changed but the division of labour and the associated role structure can change, as for instance in the design department where CAD workstations replace drawing boards and the design hierarchy becomes less apparent as detailed draughting is no longer an activity to be delegated by designers to draughtpersons.

There is then the technical aspect of skill as it relates to performing a particular task, which with computer applications, as in the case of CAD, makes the skill of drawing on a board redundant but will demand a new ability to design using a keyboard, other input devices and a visual display unit (VDU). If the managerial strategy is to retrain the existing drawing office personnel, this may give everyone the opportunity to enhance their skills and to become designers. However in practice this could be very difficult for those previously low down within the design hierarchy, whose skill is that of detailing rather than the conception of a design, and who have neither the earlier training nor the subsequent experience to facilitate such re-skilling. This can result in an elite group working with CAD and others, if they remain, becoming increasingly marginalised by being left to more peripheral activities like continuing to work on drawing boards on minor modifications to older designs.

Thirdly there is the socio/political aspect of skill which relates to the ability of organised labour to maintain recognition of a task as skilled, even when new methods of working have removed certain previously important technical components of skill in the task. Draughtspersons who for instance cannot adapt successfully to working with CAD may through union-management negotiation retain their skilled status and associated benefits and continue to work within the design area but their work has effectively been de-skilled as there is no longer a demand for their detailing skills.

Thus as automated techniques have become increasingly sophisticated following the development of microelectronics they have the potential not only to make some skills obsolete but also to create the basis for new skills and a changing structure of roles within the organisation. Where labour is organised it may for a time resist the introduction of new forms of work organisation, as occurred in the printing industry and in certain instances engineering. Alternatively negotiations may protect the jobs of members caught up in the changes but not the longer term prospects for that type of employment, as skills and tasks are made redundant by new technology.

The changes which are taking place, with the introduction of IT are therefore potentially far reaching in that they impact upon the skill components within work, the type and range of tasks demanded of the worker and the organisational structures in which these tasks are located. Task changes may be limited to certain groups within the specialism, as for instance when CAD is introduced on a limited scale, so that only certain types of specialist design work changes over to this sytem, with the bulk of the design office continuing to work in the traditional way.

In contrast, where CAD is part of a wider implementation strategy which is linked in the Computer Aided Manufacture this is likely to have far wider implications for the design of work. Here the traditional distinction between product and process design breaks down and new organisational forms are likely to be needed for effective implementation, with for instance the same design team developing a new product from conception through to execution.

CAD AND MANAGERIAL CONTROL

CAD also has implications for managerial control in that such systems can be used to increase the level of direct control over output. For instance, although the point is rarely stressed by software houses, with CAD, design office supervision can access every element of design, which every designer working on the system has produced. Further there is the capability of giving any degree of access to the total data base that is desired. For example a lower grade designer may only have access to that part of the data base that he or she has created. In turn the section supervisor may only have access to that part of the data base created within that section. Senior management on the other hand can have ready access to the whole data base, which creates the potential at least for much more detailed monitoring of work. Whereas time sheets entered manually are notoriously inaccurate and often resisted by designers, with the more sophisticated CAD systems, there is an accurate record of time taken and actions performed for all work stored in the journal file. This facilitates a much closer monitoring of performance and can lead to the intensification of work.

At the early stages of implementation of CAD systems, even if management favoured direct control methods, little may be made of such facilities, since it would be likely to prejudice acceptance by workers. In any case, management may well consider that a strategy of what Friedman (1977, 1985) refers to as 'responsible autonomy' is likely to create a more productive environment. Therefore although the technology permits such detailed monitoring, the strategy may be specifically to avoid implementing the full control made possible by the new system.

IMPLEMENTATION STRATEGY

The ways in which new technology is introduced within the organisation and implemented depend upon the particular managerial strategy. New technology opens up varying possibilities but in itself it does not determine the patterns of work or the consequences for workers. Managerial strategies for the introduction of computer-based innovations depend upon the reasons for contemplating change and a variety of other factors like existing organisational structures, management-labour and workforce relations and the control systems which are brought into operation in particular contexts.

Figure 5.1 indicates some alternative managerial strategies as they impact at the personal, technical and socio-political levels, with associated changes in skill, task and organisation, which can accompany the introduction of CAD.

In terms of skill changes, at the personal level the installation of CAD may mean re-skilling opportunities for workers, with the technology reducing the amount of tedious work. At the socio-political level these re-skilling opportunities may be offered to all members of the union whose members' jobs would otherwise be superseded. Alternatively some workers may be de-skilled, if technical change creates a new polarisation of skills. This may result in conflict, if the union whose members face de-skilling or perceive the threat of de-skilling, resist the introduction of the new technology.

In the area of task changes CAD can lead to task enlargement, with everyone in the design area being trained to use the electronic work stations and the union laying claim to the new tasks for their members. Alternatively tasks may be so reordered that some groups lose their specialism, with only an elite group using the work stations. It is also possible that the new tasks may be appropriated by another union or be undertaken by non-unionised labour. In terms of possible organisational changes accompanying the introduction of CAD, new style team working may be introduced, with everyone given designer status and rewards and the union fully consulted and involved in developing a strategy for change. An alternative approach could lead to the increasing marginalisation of certain groups of workers, e.g. those left on traditional drawing boards. This would lead to job losses over time, as the demand for work on manual boards diminishes. This situation could see a weakening of union power, especially if the marginalised groups were those previously most strongly unionised.

This typology illustrates possible alternative strategies and associated outcomes, which may be partially or more fully pursued by management, as illustrated in the discussion of the pilot fieldwork of a study of engineers and IT by the author and the findings of other researchers (see Figure 5.1).

CAD installations involve a substantial capital investment and the capital case made by management is normally in terms of the contribution to be made towards increased productivity. This may

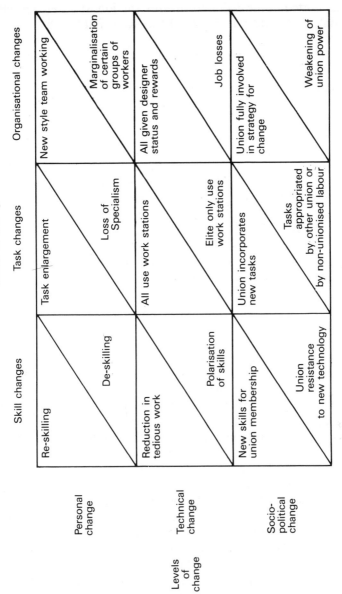

Figure 5.1 Some alternative outcomes with the installation of CAD

be supported by the claim that the installation will overcome labour shortages (Arnold and Senker 1982a & b; Baldry and Connolly, 1984).

Carnall and Medland discussing the productivity ratio, which they define as 'the time required to complete a task using CAD compared to manual methods', cite the Coopers and Lybrand and Ingersoll Engineers survey which reports productivity ratios varying from 1:1 up to 200:1. The report acknowledges that these claims are rarely supported by good evidence and estimate that in the UK it is difficult to operate a CAD/CAM system economically on a productivity ratio of less thatn 3:1 or on a single shift basis. The conclusion from Carnall and Medland is that 'benefits from CAD are too complex and interdependent to make justifications based on "productivity ratios" '(Carnall and Medland, 1984, p. 52).

For those destined to use the system, improved productivity carries with it connotations of job losses and redundancy (Arnold, 1984). The Incomes Data Services Report noted that between 1969 and 1980 the number of draughtsmen in the engineering industry had dropped by one third but argued that there were signs in some areas that the labour market for draughtsmen was becoming stronger.

The AUEW/TASS guide to negotiators on new technology makes the first priority that of protecting jobs (AUEW/TASS, 1978a). In an interview with a senior official of that union, as part of the early fieldwork of this study, the point was made that in Britain CAD has not led to redundancies, although there have been substantial declines in the size of draughting pools. A case at the Ford Motor Company was cited where the pool had reduced from 200 to 4 draughtspersons. The official acknowledged that some of his members were leaving the industry, others were absorbed through transfer, promotion within their organisation or natural wastage. The net result is that redundancies have been avoided but job losses have been substantial and the working life of all those within the design function has changed dramatically.

The views expressed by this official and by another within his union and one within ASTMS who were also interviewed are however all optimistic about the future and developments in IT, provided proper consultation takes place. The trade union movement has long been pressing employers over the need for consultative procedures in this area and white-collar trade unions in particular have been proactive concerning the implementation of new technology. AUEW/TASS produced a publication Computer Aided-Design in 1972 by Cooley. They held a conference in 1978 on the good and bad effects of micro-electronics with special reference to the impact upon employment in the engineering sector and published the proceedings. (AUEW/TASS, 1978b). The union now produces an Electronics Bulletin which monitors developments in IT.

The official cited above described his members as being 'in love with CAD'. He recounted incidents where the union had been pressing members to go for more pay if CAD was to be installed but his members 'resisted because they wanted universality of equipment – everyone wants to play with the new toy'. Whereas draughtspersons are the largest category of membership within AUEW/TASS, with professional engineers a smaller but growing membership, ASTMS claims to represent far more professional engineers than the other union. The official from ASTMS in interview also claimed that his members welcomed CAD, seeing it as making their jobs 'more efficient and interesting'. He stressed the need to see that machines are properly placed to 'meet human needs not machine needs'.

All the officials interviewed stressed the need to negotiate technology agreements in order to protect their membership. AUEW/TASS, together with ASTMS, APEX and NALGO have been at the forefront of negotiating technology agreements with employers (Williams and Steward, 1985). The NEDO Report on the introduction of new technology showed that although different benefits from technology agreements were identified by managers and trade union representatives, reactions were generally positive. The report also concluded that where consultation and information disclosure came early on in the process of change, this fostered co-operation and an improved industrial relations climate (NEDO, 1983, p. 16).

The productivity sought by management when introducing IT comes from a number of possible sources relating to task and organisational design. Cooley (1980) himself a designer and trade unionist points to ways in which the system can create a machine-centred task environment which stifles the creativity of the designer and codifies knowledge within the design process. If a machine-centred rather than a human-centred approach to implementation is taken he argues that this leads to de-skilling and the intensification of work.

Smith (1984) reports a case study of a small group of design engineers in an aerospace company in which he examines their

views on the potential impact of CAD. These designers, at the apex
of the design hierarchy, denigrated the status of drawing and saw
CAD as an opportunity to get rid of boring and routine work for
draughtsmen, freeing them for more creative tasks. In contrast
draughtsmen valued the drawing aspect of their work seeing their
task in holistic terms. Smith argues that it is the approach of such
designers towards the work of those below them in the design
hierarchy, which enables technical innovation to be pushed through
complete with negative consequences. His designers saw technical
change 'largely in straight capitalist terms of staying in the field by
keeping up with or ahead of the firm's competitors' (Smith, 1984,
p. 13). The designers saw their role as pushing for the full introduction of CAD in the face of a backward management.

The Smith study was at the very early stages of the introduction of
CAD into the organisation. The Baldry and Connolly (1984) study of
CAD and the organisation of the drawing office surveyed 7 major
CAD users in central Scotland. Like Smith, they draw upon insights
from Cooley, on the introduction of CAD systems which he predicted
would lead to the intensification of the work of draughtsmen. Baldry
and Connolly characterise the work of the draughtsman as a 'white-
collar craft'. They argue that specialisation within the drawing
process and the associated decline in the opportunity for individuals
to identify with a particular piece of work had been taking place long
before the arrival of CAD. They question whether:

> CAD should be seen as a further step along the road of functional
> specialisation, or whether it offers a means of bringing back into
> the job some of the skills and responsibilities previously lost.
> (Baldry and Connolly, 1984, p. 5)

Their empirical evidence however indicated both de-skilling and the
intensification of work, in that CAD led to further loss of autonomy
and control for the draughtsman, accompanied by an increase in the
pace of work and the introduction of shiftworking in order to
maximise the working day. They also concluded from these early
applications of CAD that craft control can be the first to go when for
instance, tape libraries of standard components are built up.

In terms of managerial strategy and control the introduction of
shiftworking with CAD helps to keep down the size of the initial
investment, as the use of workstations is shared, thus raising the
utilisation of capital. Even in an installation which has largely

replaced the use of drawing boards there is considerable potential for sharing workstations.

At one organisation visited 40 designers were sharing 8 workstations prior to the introduction of a shift system. This required a new approach to the design task and a radical change in the working environment, not least because engineers' work no longer centred on their own board, instruments, etc. The company have taken the opportunity with these changes to foster a new image of design work. Trade union organisation had broken down following a spate of earlier redundancies and has not re-established itself in the design area. The company call everyone in the design area designers and treat them as professional engineers, thus distancing them from the image of the former TASS organised draughtsmen. As part of this strategy management maintain close communications with the engineering department and ensure that they are aware of any discussion or negotiations which are taking place with union organised labour in other areas. At the time of interview they were moving towards shift working in the engineering area and the manager was confident that there would be no opposition, as they had a 'flexible' approach to pay and hours. The shift pattern would be 6–2, 2–10 and a normal day shift, with the latter not working on CAD that week. The system would provide task variety in a context of intensification of work and high capital utilisation.

Friedman (1985) articulates the concept of managerial control (which may be direct or towards responsible autonomy) in terms of task organisation, control structures, employment relations and lateral relations. In terms of Friedman's typology, managerial strategy in this company was in the direction of responsible autonomy, with changes in the task organisation, some aspects of the control structure, industrial relations and lateral relations. The nature of the task had changed, as had its organisation, the control structure emphasised the professionalism of engineers and collective consciousness had given way to an elitism which distanced the engineers from organised labour within the firm.

The introduction of CAD in the above instance contrasted strongly with the situation in another organisation, which had a much longer experience of the use of CAD. Here the installation had been made in a room off the main drawing office. Under agreements with AUEW/TASS all their members were to be trained on the system but the utilisation level was low and the organisation of the design area remained largely unchanged. There appeared to be a lack of commitment to the system at the level of supervision and therefore little encouragement to extend usage beyond those who were attracted to the new medium. At one stage the company had considered shift working but union demands concerning the level and extent of shift premiums were seen as making implementation unviable. In this company CAD existed alongside traditional design activities and had brought little or no changes in work organisation.

In a third organisation where interviews took place, CAD had been up and running for a number of years but is now beginning to integrate with CAM to establish a system of what the company described as computer integrated engineering (CIE). Previously tool engineering and assembly design had been separate tasks with designers specialising in one or the other area. The rhythm of the work was different between the specialisms, especially in terms of the peaks in demand for tool work compared with assembly. At that time, there was no shift system in operation in design engineering.

A major change in work organisation has come with the introduction of CAD cells consisting of 4 workstations used by 6 designers per shift. The cell covers both tool and assembly design with engineers moving towards a situation where they design in either area instead of specialising. From the management standpoint there is clearly much better utilisation of capital but there has also been a major change in the utilisation of labour, with the new system fostering polyvalent skills rather than the de-skilling of engineers. The sharing of tasks within the cell enlarged the job of designers and fostered a team approach. Peaks in demand which previously involved uneven work demands are now absorbed within the pattern of working of the cell. These changes have involved an extensive programme of training which has enhanced the skills of design engineers. As a result it has improved the market position of the engineers and the company lose a proportion of these trained people to other manufacturers and to the software houses.

The introduction of the CAD cells has not just changed the task and organisational environment of design engineers. One of the managers interviewed described the cell as 'like a magnet pulling all other things to it'. Process planning used to be a separate department and prior to these developments career progression for design engineers meant moving 'up' into process planning but now process engineers are joining the cell. Also NC programming is being done in the cell and estimating is foreseen as becoming part of the cell too in the near future.

This approach to the implementation of CAD has certainly enlarged the job of engineers and could be seen as having enriched the work as well. It has improved their place within the external labour market but does not appear to have altered their position within the internal labour market substantially, although there has been some upgrading of engineers as a result of CAD developments.

The major organisational change has been in the breaking down of boundaries between specialist tasks through the team working concept of the cell and other associated roles. Not everyone has moved into the cells, as there are also specialist design teams servicing four cells, consisting of experienced people who do not have CAD skills but who, from their experience in design over the years, are able to advise the cell engineers on certain aspects of design. This is essentially a mechanism for ensuring that components of design skill, many of which are least easily codified, are retained as new skills develop out of the task reorganisation and the utilisation of new technology.

The industrial relations aspects of this reorganisation appear to point to a weakening of union influence, as the union were attempting to negotiate better terms for the introduction of shift working but their members signed up and moved over to shift working before the negotiations were completed. Since that time the centrality of union influence appears to have diminished, reflected for instance, in a comment that the negotiating committee were 'no longer mixed up in the day to day issues'.

A study of the implications of CAD in firms in Germany by Wingert, Duus, Rader and Riehm considered both technical and human resource aspects of the applications. The English summary of the book together with earlier articles provide a number of insights into strategies of implementation and the consequences of CAD for job design (Rader 1982a & b; Rader and Wingert, 1983;Wingert, Rader and Riehm, 1981; Wingert, 1983; Riehm and Wingert 1983; Duus and Radar, 1983). Commenting upon managerial strategies, these researchers state that in only four cases were there what could be called 'long-term and deliberate approaches to introduction and the decisions involved' (Wingert, Duus, Rader and Riehm, 1984, p. 3 summary). They also pointed out that training schemes were unmethodical and there was an underestimation of the time and organisational effort required before the scheme was fully operational. Looking at industrial relations aspects, in many cases they found strained relationships with Works Councils and what they identified as misapprehensions on both sides of the other's position.

In terms of job and organisational design, the German researchers found considerable variability. For instance:

> If a CAD-programme with a limited function is applied within a context where the CAD application is a service for design groups, the range of activities grows narrower and requirements regarding knowledge and experience are reduced. Difficulties in the application of programmes lead to 'better' staff being trained as CAD-users. Minimal changes in activities and qualifications may be observed when CAD merely supports segments of existing activity and no new organizational forms are created for the application. (Wingert *et al.*, 1984, p. 6 summary)

These findings reinforce the argument that the likelihood of de-skilling is dependent upon the approach to implementation but their statement appears to imply that the absence of organisational change accompanying implementation may avoid de-skilling. In the cell development cited above however, organisational change is clearly in the direction of enlarging the skills of the whole design office but again this depends upon the wider context in which technological change takes place.

In a number of areas of engineering in Britain there has been a tradition of sub-contracting design work and of self employed designers and draughtpersons. The adoption of CAD systems introduces another dimension to these arrangements, especially where systems have to be compatible with client firms, as the capital cost is very high, especially for small operations.

A design agency studied during the current research operates on the 'flexible firm' principle, with core and peripheral workers (Loveridge, 1983a & b; Atkinson, 1985). The agency has designers working on CAD together with a traditional design office. Whereas the CAD designers are employees, those in the traditional drawing office are all self employed and manual workers in other parts of the company are also contract labour. This system enables the agency to keep down their operating costs, to tender successfully in a very competitive market and to develop further their CAD investment. In the case of their primary internal workers, the CAD designers, half of them had been trained by the company. The national shortage of CAD trained designers led this agency to find ways of keeping its core workers after training and they did so by holding back a proportion of the CAD designer's salary for eighteen months which if they stayed with the company they would receive in a lump sum. The designers accepted the scheme as a means of enforced saving and the company gained working capital to finance the business.

Whereas the subcontract employees worked normal days, the CAD designers were employed on shifts to avoid expensive capital equipment lying idle. The manager interviewed made the point that whereas depreciation on a drawing board runs at 50p per hour, on a CAD workstation it is £50 per hour, hence they cannot afford to have one idle. Managerial strategy in this organisation has created a highly segmented labour force which relies heavily upon the cash nexus to keep its employees, with the flexibility apparently required by management to respond to the market, bought at the price of the loss of job security for the majority of employees.

CONCLUSIONS

The case for the adoption of IT pressed by government and equipment suppliers gives little recognition of the implications of adoption for the actual users or for the significance of such aspects for successful implementation. This chapter has considered these issues in the context of engineering, drawing on a growing body of social science literature concerned with the impact of this new technological revolution, together with some findings from a pilot study of engineers and IT.

The apparent slow take up of IT by British management in comparison with overseas industrial competitors has been considered in relation to the human capital consequences of such innovations. The issues have been conceptualised in terms of managerial strategies and their impact upon the labour process and explored in the context of the introduction of CAD and the work of engineers.

The implementation of CAD requires a substantial capital investment, and a technology driven managerial strategy towards such innovation leads to a machine-centred rather than a human-centred approach. Engineers, particularly those at the higher levels of the technical hierarchy, are key providers of technical knowledge to inform implementation decisions. Also management hierarchies have traditionally provided career advancement for engineers in industry. Consequently as an occupational group they are strategically placed within the ranks of capital to influence the ways in which IT is implemented, whilst others lower down the technical hierarchy are at the forefront of those faced by changes in the organisation of their work, due to the introduction of computerised systems.

Here the strategy behind implementation decisions has been considered in relation to new forms of work organisation, which vary in their impact upon skills, tasks and the design of work and the implications of the strategy for managerial control and the responses of labour. Neither de-skilling, job losses, the intensification of work nor indeed worker resistance are the inevitable consequence of computerisation in engineering but a function of managerial strategy and hierarchical and lateral relationships within the organisation.

For those working in design, CAD may provide the opportunity for re-skilling, task enlargement and flexible specialisation within a new structure of work organisation. These changes may be open to all those within the design office or they may be restricted to an elite group, with others experiencing deskilling, loss of their specialist tasks and a position of increasing marginalisation, as work shifts away from traditional draughting. CAD removes many of the more tedious and routine tasks within design but it can also lead to the intensification of work, with expectations of higher productivity to justify the investment.

In the field of engineering design, the major union AUEW/TASS (now TASS) has generally accepted the introduction of CAD, negotiating for all their members to be trained in the necessary skills to work with the new system. Where a union resists the introduction, members may leave, if they themselves favour the innovation, which will weaken or destroy union power in that setting. There is also the possibility of a rival union taking over the work, which is a further factor which favours acceptance.

Material from a series of cases has been used to illustrate some of the processes involved with the introduction of CAD and the variability of outcomes. In some organisations, for instance, introducing CAD has only affected the tasks of a minority of designers and draughtspersons and control structures, work organisation and employment relations have been little disturbed.

This approach to innovation contrasts with that of another organisation where the introduction of CAD has been part of a control structure which fosters 'professionalism' amongst designers as part of a strategy to avoid reunionisation. Here there is little distinction in terms of a design hierarchy, with everyone treated as designers and using workstations instead of drawing boards.

This differs from more traditional design offices where the tasks of designers and draughtspersons are clearly delineated and yet again with the CAD agency cited where CAD designers had quite different employment contracts to those in the traditional drawing office, which provides a further dimension to segmentation within design.

The impact of computerisation has differed between engineering specialisms. The spread of CAD in tool design has generally been more rapid than in the area of product design but the most radical influence of IT so far has come with the introduction of computer integrated manufacturing, which integrates design and production. Winch (1984) has argued for a matrix organisational structure to accommodate the linking of CAD and CAM. However, whilst the matrix allows for a cross-cutting of activity, it does not necessarily provide the flexibility that CIM demands. The cell concept described earlier offers an alternative and potentially more radical approach. A development of this sort challenges the whole concept of traditional functional boundaries, changing job and task design and fostering flexible specialisation.

Despite apparent concern by management over worker resistance to IT, it is argued here and elsewhere that with certain exceptions, particularly in the early days of the introduction of CAD, the trade union approach to new technology has been generally positive, provided certain safeguards are incorporated. The movement presses for consultation at the planning stage of an implementation strategy and a cogent case can be made for the involvement of the end user at this stage to heighten acceptance and to draw upon the tacit knowledge and skills of the workforce. This however, is not easy to achieve, unless management is ready to recognise the value of this contribution, as unions may lack the resources to prepare a detailed alternative strategy. There can also be difficulties for the labour movement in presenting a cohesive approach, when the impact differs for members of different unions within a plant.

Whilst the evidence of job losses associated with the introduction of IT is now well documented, some respondents in this study made the distinction between job loss and 'people loss' in their organisation. The introduction of computerisation in both design and production has raised the productivity of individuals and therefore fewer are required for the same level of output. In some organisations 'people loss' is avoided however, by increasing output and creating jobs in other areas.

Where the capital cost of new technology is high, as in the case of CAD, the pressure for intensification of usage is considerable and this has led to the introduction or reintroduction of shift working. In a number of cases this has been resisted by engineers through collective action but the opportunity for higher earnings and or the attractions of a 'high tech' working environment has tended to lower resistance to these changes in work organisation and the practice of shift working in the computerised design area is growing.

The review of research literature and commentaries together with preliminary field work all point to the potential for variable approaches to the introduction of IT in engineering. Whilst there are threats to the quality of working life, these are not the inevitable consequences of a particular technology. Rather they depend upon the approaches of capital and labour in particular historical and cultural contexts. There are choices to be made but these have to be recognised and articulated and professional engineers in senior technical posts and in management, are an occupational group well placed to make explicit the choices open to management. This would require an interventionist role by engineers as work organisers in both corporate and company strategy, which went beyond technical rationality to combine a human centred perspective, with their more traditional machine centred approach, recognising the implications for both lateral and hierarchical relationships and the impact of job and task design upon the end user.

References

Advisory Council for Applied Research and Development (1983) *New Opportunities in Manufacturing – The Management of Technology* (London, HMSO).
Arnold E. (1981) 'The Manpower Implications of Computer Aided Desgn in the U.K. Engineering Industry' in *BCS '81: Information Technology for the Eighties,* proceedings edited by Parslow R. D. (London, Heyden & Son) pp. 148–58.
Arnold E., Senker P. (1982a) *Designing the Future – Implications of CAD interactive graphics for employment and skills in the British Engineering Industry,* Engineering Industry Training Board Occasional Paper, no 9.

Arnold E., Senker P. (1982b) 'Computer-aided Design in the U.K. Engineering Industry' in *CAD '82 Proceedings of the 5th International Conference on Computers in Design Engineering* (IPC, Science and Technology Press).

Arnold E. (1984) 'The Draftsman's Contract', *CADCAM International*, Feb. pp. 20–21.

Atkinson J. (1985) 'The Changing Corporation' in Clutterbuck D. (ed.) *New Patterns of Work* (Aldershot, Gower) pp. 13–34.

AUEW/TASS (1978a) *New Technology; A Guide for Negotiators* (Richmond, AUEW-TASS) October.

AUEW/TASS (1978b) *Computer Technology and Employment* (NCC Publications and AUEW/TASS).

Baldry C., Connolly A. (1984) 'Drawing the Line – Computer Aided Design and the Organisation of the Drawing Office', *UMIST/ASTON Organisation and Control of the Labour Process, Second Annual Conference*, March.

Buchanan D. A. (1985) 'Canned cycles and dancing tools: who's *really* in control of computer aided machining?' *UMIST/ASTON Organisation and Control of the Labour Process 3rd Annual Conference*, April.

Carnall C. A. and Medland A. J. (1984) 'Computer-Aided design: social and technological choices for development' in Warner M. (ed.) *Microprocessors, Manpower and Society* (Aldershot, Gower) pp. 49–65.

Child J. (1987) 'Organizational Design for Advanced Manufacturing Technology' in Wall T. D., Clegg C. W. and Kemp N. J. (eds.) *The Human Side of Advanced Manufacturing Technology* (London, John Wiley) pp. 101–33.

Cockburn C. (1985) 'The nature of skill: the case of the printers' in Littler C. R. (ed.) *The Experience of Work* (Aldershot, Gower) pp. 132–40.

Cooley M. (1972) *Computer aided design* (London, AUEW/TASS).

Cooley M. (1980) *Architect or Bee? The Human/Technology Relationship* (Slough, Langley Technical Services).

Duus W. and Rader M. (1983) 'The tightrope act of proving effectiveness – some results on CAD'. Paper presented at the *First International Conference on Computer Applications in Production and Engineering CAPE '83*, Amsterdam, April.

Friedman A. L. (1977) *Industry & Labour, Class Struggle at Work and Monopoly Capitalism* (London, Macmillan).

Friedman A. (1985) Managerial Strategies, Activities, Techniques and Technology: Towards a Complex Theory of the Labour Process, *UMIST/ASTON Organisation and Control of the Labour Process Third Annual Conference*.

Harrison M. and Dunn J. (1986) 'AMT; failing to redraw the map of UK industry', *The Engineer*, 20 Feb., pp. 22–23.

Hartmann G., Nicholas I. J., Sorge A., Warner M. (1984) 'Consequences of CNC Technology: a study of British and West German manufacturing firms' in Warner M. (ed.) *Microprocessors, Manpower and Society: A Comparative Crossnational Approach* (Aldershot, Gower) pp. 3ll–25.

Incomes Data Services (1983) *Draftsmen and CAD*, Income Data Services Study, no. 301, Nov.

Ingersoll Engineers (1985) *Integrated Manufacture* (London, IFS Publications).

116   *Strategies, Information and Engineers*

Johns T. (1985) 'Strategic Planning for AMT', *Innovation and Management,* Autumn pp. 23–29.

Jones B. (1983) 'Destruction or redistribution of engineering skills: the case of numerical control' in S. Wood (ed.) *The Degradation of Work?* (London, Hutchinson) pp. 179–200.

Kelly J. (1985) 'Management's Redesign of Work: Labour Process, Labour Markets and Product Markets' in Knights D. *et al. Job Redesign: Critical Perspectives in the Labour Process* (Aldershot, Gower) pp. 30–51.

Loveridge R. (1983a) 'Labour Market Segmentation and the Firm' in Edwards J. *et. al. Manpower Strategy and Techniques in an Organizational Context* (London, John Wiley) pp. 155–75.

Loveridge R. (1983b) 'Sources of diversity in internal labour markets', *Sociology* 17 (1) Feb. pp. 44–62.

National Economic Development Office (1983) *The Introduction of New Technology,* Electronics Economic Development Committee, Employment and Technology Task Force (London, National Economic Development Office).

National Economic Development Office (1985) *Advanced Manufacturing Technology; The Impact of New Technology on Engineering Batch Production* (London, National Economic Development Office).

Northcott J., Marti J., Zeilinger A. (1981) *Microprocessors in Manufactured Products* (London, Policy Studies Institute) Nov.

Northcott J., Rogers P. (1982) *Microelectronics in Industry: What's Happening in Britain* (London, Policy Studies Institute) Mar.

Northcott J., Rogers P. (1984) *Microelectronics in British Industry: the Pattern of Change* (London, Policy Studies Institute) Mar.

Northcott J., Fogarty M., Trevor M. (1985) *Chips and Jobs: Acceptance of New Technology at Work* (London, Policy Studies Institute).

Northcott J., Rogers P., Knetsch W., De Lestapis B. (1985) *Micro-electronics in Industry – An International Comparison, Britain, Germany, France* (London, Policy Studies Unit).

Rader M. (1982a) 'The Social Effects of Computer-Aided Design: Current Trends and Forecasts for the Future' in Bannon L., Barry U. and Holst O., (eds) *Information Technology Impact on the Way of Life* (Dublin Tycooly International Publishing Limited) pp. 168–81.

Rader M. (1982b) 'Managing the Introduction of CAD into the Design Office' *Second European Conference on Computer Aided Design (CAD) in Small and Medium Size Industries,* Paris.

Rader M., Wingert B. (1981) *Computer Aided Design in Great Britain and the Federal Republic of Germany – Current Trends and Impacts* (Kernforschungszentrum, Karlsruhe) Sep.

Riehm U., Wingert B. (1983) 'Technology induced morphogenesis of skills: the case of CAD' *First International Conference on Computer Application in Production and Engineering,* Amsterdam, Apr.

Senker P. (1984) 'Training for Automation' in Warner M. (ed.) *Microprocessors, Manpower and Society : A Comparative Cross National Approach* (Aldershot, Gower) pp. 134–46.

Smith C. (1984) 'Design Engineers and the Capitalist Firm' *Work Organisation Research Centre Working Paper Series.* Aston University, Nov.

Sorge A., Hartmann G., Warner M., Nicholas I. (1983) *Microelectronics and Manpower in Manufacturing* (Aldershot, Gower).

Streek W. (ed.) (1985) *Industrial Relations and Technical Change in the British, Italian and German Automobile Industry, Three Case Studies.* International Institute of Management Labour Market Policy Discussion Paper 83–5 Berlin, Aug.

Streek W., Hoff A. (1983) 'Manpower Management and Industrial Relations in the Restructuring of the World Automobile Industry', *International Institute of Management Labour Market* Policy Discussion Paper 83–5 Berlin, Dec.

Technical Change Centre (1986) *Advanced Manufacturing Technology in the Small Firm* (London, Technical Change Centre).

Voss C. A. (1984) 'Management and the new manufacturing technologies', unpublished paper, *Australian Graduate School of Management* (Kensington, New South Wales).

Warner M. (1984) *Organizations and Experiments: Designing New Ways of Managing Work* (Chichester, John Wiley).

Wilkinson B. (1983) *The Shopfloor Politics of New Technology* (London, Heinemann).

Williams R., Steward F. (1985) 'Technology agreements in Great Britain: a survey 1977–83,' *Industrial Relations Journal* 16 (3) Autumn, pp. 58–73.

Wilson F. (1985) 'Computer Numerical Control and Constraint', *Organisation and Control of the Labour Process – 3rd Annual Conference Report.*

Wilson R. A. (1984) 'The Impact of Information Technology on the Engineering Industry', *University of Warwick Institute for Employment Research, Coventry.*

Winch G. (1984) 'Organisation design for CAD/CAM' in Winch G. (ed.) *Information Technology in Manufacturing Processes, Case Studies in Technological Change* (London, Rossendale) pp. 57–71.

Wingert B. (1983) 'Old Imperatives for the Design of CAD Systems and Recent Applications – Some Empirical Evidence for a Gap'. Paper presented at the *APS Workshop on Humanisation of Working Life* (Stavanger, Norway) Nov.

Wingert B., Duus W., Rader M., Riehm U. (1984) *Computer Aided Design in Mechanical Engineering: Impacts, Potentials and Risks* (Heidelberg, Berlin, Springer-Verlag).

Wingert B., Rader M., Riehm U. (1981) 'Changes in Working Skills in the Field of Design Caused by the Use of Computers' in Mermet J. (ed.) *CAD in Medium Sized and Small Industries* (Amsterdam, North-Holland Publishing Company).

6 Information Technology and the Control Function of Supervision

Patrick Dawson

INTRODUCTION

The ability of computer systems to rapidly process and transmit large quantities of operating information over dispersed geographical areas has important implications for supervision and management control of the labour process (Child, 1984, p. 258). The characteristics of this technology provide management with the opportunity to incorporate into the machine elements of control associated with directing, monitoring and evaluating production operations (Edwards, 1979, pp. 18–162). Such an application of new technology may serve to reduce managements' dependence on hierarchical control structures, and thereby alter the dimensions and combination of other control systems within the organisation (Thompson, 1983, p. 152). The options open to management include: devolving additional elements of control to the local level and enhancing the role of the supervisor; concentrating control at a higher level of management and eroding personal supervisory control mechanisms; replacing the traditional role of the supervisor with a computerised system of control (Dawson and McLoughlin, 1986). It has thus been suggested that computer technology may necessitate a reconstruction of line management (Buchanan, 1983, p. 79) and a redefinition of the supervisory function (Dawson, 1986a).

This chapter considers the implications of information technology for the control function of supervision. The first section reviews the debate on the relationships between management control systems and supervision. In section two the concept of supervision is reappraised, and the criteria for identifying and defining supervisors are outlined. This revised concept of supervision is then used in an empirical case study which examines the effects of information

118

technology on supervision, work organisation and management control in a number of railway freight marshalling yards. The chapter concludes by claiming that computer technology is likely to lead to a far more complex redefinition of supervisory control than is implied by simply pointing to changes in the traditional labour control function of first-line supervision.

MANAGEMENT CONTROL SYSTEMS AND SUPERVISION

Since Braverman (1974), a number of labour process theorists have noted a continual erosion of supervisory decision-making responsibility within the management function (e.g. Armstrong, 1983, pp. 339–50; Child, 1985, p. 115; Knights and Collinson, 1985, p. 213). The diminution of the role of the supervisor as a shopfloor disciplinarian and labour controller is seen to stem from changes in the functional organisation of work, and the post-war growth in the collective organisation of employees and the power of the shop steward (Child, 1975, pp. 73–4). The tendency for the traditional labour control function of supervision to become increasingly peripheral to production is seen to be reinforced by the actions of senior management who introduce more sophisticated mechanisms of control into the labour process (e.g. Edwards, 1979). These refined and less obtrusive control systems provide alternative forms of work organisation in which supervisors are no longer the main instrument of management in the direct control of labour activities, as the labour control function of capital is increasingly incorporated into bureaucratic and/or technical systems of control (Braverman, 1974, p. 195). Essentially, it is claimed that:
• the variability of labour poses itself as a recurrent managerial problem, and increasing control over the predictability of labour is a central managerial objective (Clegg and Dunkerley, 1980, p. 364);
• new technologies are introduced and used by management as systems of control which replace traditional modes of supervision. New technology is thereby seen to eliminate and/or erode the traditional function of supervision (e.g. Child and Partridge, 1982; Leavitt and Whisler, 1958).
If these claims are justified, then it poses the question as to whether there is a role for the supervisor following the application of information technology to the control of the labour process. To illustrate this it is worth looking in some detail at Edwards (1979), who identifies

three elements essential to the control of labour, namely:
- directing the activities of labour;
- monitoring the activities of labour;
- disciplining the non-compliance of labour (1979, p. 18).

According to his historical analysis, the systems of control used by management to co-ordinate these three elements have undergone fundamental changes. Edwards argues that it is possible to discern a typology of systems of control which have evolved as a result of conflict and contradiction in the capitalist enterprise, that is, from simple forms of personal control systems (entrepreneurial control and hierarchical control) to structural systems of control (technical control and bureaucratic control) (1979, pp. 25–162).[1] He suggests that under the personal control systems of the nineteenth century, the supervisor held a pivotal position as a managerial agent of labour control. The main function of supervision was to direct, evaluate and discipline labour with the objective of ensuring that workers worked. As Edwards (1979, p. 33) noted: 'power was unmistakably vested in the person of supervisor'.

With the growth in the size of businesses in the twentieth century and the increased need to co-ordinate spatially dispersed areas of operation, more formalised methods of control were developed. Management formulated and implemented sets of rules and disciplinary procedures. These impersonal bureaucratic control methods had the advantage of being less visible to workers whilst resolving the problem of shopfloor conflict between workers and their autocratic supervisors. The other structural method which management have employed is technical control through the introduction of modern technologies. For example, Edwards (1979, p. 119) argues that the introduction of assembly-line technology enabled management to eliminate direct supervision which had highlighted the class division at the workplace:

> The substitution of technical for human direction and pacing of work simultaneously revolutionised the relation between foreman and workers . . . In effect, the line eliminated 'obtrusive foremanship', that is close supervision in which the foreman simultaneously directed production, inspected and approved work, and disciplined workers.

Whilst technical control incorporated the elements of direction,

Edwards (1979, pp. 120–2) recognised that foremen on the assembly-line still held important positions as 'inspectors', with responsibility for maintaining product standards and detecting inadequate work. He claims that the job of the foreman was transformed to a monitoring job and hence, was no longer concerned with the initiation and control of job tasks (the pace and pattern of work being set by the machinery). As Braverman (1974, p. 195) also suggested: 'Machinery offers to management the opportunity to do by wholly mechanical means that which it had previously attempted to do by organisational and disciplinary means.'

Edward's conclusion that the function of supervision is becoming increasingly peripheral to production rests on the claim that impersonal control mechanisms have replaced supervisors as the main instrument for controlling staff. The position of foreman is examined and defined in terms of the labour control function of capital. Essentially, the role of the supervisor is seen to centre on extracting surplus value from the workforce and transforming labour power into labour (see Thompson, 1983, pp. 38–64).[2] Although changes in the methods employed by management to control labour are noted, the predominant theme is that there has been a 'peripheralisation' of the direct supervisor of labour. It is argued that developments in systems of bureaucratic control have relieved the supervisor of the task of disciplining staff, and developments in technical control systems have incorporated the element of direction. Moreover, the recent advances in new technology and in particular information technology, are seen to offer management the opportunity to wholly incorporate the traditional labour control function of supervision into technical systems of control. Edwards (1979) suggests that the ability of modern computer systems to monitor and evaluate work performance may bring about an erosion of the remaining supervisory tasks of detection, inspection and evaluation. He claims that this may bring in its wake the demise of the traditional function of supervision:

> As with real foremen, these mechanical foremen ... are themselves directed, evaluated and corrected by higher level ... mini-computers that control and direct many processes at once ... Computer technology gives a giant boost to the earlier methods of technical control. (1979, pp. 124–5)

A major weakness of Edwards' study is that it neglects the fact that supervision can be concerned with aspects of production control other than those associated with the direct control of labour. Whilst his claim that the traditional function of supervision has been eroded may be correct, this does not necessarily indicate that there will not be an important role for the supervisor under more advanced systems of production. The role of the supervisor may be eroded, replaced or redefined under new forms of work organisation and management control of the labour process. It is argued here that to understand this, supervision needs to be reconceptualised to account for changes in the traditional labour control function of supervision.

RECONCEPTUALISING SUPERVISION

A major difficulty in trying to present a 'universal' concept of supervision stems from the variety of situations in which individuals can be identified as holding a 'supervisory relationship' within an operating system. In order to take into account the variety of supervisory tasks, status levels, and job titles which may exist within the supervisory genre, the term 'supervision' needs to be very broadly conceived. *Direct control of workplace operations* is a useful starting point as it locates supervision within the context of overall control of workplace operations.

The supervisory control functions which may be identified and differentiated at the workplace are:
• planning and directing workplace operations;
• monitoring and evaluating workplace operations;
• correcting and adapting workplace operations.
However, these three functions of direction, appraisal, and regulation may be achieved through a number of differing personal and impersonal methods of control. Three examples previously discussed are: firstly, through incorporating elements of control into the actual machinery of production; secondly, through administrative or bureaucratic means by formulating a comprehensive series of operating rules and procedures; and thirdly, through the formation of 'self-supervising' autonomous work groups (in the sense of having control over their own job tasks).

If supervision is thus conceptualised, it is then possible to discuss the ways in which day-to-day control functions have been redistributed with the introduction of new technology. It allows for the possibility of the redefinition of the control function of supervision under computer-aided production systems, for example, from being primarily concerned with the activities of labour, or machine and process supervision, to being concerned with a far wider area of production operations control. Alternatively, it is possible to envisage a situation where the role of the supervisor is abolished altogether through the development of fully automated production systems. In such a case, although the supervisory control elements would remain important, they would no longer be carried out by individuals who could be identified and defined as 'supervisors', for the control function of supervision would be wholly incorporated into the machinery of production.

In the following section, this broader concept of supervision is utilised in a case study examination of the effects of information technology on the control function of supervision in British Rail marshalling yards. Individuals are designated as holding a supervisory relationship to the operating system in cases where: firstly, they are in direct control of some aspects of workplace operations; and secondly, authority is invested in their position by management and/or the workforce. These criteria are used to delimit a structure of supervision comprising a hierarchy of supervisory roles. At the apex of the hierarchy are individuals who hold 'mixed' managerial-supervisory roles. These individuals can be distinguished from management on the basis that they are *directly* involved in the day-to-day control problems of an operating system (Betts, 1980, p. 28). At the bottom of the supervisory hierarchy are individuals who are afforded authority by their work group, and are performing supervisory tasks; they hold 'mixed' supervisory-operative roles. Between these two types there is the 'pure' type of supervisory role, this is occupied by individuals who are formally recognised as being involved in the control of marshalling yard operations (Thurley and Wirdenius, 1973, p. 25). The day-to-day liaison between, and interaction of, these individuals is taken into account by employing the concept of a 'supervisory system of control' developed by Thurley and Wirdenius (1973, p. 28). The redefinition of supervision is also explained within the context of changes in work organisation and the system of management control (see Dawson, 1986a, pp. 70–5).

THE BRITISH RAIL CASE STUDY

In 1971, British Rail decided to invest £13 million in a new computer information system to improve management's control over freight operations. The system, known as Total Operations Processing System (TOPS), has been in operation since 1975 and constitutes one of the first large-scale ventures by British industry in the application of an on-line real-time computer information system.

While numerous studies exist on signalmen, permanent way staff, drivers, guards, engineers, station masters, and porters, in addition to the broader studies on British Rail management and industrial relations (e.g. Bonavia, 1981; Farrington, 1984). The literature on technical change and marshalling yard operations is generally only concerned with automatic marshalling techniques (e.g. Bowick, 1975). The industrial life of marshalling yard communities is one aspect of railway history which has not been well documented. Furthermore, although TOPS has been called 'the most sophisticated of all innovations which brought freight handling more completely into the age of electronics' (Bagwell, 1982, p. 67), analysis of this change has largely been in the form of internal BR reports.

The Study of Marshalling Yards

The main body of research was conducted between 1981 and 1983, as part of a programme of research being conducted by the New Technology Research Group at Southampton University. It involved a retrospective study of management strategy and industrial relations issues in the implementation of the TOPS system (see McLoughlin, Smith and Dawson, 1983), and a more detailed study of the effects of change on local supervision based in railway marshalling yards (see Dawson, 1986a). This chapter draws primarily on the latter research which involved an in-depth study of the effects of change in five traditional British Rail marshalling yards. Four of the yards were principal marshalling facilities and the other was a smaller specialist traffic yard. Each of the principal marshalling yards comprised at least three distinct sub-yards and covered an area of one or more square miles.

During the study, interviews were conducted with 80 British Rail employees at:

- national and regional headquarters
- two British Rail training centres
- a number of British Rail marshalling yards

In the five marshalling yards which formed the basis of the study interviews were conducted with 10 local managers, 12 senior supervisors, 17 first-line supervisors, 12 deputy supervisors, and 10 working supervisors. The interview schedules covered topics such as job content, working and personal relationships with other supervisors, management and yard staff, and the way these had been changed by computerisation.

A questionnaire was designed solely for use with supervisory graded staff, who at the outset of the study claimed that they might not have enough time to be interviewed. The questionnaire was therefore intended either to provide data which could not otherwise be obtained, or to act as a supplement to interviews conducted with the supervisors. As it turned out, data elicited by questionnaire was largely used to supplement other methods of data collection. Questionnaires were completed by fourteen senior supervisors and ten first-line supervisors from a sample taken in five marshalling yards and two supervisory training centres.

A key research method used throughout the study was non-participant observation. In each of the five marshalling yards periods of between two to five weeks were spent observing the working practices of staff. Full ten hour day and night shifts were spent with individual supervisors and 'shunting gangs', observing and informally discussing the work of yard staff. Particular attention was paid to the use that was made of information from the computer system by supervisors in making operating decisions. In addition, the nature and number of contacts with other supervisors and yard staff were monitored. Such a detailed programme of observation made it possible to ascertain the nature of supervisory tasks and the roles of individual supervisors. Furthermore, from interviews and discussions, it was possible to construct a picture of working practices prior to computerisation.

Data elicited through these methods was supplemented by documentary material from the local marshalling yard (this included job descriptions of marshalling yard staff) and from national and regional headquarters.

Finally, further attempts were made to understand the operational use of the computer by briefly visiting and examining systems on

Victoria Railways (Australia) and New Zealand Railways, and by attending courses held on the TOPS system for supervisors at British Rail's training schools.

In the section which follows, the importance of information to operations management in the control of railway freight transits is discussed, and the key features of railway freight systems are identified in order to provide the context for the subsequent comparison of freight operations control and marshalling yard supervision prior to computerisation, and after the introduction of the TOPS computer system.

Railway Freight Operations and the Importance of Information

British Rail's Working Time Table (WTT) provides an official plan of the freight train services scheduled to run on any given day. The WTT lists all outbound scheduled services, all inbound scheduled services, and all those services which are scheduled to connect onto other booked freight trains. Any formal alterations to the WTT are sent from regional headquarters to local operating staff in the form of weekly and daily freight train notices. However, the actual running of freight services is complicated by the regular occurence of contingencies, such as, derailments, resource shortages, locomotive failures and fluctuations in the level of freight. Essentially, the problem of management control centres on the task of providing an adequate supply of resources (wagons, locomotives, train crews) to meet changing customer demands, and then to integrate freight transits over a national rail network. Information has to be captured, transmitted, processed and disseminated on the location and disposition of British Rail's freight resources. This information then has to be utilised in the control and integration of a number of interdependent sequence of events, for example, about the route to be taken, the provision of train crews (and relief), the type of locomotive required, the compatibility of wagons, and their integration into existing and planned passenger and freight train services. Six essential elements of railway freight operations are illustrated in Figure 1.

An important element in freight operations is the actual shunting and marshalling of freight wagons (see Dawson, 1986b, pp. 2–3). Over the past few years, the policy of British Rail has been to concentrate these operations in high capacity marshalling yards located at nodal points on the railfreight network. These high capacity

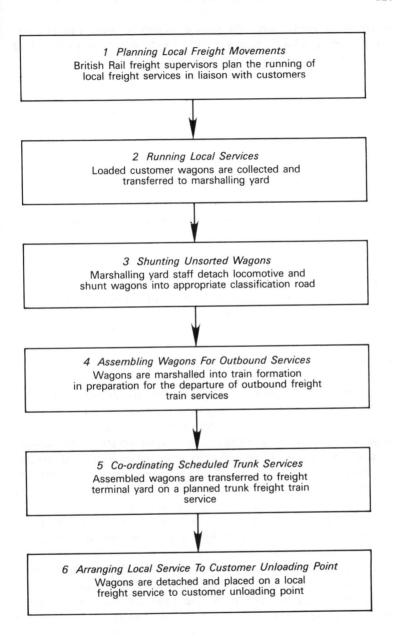

Figure 6.1 The basic sequence of operations in freight transits

marshalling yards normally consist of two or more distinct sub-yards, each of which comprise 30 to 60 classification roads which collect traffic for a number of destinations. Unsorted trains are received by marshalling yard staff (see Figure 2), who uncouple and marshall wagons ready for final assembly on outbound freight train services. Once a freight train is assembled, the train proceeds to a freight terminal yard in the proximity of the customer unloading point. The wagons are then shunted ready for a local transfer to their destination.

Information is a key resource in the control and co-ordination of these operations, and since the early 1960s there have been three main stages in the development of freight information control systems within high capacity marshalling yards. These are as follows:

• a manual system
• a telex based system
• a computerised system

Each of these stages is examined in terms of its effects on the jobs of yard staff and the traditional control function of marshalling yard supervision.

The Manual System of Freight Operations Control

Under the manual system of freight operations control information on the disposition of marshalling yard resources would be transmitted from local supervisors to central headquarters staff through a manual hierarchical reporting and command structure. Marshalling yard supervisors would deal directly with one of 20 or so divisional control offices in arranging the local movements of freight and initiating changes to scheduled servies. Reports at divisional control would then be forwarded to one of five regional control offices who would collate this inforamtion and inform national headquarters of the current state of railway freight operations over the entire rail network.

From interviews and informal discussions with local supervisors, and from the analysis of documentary material, it became evident that under the manual system of freight information control, supervisory tasks were undertaken at four different status-levels in the occupational structure within high capacity marshalling yards. These status-levels were:

- *senior supervisors* (movements supervisors) responsible for the control of all marshalling yard operations;
- *formally defined first-line supervisors* (yard supervisors) responsible for the day-to-day control of freight operations within the separate yards which make up a marshalling yard;
- *deputy supervisors* (chargemen) responsible for the control of freight train movements into and out of the yard, and for overseeing yard operations in the absence of a yard supervisor;
- *working supervisors* (head shunters) in charge of shunting gangs within sub-sections of the yard.

The individuals holding these positions would work together on common problems in the direct control of marshalling yard operations. A supervisory hierarchy of a typical high capacity marshalling yard is shown in Figure 6.2. However, it should be noted that this structure would vary according to local conditions, and in particular, to the nature of traffic flow and the layout of the marshalling yard.

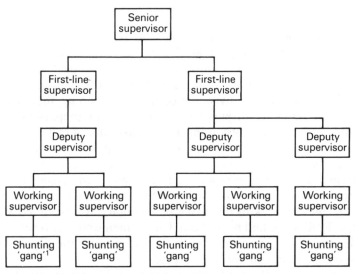

A shunting 'gang' is normally composed of two or three under shunters who work closely with their head shunter (working supervisor).

Figure 6.2   An example of a supervisory hierarchy in a high capacity marshalling yard

Prior to computerisation, the movements supervisor held a 'mixed' managerial-supervisory role with a fairly wide span of control. His main task was to oversee marshalling yard operations as a whole (including for example, the supervision of staff in the locomotive shed), and to ensure that effective action was taken in the case of any of a number of marshalling yard contingencies. A retired movements supervisor summarised the job as follows:

> As a movements supervisor you were concerned with everything ... you would see if there were any sort of problems, you know, that were going to happen within the next few hours. Then you would go out around the yard and check your wagons, and have a word with your supervisors, and check the cripples [wagons which are in need of repair], and see if things were on the move ... As a movements supervisor you were in the yard continually walking from one yard to another, back and forth to the diesel depot and all that.

The labour control function of supervision was carried out by the movements supervisor who would monitor the performance of yard staff and discipline misdemeanours. His immediate subordinate was the yard supervisor who held a 'pure' supervisory role in the direct control of operations within the yard. His main concern was to avoid yard congestion and keep local customers satisfied (see Dawson, 1987, pp. 49–52). Yard supervisors would deal with local fluctuations in the levels of freight through running additional services in liaison with divisional control. In so doing, they would often order wagons surplus to requirements in preparation for possible future operating contingencies. Their main function was to plan and direct the yard throughput of freight. Daily operating decisions were made on the basis of their knowledge and experience of local freight train movements. Furthermore, in directing yard operations they would liaise closely with their chargemen who were responsible for checking that assembled freight trains accorded with British Rail's rules and regulations. Chargemen would also deputise in the absence of the yard supervisor and monitor the day-to-day movements of freight within the yard.

Located at the bottom of the supervisory hierarchy were head shunters. They held 'mixed' supervisory-operative roles and would carry out operative type tasks (such as, the shunting and marshalling of freight wagons), and yet they would also be directly involved in the daily supervision of these operations. Head shunters were responsible for planning and directing *shunting* operations within their allocated section of the yard, that is, making operating decisions on the yard placement of freight wagons from the information provided by a label on the wagon indicating customer destination. They would also make decisions on the *marshalling* of trains, that is, the final formation of wagons on freight services due to depart from the yard. These decisions were made on the basis of their accumulated knowledge and experience of railway geography and the routing of outbound freight train services. Their ability to minimise the movements of freight in assembling trains earned them a position of authority and status within the yard.

The Telex-Based System of Freight Operations Control

Prior to the introduction of TOPS, the position of movements supervisor had either disappeared as a result of local work reorganisation schemes, or it had been redefined as a consequence of the introduction of a telex-based system of freight information control called Advance Traffic Information (ATI). In some of the smaller yards, the traditional tasks associated with the job of movements supervisor were incorporated into other supervisory and managerial positions. The task of dealing with contingencies for example, was in many instances incorporated into the job of the first-line supervisor (as a result yard supervisors were upgraded within the formal supervisory grading scheme). In the case of high capacity yards where fairly large supervisory structures existed and where the volume of local traffic was 'sufficiently intensive', the introduction of ATI brought about a re-location of the movements supervisor into the ATI office: 'The supervisor must be located next to the traffic clerk . . . He is responsible for organising the clerks working for him and integrating yard and office activities' (British Railways, 1971, para. 3.3.).

However, the ATI system did not have any major effects on marshalling yard supervision. It did not provide accurate and current information which meant that it was not possible to delegate control of the area movements of freight to the local level. Thus, the day-to-day control of resources in the provision of freight train services continued to be exercised at a number of organisational levels. This created three principal problems for management in the control of railway freight operations. Firstly, management relied for its information about the disposition of resources on daily physical

checks. At headquarters, day-to-day decisions about resource allocation (especially the supply of empty wagons to meet customers'
loading requirements) were contingent upon the provision of information through hierarchical manual reporting procedures which
listed the location and status of wagon and locomotive fleets.
Secondly, the effectiveness of manual reporting procedures and
information flows were undermined by a combination of the
parochial attitudes of railway freight supervisors and the impossibility
of validating the information provided by staff responsible for
checking wagons. The need to satisfy local requirements and
respond to fluctuations in customer demands meant that 'figure
adjusting' in daily returns was widespread and that stores of
unreported wagons and 'spare' locomotives were accumulated in
individual local areas as a matter of course. Thirdly, customers had
no knowledge of the whereabouts of their consignments. Once des-
patched, their wagons were 'lost' until such time as they arrived at
their destination. Despite the attention of a small army of wagon
inspectors it was estimated that only 80 per cent of the wagon fleet
was accounted for in each daily distribution report (McLoughlin,
Smith and Dawson, 1983, p. 8). Customers were also inclined to
engage in wagon hoarding, and were able to use British Rail wagons
within their own private rail networks with impunity. To improve the
efficiency of a largely labour based freight traffic control system,
headquarters management were forced to direct their efforts towards
physical inspections of marshalling yard wagon stocks and 'post-
mortems' of freight operations.

In an attempt to combat the management control problems
associated with this manual infomation system and hierarchical
command structure, British Rail management decided to introduce
a computerised system of freight information control (TOPS). This
system has been in operation since 1975 following a four-year
implementation programme. In the section which follows, the longer
term effects of computerisation on the control function of supervision
are examined.

The Computerised System of Freight Information Control (TOPS)

There were three main intentions behind management's decision to
introduce the TOPS computer system. Firstly, it was hoped that computerisation would improve the market position of railway freight by
offering a better quality service to customers, in particular, faster and

more reliable freight transits. Secondly, computerisation was expected to reduce operating costs by improving the utilisation of wagons and locomotives. Thirdly, it was anticipated that computerisation would make operating conditions and performance more visible to management by providing real-time information at headquarters level.

The main element of management's strategy to achieve these objectives concerned the re-organisation of the existing rail freight operations control structure. The computer system obviated the need for a hierarchical reporting and command structure, since information could now be transmitted from remote locations direct to headquarters level. Furthermore, the computer data base could be used directly at local as well as headquarters levels, so that real-time information was available at the point of operations. As a result, there was no longer a need for divisional involvement in many of the operating decisions at local level. Computerisation therefore offered the possibility for management to transform the existing operational control organisation. As it turned out, British Rail were able to both centralise overall control of operations at regional and national headquarters, and delegate day-to-day operating decision-making responsibility to locally based supervisors.

The centralisation of control enabled the remote monitoring and evaluation of area level operating performance by headquarters management at regional and national levels. Using the new information generated by TOPS, headquarters management are able for the first time to effectively co-ordinate freight resources. TOPS provides up-to-date information on the current operating situation; the disposition of resources; and the operating performance of every operating area on the entire network. This enables headquarters management to make rapid decisions on traffic priorities, and respond to changes in customer demands.

The delegation of operations control involved the creation of locally based Area Freight Centres (AFCs) to act as the main reporting points for all activities required to be known by TOPS. In 1984, there were approximately 100 AFCs acting as 'data traps' for information from 5000 individual locations (in 1975 there were 152 AFCs, and by 1979 this figure had been reduced to 138). Each AFC is normally staffed by a senior supervisor (area freight assistant) and a number of clerical staff (TOPS clerks) who are responsible for reporting TOPS information by entering data on mini-computer terminals which are linked to a central computer. At each location where an event occurs (knowledge of which is required by TOPS), the staff concerned (guards, shunters, supervisors) report details to the AFC for input to the central computer. In this way the central computer is able to keep on its files a continuously updated 'real-time' picture of the location and disposition of the wagon and locomotive fleets throughout the entire rail freight network.

The delegation of control has resulted in a redefinition of the control function of marshalling yard supervision. On the basis of TOPS generated information railway freight supervisors are now able to control and co-ordinate freight operations over a wider geographical area and arrange additional services in liaison with other operating staff. The availability of information on the future movements of freight has also made it possible to pre-plan marshalling yard operations to accommodate alterations to the WTT. In addition, the TOPS computer system has enabled local supervisors to deal more effectively with daily operating contingencies through providing accurate information on the disposition of British Rail's freight resources.

A new senior supervisory position, the Area Freight Assistant (AFA), has been created to exploit the control potential of the new technology. Working from a desk in the local area freight centre, AFAs utilise computer generated information in assessing, planning, and co-ordinating freight train movements within their TOPS Responsibility Area (TRA). Their primary aim is to ensure the efficient utilisation of resources in the provision of local and trunk freight train services. In order to achieve this objective, AFAs will monitor area freight operations, deal with operating contingencies, and plan the future movements of freight in close liaison with other supervisors and senior yard staff. In planning, monitoring and correcting area freight operations the AFA also acts as a crucial communications link within the railway freight operating system, and holds a key role in the hour-by-hour management of area freight operations.

However, although there has been an extension in the operational control of the responsibilities of local supervisors (see Figure 6.3), there has also been a displacement of a number of traditional practices associated with marshalling yard operations. The ability of local supervisors to assess the local disposition of freight resources and the loads of potential freight trains is no longer necessary as the computer provides detailed information on what is in the yard, what is coming towards the yard, and what is due to leave the yard. Yard supervisors can no longer adopt a parochial attitude to freight yard operations; chargemen no longer require a detailed understanding of British Rails rules and regulations; and head shunters no longer need to accumulate years of experience in order to assess correct train formations. As one yard supervisor commented:

> It's made the job of the head shunter much easier than it was in pre-TOPS days, because in pre-TOPS days the head shunter had to know the geography of the system. You had wagons coming into the yard for all the destinations on the Western Region and he had to know what trains they went on. But now under this TOPS system and the tag numbers everything's done for you, you know, all the thinking is done for you. It's taken a hell of a lot off the burden of training a shunter to work in the yard, you know, it took years and years to get to do the job properly.

With TOPS, if the formation of a train does not meet the safety standards laid down in British Rail's regulations then it will be rejected and a reason provided:

> REJECTED – 37 FT BARR REQ BETWEEN WAGON 01 & LOCO 47119. (TOPS printout)

In the example above, a dangerous goods train has been rejected because a barrier wagon has not been placed between the locomotive and the wagon load. The TOPS system will also check the loading of the train and ensure that sufficient brake force is available for the safe running of the service. This is illustrated by the comment of one yard supervisor who noted:

> As far as the yard working is concerned, the introduction of TOPS has made life much easier for the supervisor and chargemen. Chargemen before the introduction of TOPS had to calculate their trains and so on. But, since the introduction of TOPS you are greatly assisted ... which makes things so much easier for you.

It is no longer necessary for yard supervisors and chargemen to manually check that train formations comply with the rules and regulations laid down by British Rail, nor do they need to calculate the brake force of their outbound freight train services. All these

Supervisory classification →	The supervisory system c. 1960	The supervisory system c. 1970	The supervisory system c. 1980
Senior supervisor:	Movements supervisor	A.T.I. supervisor	Area freight assistant
First-line supervisor:	Yard inspector	Yard supervisor	Yard supervisor
Deputy supervisor:	Foreman	Chargeman	Chargeman
Working supervisor:	Head shunter	Senior railman	Senior railman
Changes in operational control responsibilities	Day-to-day control of marshalling yard operations	Marshalling yard operations and local movements of freight traffic	Day-to-day control of area freight operations
Changes in the control of freight train running	The running of freight services is the responsibility of the divisional control organisation	Where local freight traffic was sufficiently intense, control was devolved to local supervision	AFAs control the running of area freight services and divisional movements in liaison with other AFAs

Figure 6.3 Examples of supervisory systems within high capacity marshalling yards: c. 1960-85

details (the number of the vehicle, its weight, brake force, brake type and destination) are listed on the computer printout (usually referred to as the 'TOPS train list'). Thus, TOPS has reduced the amount of knowledge required of yard supervisors and chargemen in ensuring correct train formations of outbound freight train services.

The availability of real-time information has also made the function and performance of local management and supervision far more open to senior management control. The area manager of a principal marshalling yard in South Wales summed up the managerial implications of TOPS as follows:

> There's one very big 'disadvantage' of TOPS ... and that is they can monitor the area manager ... Sir Peter Parker if he wishes can press a few buttons and he can say: 'Christ! There's been twelve wagons at yard x now for fourteen days, what's the area manager doing about that.' ... We've created a 'Big Brother' effect, now everyday's an 'open day', everybody knows what we're doing.

Thus, whilst computerisation has not resulted in a simple erosion of the control function of supervision, it has brought about a substantial transformation in the nature of local operating practices. Supervisors are now more fully integrated into the wider system of management control and are unable to adopt a parochial attitude to their work. For example, yard operations can now be monitored by central headquarters staff who are remote from the location in which these events take place. Moreover, supervisors no longer require years of 'hands-on' experience in order to make daily operating decisions since these decisions can now be made on the basis of computer generated information. Finally, it is worth stressing that the control potential of this new technology has not only influenced the work of operatives and supervisors, but also the function of operations management in the day-to-day control of freight transits over the national railway network.

CONCLUSION: INFORMATION TECHNOLOGY AND THE CONTROL FUNCTION OF SUPERVISION

The TOPS system has enabled management to centralise operations and devolve additional elements of control to the local level. As a result, computerisation has not merely led to an extension in technical control but also to a change in techniques and combinations of structures of control. Within this reconstruction, manual hierarchical structures of control no longer play such an important part in the operating system. Tasks previously carried out at divisional level have been incorporated into the machine, concentrated in higher managment, and devolved to a new supervisory system of control.

British Rail's decision to create a new type of 'mixed' managerial-supervisory position to exploit the information made available by the TOPS computer system has resulted in a redefinition of the control function of local supervision. From making a few simple TOPS enquiries AFAs are able to acquire accurate real-time information on both the disposition of freight resources within their TRA and on the composition of approaching freight traffic. This information is used to make daily operating decisions on the running and canellation of freight services. With TOPS, it is thus AFAs (rather than divisional controllers) who occupy a central position within operations management in the day-to-day control of railway freight services.

In contrast, the autonomy and control previously associated with the position of yard supervisor has been substantially reduced. Prior to computerisation yard supervisors would initiate the running and cancellation of freight services. With TOPS, it is thus AFAs (rather (paradoxically, although divisional controllers had overall decision making responsibility, effective decision-making depended upon the accuracy of yard supervisors' reports about current operating circumstances). Under the routine operation of TOPS, it is now the job of the AFA to initiate alterations to scheduled rail freight services. Furthermore, yard supervisors no longer need to spend the first hour of each turn of duty taking stock of the wagons in the yard and telephoning the details to divisional control. Any wagon movements into and out of the yard are immediately reported to the TOPS computer via terminals in the local AFCs. By recording every wagon movement, the TOPS computer system is able to maintain a continuously up-dated picture on what is in the yard, what is due to arrive in the yard, and what is due to depart from the yard. In automatically generating routing information for the distribution of empty wagons over the entire rail network, the TOPS computer system has also obviated the need for yard supervisors to hoard and over-order empty wagons to meet variable customer demands.

In the case of chargemen, their accumulated knowledge and experience is no longer required in making daily operating decisions on the formation of freight trains. They no longer need to check manually that the total brakeforce of outbound freight train services conforms to British Rail's rules and regulations, as the TOPS computer system automatically validates correct train formations. The main duties of the chargeman are to ensure the safe movements of all freight trains on their arrival and departure from the yard, and to deputise in the absence of the yard supervisor.

A similar erosion of the need for traditional marshalling yard skills has occurred with the position of head shunter. A detailed knowledge of railway geography is no longer used in the marshalling of outbound freight train services. The TOPS computer system automatically generates a sorting code which details the required formation of trains prior to their departure from the yard. However, although the formation of trains (the marshalling of wagons) is now determined by a TOPS computer printout, head shunters have maintained decision-making repsonsibility over the yard placement of inbound freight wagons (the shunting of wagons). Consequently, management's strategic objective to control shunting operations through the implementation of a TOPS Allocation Program has not been successful (this program cannot adequately deal with the continual adjustments required of a localised road plan allocation of wagons) (see Dawson, 1986a).

Whilst the introduction of a computerised system of freight information control has displaced many of the traditional practices associated with marshalling yard supervision, this has not resulted in a concomitant erosion of supervisory roles and functions. Although some supervisory tasks have been eroded and replaced, others have been created and enhanced. This has resulted in a complex redefinition of supervisory functions which currently comprise a mixture of traditional tasks and new computer based activities. This highlights a major weakness in studies which attempt to explain changes in the role of the supervisor in terms of changes in the traditional labour control function of supervision. When evaluating the implications of computer technology for supervision, a broader definition of supervisiory control is required to account for the restructuring and redefinition of decision-making responsibilities within operations (or production) management.

In the case reported here, the emergence of a new type of supervisory position raises a number of interesting questions, for example: would the creation of computer-oriented positions in other industries differ from the type examined in British Rail, or does the emergence of this new supervisory position (whose job is to exploit computer generated data) signal the possible convergence in the general function of supervision across different industries? For the moment these questions cannot be answered. Nevertheless, if management decide to introduce computer technology as a means of extending the operational control responsibilities of local supervisors then it is possible to envisage the creation of new computer-oriented supervisory positions, whose role is to control and co-ordinate previously diverse areas of production or service operations. It is also plausible to suggest that these supervisors will exhibit characteristics which contrast with both machine and labour-oriented supervisors. In any event, computerisation is likely to result in a far more complex redefinition of the supervisory control function than is indicated by simply pointing to the erosion of traditional supervisory roles.

Notes

1. The four systems of control which Edwards (1979, pp. 25–162) develops are:

    (i) *Entrepreneurial control*: this refers to the simple forms of control which existed in the majority of small firms in the second half of the nineteenth century. It basically involves personal direct control by the employer.

    (ii) *Hierarchical control*: this refers to the military model of a giant pyramid of control with a chain of command, which emerged at the turn of the century with the growth in the size of organisations (according to Edwards the supervisor had 'despotic rule' at this time).

    (iii) *Technical control*: this refers to the achievement of control through technical means which are built into the physical structure of the labour process, for example, the assembly line.

    (iv) *Bureaucratic control*: this is a form of structural control achieved through bureaucratic means in building in formalised rules and procedures into the social structure, for example, personnel policies, disciplinary procedures, formal job descriptions and so forth.

2. Basically, the control function of capital is concerned with combining the labour process with the creation of value. The worker is employed as a form of variable capital and does not become a realised asset until his potential productive output (labour power) has been transformed into the creation of goods or services (labour).

References

Armstrong, P. (1983) 'Class Relations at the Point of Production: A Case Study', *Sociology*, vol. 17, no. 3, pp. 339–59.

Bagwell, P. S. (1982) *The Railwaymen Volume 2: The Beeching Era and After* (London, Allen & Unwin).

Betts, P. W. (1980) *Supervisory Studies*, 3rd edn (McDonald & Evans).

Bonavia, M. R. (1981) *British Rail: The First 25 Years* (London David & Charles).

Bowick, D. M. (1975) 'Computer Systems Impact on Railways', *The Chartered Institute of Transport Journal*, vol. 36, no. 8, pp. 179–85.

Braverman, H. (1974) *Labor and Monopoly Capital: The Degradation of Work in the Twentieth Century* (New York, Monthly Review Press).

British Railways Western Region (1971) *The ATI Investment Report* (British Railways Western Region).

Buchanan, D. (1983) 'Technological Imperatives and Strategic Choice' in G.Winch, (ed.), *Information Technology in Manufacturing Processes: Case studies in Technological Change* (London, Rossendale).

Child, J. (1975) 'The Industrial Supervisor', in G. Esland, G. Salaman, M. Speakman (eds), *People and Work* (London, Holmes McDougall), pp. 70–87.

Child, J., B. Partridge, (1982) *Lost Managers: Supervisors in Industry and Society* (Cambridge, Cambridge University Press).

Child, J. (1984) *Organisation: A Guide to Problems and Practice*, 2nd edn (London, Harper & Row).

Child, J. (1985) 'Managerial Strategies, New Technology and the Labour Process' in D. Knights, H. Willmott, D. Collinson (eds), *Job Redesign: Critical Perspectives on the Labour Process* (Aldershot, Gower).

Clegg, S., D. Dunkerley (1980) *Organization, Class and Control* (London, Routledge & Kegan Paul).

Dawson, P. M. B. (1986a) *Computer Technology and the Redefinition of Supervision* (Ph.D. Thesis, University of Southampton).

Dawson, P. M. B. (1986b) 'How Computers Affect Supervisory Systems of Control' in A. Roff and D. Brown (eds), *Business Case File in Information Technology* (London, Van Nostrand Reinhold).

Dawson, P. M. B., I. P. McLoughlin, (1986) 'Organisational Choice in the Design of Supervisory Systems'. Paper presented to the European Conference on the implications of information technology for the role of management at the European Institute for Advanced Studies in Management, Brussels, Sep. 1986.

Dawson, P. M. B. (1987) 'Computer Technology and the Job of the First-Line Supervisor', *New Technology, Work and Employment*, vol. 2, no. 1, pp. 47–60.

Edwards, R. (1979) *Contested Terrain: The Transformation of the Workplace in the Twentieth Century* (London, Heinemann).

Farrington, J. (1984) *Life on the Lines* (Moorland).

Knights, D., D. Collinson (1985) 'Redesigning work on the Shopfloor: A Question of Control or Consent?' in D. Knights, H. Willmott, D. Collinson (eds), *Job Redesign: Critical Perspectives on the Labour Process* (Aldershot, Gower).

Leavitt, H. J., T. L. Whisler (1958) 'Management in the 80s', *Harvard Business Review*, vol. 36, Nov.–Dec., pp. 41–8.

Littler, C. R. (1982) *The Development of the Labour Process in Capitalist Societies* (London, Heinemann).

Marglin, S. A. (1976) 'What Do Bosses Do? The Origins and Function of Hierarchy in Capitalist Production', in A. Gorz (ed), *The Division of Labour: The Labour Process and Class Struggle in Modern Capitalism* (New York, Harvester Press) pp. 13–53.

McLoughlin, I. P., J. H. Smith, P. M. B. Dawson (1983) 'The Introduction of a Computerised Freight Information System in British Rail – TOPS', New Technology Research Group, University of Southampton.

Thompson, R. (1983) *The Nature of Work. An Introduction to Debates on the Labour Process* (London, Macmillan).

Thurley, K. E. and H. Wirdenius (1973) *Supervision: A Reappraisal* (London, Heinemann).

7 How Much Change at the Store? The Impact of New Technologies and Labour Processes on Managers and Staffs in Retail Distribution*

Steve Smith

INTRODUCTION AND METHOD

Here I will look at the labour process implications of the introduction of new technology in retail distribution, largely on the basis of evidence from interviews with middle and senior managers in a cross-section of UK companies.

The most important recent innovation in retailing is Electronic Point of Sale (EPOS). EPOS systems 'drive' stock control, financial control and stock re-ordering functions from data captured at the checkout. Although EPOS offers a great deal of scope in design and utilisation, in fact it is being fitted into organisations which are already either highly Taylorised, or alternatively, organisations which have remained firmly attached to craft forms of work and organisational control. These lead to two rather distinct alternatives in the way the technology is used as we will see. Indeed, for purposes of argument, one is inclined to reverse our nominal interest in the 'impact of new technology on organisations' and think instead in terms of the 'impact of organisations on new technology'.

*This chapter is based on a paper read to the *4th Aston/UMIST Conference on Organization and Control of the Labour Process.* Birmingham, April 2nd–4th 1986. It arose out of research at the Open University's Faculty of Technology on technical and employment change in banking and retailing with reference to greater London, directed by Dr David Wield.

I hope that this paper will contribute towards correcting two imbalances in labour process research. First there is a recognisable emphasis in labour process research upon what we have come to call 'manufacturing' or 'industrial' employment, though there has always been a minority interest in 'office' and 'service sector' workers and their work organisation. While these categories are rather vague in distinguishing objects of study there is nevertheless an understanding that we are drawing a broad distinction between male and female employment, between different kinds of commodities and between different worker ideologies. Although we are in a position to say that these divisions are artificial and that, in strictly economic terms, the service sector does not exist as an objective second category of activity, the tendency is still to concentrate on 'factory jobs' in the popular sense of what this means, and to assume that they are in *some* sense different. Any special qualities of service sector labour have tended to be left to grand theorists.

Second, although recent conferences on the labour process have shown a redirection in research activity (e.g. Knights and Willmott, 1986), we persist in directing most of our immediate research effort towards the shopfloor. This may be for ideological reasons. But this bias also stems from anticipated research access difficulties. It is frequently believed that managers are difficult to reach in connection with labour process research, and that this is particularly true of strategic decision makers. Similarly, introductory textbooks in sociology refer to the 'problems of studying the powerful'. This disposition in and beyond labour process research is one which I refute.

I have arranged this account into two ideal-typical polarities, which roughly correspond with two respective management control strategies: Friedman's categories of 'direct control' and 'responsible autonomy' (Friedman, 1977). EPOS provides evidence that supports the use of either strategy depending on circumstances but also demonstrates how they are not necessarily mutually exclusive in practice.

What follows is mostly based on extended part-structured interviews with store managers and HQ managers in several UK companies. Additional interviews with equipment suppliers, an industry association and with shopfloor workers have been helpful; however, the bulk of the evidence was collected through visits to managers in stores and head offices. Evidence was also gathered from a leading consultancy in retail distribution which helped generously with documentary material.

My fieldwork began with random interviews of retail managers and their technology suppliers at two large commercial conferences on new technology in retailing, followed by those at later conferences. Approximately thirty-five interviews were conducted in this way. From these I gained an overview of trends in retail technology supply and of potential user-interest which covered most of the important names in the high street. An informal Delphi survey of these groups indicates a steady take up of EPOS, accelerating over the next five years. The core material for this paper, however, came from a more detailed record of fourteen retailers. These had all implemented EPOS, although many had only reached pilot projects in a small number of their branches.

In all cases I introduced myself as an 'independent researcher' from the Open University who was 'interested in the sorts of impact which new technologies are having on people's jobs in [banking and] retailing. I am specifically interested in what jobs are lost, what new jobs are created, the effect of new technology on skills and on how managers do their jobs.'[1]

THEORIES OF CONTROL AND THEORIES OF TECH-NOLOGY

Harry Braverman's classic, *Labour and Monopoly Capital* (1974) provides the theoretical framework for this research. The reader will recognise Braverman's work as a Marxian theory of direct control by management over non-managerial wage labour through the technical division of labour, and especially through a technology strategy which destroys craft skills and absorbs organisational intelligence into the apex of corporate hierarchies.

According to Braverman, retailing will be characterised by Taylorism: machine control (monitoring, pacing) of workers, and that, through de-skilling, workers will experience the hegemony of a collective organisational machine which frustrates their interests in controlling their own labour. According to Braverman, work is thus experienced as a double alienation – of both the products of labour and of the control of the labourer over his or her mental and manual activities. This is seen as a prerequisite to the successful extraction of surplus value from the 'collective labourer'.

Braverman's 'de-skilling thesis' is readily translated into the retailing context by hypothesising that EPOS is intended as a 'control tool for capital', and that data-processing betrays a Taylorian strategy: the intensification of the division of labour, centralisation and so on (see Braverman, 1974, 371–3).

Several writers within the Aston/UMIST standing conference on the labour process have challenged Braverman and presented a range of more open alternative possibilities. For example Teulings and others have argued that managements are often incapable of producing coherent strategies because management has also been compromised by its own division of labour (Teulings, 1986). Friedman (1977) has pointed out that over time, managements will pursue either (Taylorian) 'direct control' strategies or, alternatively, 'responsible autonomy' strategies which approximate, in varying degrees, to craft autonomy for expert workers. The choice of one or the other is, he argues, a matter of the historical circumstance of the industry: its markets, industrial relations, labour demand, profitability and company idiosyncracies.

Wilkinson (1983) has shown that workers have a range of counter-management strategies which qualify and moderate managerial control attempts, and that the shopfloor politics of technical change are rarely decisively settled one way or the other.

Burawoy (1985) and Reed (1986) have also drawn attention to what Reed terms the

> underestimation of the diversity ... complexity ... [and] inherent contradictions of different managerial control strategies and structure, the ... [inadequate] attention to the 'subjective' components of work and the economic determinism which tends to flow from this neglect. (Reed 1986, p. 5)

The revisionists would lead us to expect some diversity of outcomes in the field.

But in a quite different vein, Hochschild (1983), has generated interest in forms of labour process control which cut right across these debates. In her book *The Managed Heart*, Hochschild establishes that for the large part of the US population which is employed in the production of 'emotional work products', the workforce is engaged in a potentially more deeply estranging, emotional self-management process. Many of these kinds of jobs will be found in branches of what we call service employment. Hochschild argues that unlike the production of say, wallpaper, the production of an airline flight 'experience', or of a successful debt collection, depends on the producers acting on their own 'deep emotions', and through 'deep acting', carrying off an effect which is required by the market for these commodities. Some service workers thus trade in emotional 'use-values'; emotions which may be measured in commercial terms forming a part of commodified exchange relations.[2]

Airline flight attendants must 'really mean' their smiles if they are to convey the emotional product successfully. As one advertisement declared, their smiles were 'not just painted on'. By' performing' [sic] emotional labour successfully, Hochschild is certain that they are implicated in the management of their own personalities. This 'commercialisation of human feeling' may be attempted within any kind of organisation which embodies emotional labour in the commodities it exchanges with the purchaser.

It takes us beyond Braverman, because such an organisation may have a high or a low technical division of labour and may be decentralised or centralised. In other words there is no simple relationship between the intensity of the division of labour (specialisation) and the extent to which emotional labourers engage in autonomous self-management. Airlines do exhibit an intense division of labour and flight attendants are one set of workers among many others in the industry. Airline managements are often quite coercive in management style *qau* Friedman's concept of 'direct control' yet what flight attendants are coerced into is in fact very much a 'performance of the self'; literally 'self-control' *qua* 'responsible autonomy'. Here Friedman's dichotomy between 'direct control' and 'responsible autonomy' begins to break down for they are not mutually exclusive nor decisive terms in describing the labour process of airline flight attendants, nor indeed of many other service sector workers. *The Managed Heart* offers a way forward by linking the social psychology of emotion with the sociology of work and, in particular, how there can be an extension of the economy into the self.

Turning to insurance sales workers, Mills (1951), Howton and Rosenberg (1965), Knights (1975) and Evans and Blase (1984) also refer to the personal subversion which selling may cause. The 'indescribable thrill yielded by creative selling . . . this psychic income' (Howton and Rosenberg, 1965, p. 282) is potentially more coercive than the controls experienced by workers whose emotions do not become the objects of their labour. After a certain point it may be meaningless to ask whether they like work, for workers may no longer be capable of distinguishing between their selves and their work. Such absorption of the one by the other is often welcome among those who choose their careers and who are protected by professional organisations. But many emotional labourers have much less choice. Even formal power-holders – managers in all industries, service or otherwise, are emotional workers *par excellence* in so far as they have to produce displays which define them as managers in order to be able to carry out their jobs.

Finally however, Hochschild reminds us that there are limits to the extent to which managements can force workers to give 'service'. An example would be to compare retailing with a car factory. The deployment of a coercive and de-skilling technology in a car factory may create a 'couldn't care less' attitude among workers and this may or may not precipitate a spiral of direct control met by direct and indirect resistance leading eventually to lost production. But in retailing a 'couldn't care less' attitude may compromise business objectives in a quite immediate way. As indeed was the case in banking (Smith, 1985; Smith and Wield, 1988), the proletarianisation of white collar workers which is caused by a rapid substitution of direct control in place of responsible autonomy creates motivation problems. This is the cost to management of its own policies.

Logically therefore one might expect managers to be sensitive to the contradiction within serviced-based industries in particular. This phenomenon affects profits in a bigger way for some retailers than for others, for a variety of reasons. At one extreme, cash and carry companies are clearly not in the market place for emotions. At the opposite extreme, the famous Regent Street and Bond Street stores sell ambience and service. They refer to the 'art' of their work; they reflect the value of this labour-of-love in the higher prices they charge, and their customers expect both the art and the higher prices. These stores are constrained to avoid extremes of direct control.

In the next two sections I will explore these extremes. This will provide the basis for a modification of the notion of the labour process for use in some parts of the service sector.

TAYLORISM FOR RETAILERS

This research was taken against the background of a developing interest in corporate culture and a realisation that it may be possible to manage culture (ideology and symbols) with the conscious aim of increasing profitability. The Standing Conference of Organisational Symbolism (SCOS) provides a forum for this debate.

Many companies have experimented with culture management programmes. However for most UK retail chains there is a divide between corporate expectation of what may be reasonably expected from an employee, and what rightfully belongs to the unmanaged culture of the company and the private life of the individual. These involve minimal efforts to manage the outlook of employees. In my research these *tended* to be companies which had a higher division of labour. The alternative type of retailer demands more emotionally-committed work from its employees.

Certainly the majority of retailers which I visited tend to cluster around the Taylorian ideal type. They practise an intense division of labour, a pronounced centralisation of control and a lack of discretion among not only shopfloor personnel, but also among store managers too. The way in which this type of retailer manages information provides a transparent indication of the organisational logic: most of the main features of store performance were centrally determined from locally supplied sales data.

Typically I found that store managers therefore had little or no say in any of the following: number of lines carried, selection of lines carried, store layout of lines carried, promotions, price, window display, staff budgets, marketing, store design and decoration and delivery dates. This left them with responsibility for staff punctuality and presentation – usually devolved to the senior store supervisor and some control over day-to-day staff deployment. The store manager, (like the bank manager) will have some effect on the 'tone' and morale of the branch, and will make sure that tidiness is maintained. In one leading chain the manager hands out detailed work schedules to individual staff which he receives from the headquarters mainframe. These will indicate what tasks each worker should be doing for each hour of each working day. The manager has little part to play at all and has already been automated-out to a considerable extent.

The store manager will devolve training to the training supervisor, who may in any case be a periodic visitor from regional head office. The content of the training will again be set centrally in order to ensure consistency throughout a national chain.

Finally the store manager will be expected to control 'shrinkage' (theft) and to ensure that the necessary trading information is communicated to the centre for stock control and auditing purposes. With the gradual diffusion of EPOS systems even the latter functions are eroded within the Taylorian ideal type, as data may be transmitted without intervention by store personnel.

Below the store manager there is a highly casualised workforce – perhaps forty per cent of the staff will be women part-timers and staff turnover is high. The Saturday workforce may include only a handful of the weekday workforce. There is a marked sex-segregation of roles. For example, where a woman manages other women her job is likely to be classified as 'supervisory' rather than managerial.

Above the store manager one will typically find a division of labour between buying and retail operations. Careeer options and entry points conform to this division, and entrepreneural skills will be concentrated among the senior buyers. Sideways shifts between functions are unlikely, and there is an attenuated apprenticeship system.

CENTRALISATION WITH EPOS

In high volume, low value retailing it is very important to maximise information about the sales performance of all lines. This objective is the primary aim of EPOS in the UK. Several senior managers were aware that the UK differed from the USA where EPOS was first justified not by the information it generated but by staff productivity at the checkout and by the claimed elimination of several back office and headquarters data-processing jobs. It was the suppliers who had stressed that direct data-capture, usually through laser-scanning of bar-codes attached to each sale item, would speed up throughput at the checkout.

European retailers have found no significant increase in checkout speeds, although EPOS systems can be used to monitor individual staff performance in detail. Management can measure the average time it takes for each checkout operator to handle the average individual item; how long they take to deal with each customer, the amount of time taken between scanning the last item and taking payment for the transaction, the amount of down-time between customers, takings per hour per operator, number of miss-scans and so on.

Although this means that in theory management can use EPOS to plan its weekly checkout staff rota, and to introduce piecework, I am not aware of any retailer which intends to utilise these facilities. There is also some evidence in the insurance industry that the new technology is not being used directly for purposes of management control (Storey, 1986). At the most, staff monitoring will be used typically only to measure the extremes of worker productivity and might be used as a basis for a request that individual operators speed up. Managers were reluctant to exploit this 'big brother aspect' as they called it, for fear of precipitating a backlash at the checkout. This is a very vulnerable point, especially at peak trading hours. 'A stoppage there could cause a riot!' said one manager, 'and we don't want our girls to find out that we can monitor them.' Nor could EPOS be used to measure 'service' which cannot be directly linked to the pace of work.

In this (as in previous designs of conventional electronic till) there had been some de-skilling. Operators were inclined to lose their powers of mental arithmetic. Now that the price had been replaced by an unintelligible code, it was harder to rearrange a customer's order when it had totalled more than the customer expected. A 'price look-up' (PLU) facility did not necessarily eliminate this difficulty once the operator's sense of what she/he was doing had atrophied.

Looking further into the store, EPOS does eliminate some manual data entry work, though not all. Only two companies had reduced their store staff as a result of EPOS. The preferred option was to redeploy staff to the selling function. At headquarters I found extensive evidence of small to moderate job losses, again among data entry clerks. In a total company workforce of two and a half thousand this might translate into five to fifteen redundancies, invariably of women workers.

The main effect of EPOS was to enable retail operations managers to carry lower inventories, and to concentrate on the fastest selling or most profitable lines carried. Usually this meant a reduction in the number of lines and some experimentation with new lines. One chain store had changed forty per cent of its lines in twelve months, and was taking a 'brute force' computing policy to finding out what sold best. This suggested some de-skilling of the buyer's craft, as well as a shift in the kind of skills needed.

EPOS data also enables operations managers to monitor regional and seasonal trends, the effects of price changes on sales and to compare the sales of similar goods (by value and by nature). The preferred monitors of overall performance appeared to be volume and value of sales per square foot and value of average customer sales.

Efforts were continuing in order to establish an interface between the EPOS systems and warehouse computers, again with similar objectives, i.e. reducing inventories and maximising throughput.

What follows is a series of typical accounts of what managers in this kind of retail distributor wanted to achieve, and of where the main weaknesses lie. A DP manager:

> Till about four years ago our stock control data was always about eight or nine weeks out of date. This meant that we didn't know what had happened in the Christmas rush until much too late.

He explained that stock control, auditing and re-ordering had previously been 'driven' by a complex system of item-tag collection and data entry. This data was unreliable because shop workers would often forget to detach the tags from goods as they were sold, and cumulative errors would build up in the inventory record. Eventually the only way of knowing what was in a store was to go and count it. This they used to do frequently.

He and other managers complained that with EPOS they were in contrast 'deluged with data which they did not know what to do with'. Gradually they were learning how to use it for strategic management purposes.

Other chains had used EPOS to virtually automate the reordering process. As long as they knew how many lines a given store carried, and how fast each line was selling they could replenish the shelving (which was of known dimensions) at a rate to match. These 'hard benefits' had been used to justify installing EPOS. The 'soft benefits' of how to interpret sales trends took longer to reach and were not usually part of the initial project justification.

EPOS had caused an increase in store workload in many cases because item codes, or machine readable labels (magnetic strips or bar-codes) had to be attached to every item. In some more economically concentrated branches of retailing, manufacturers had been forced to print bar-codes on packaging, but where they did not this could involve a 'nightmare demand on shop staff'. Where item code numbers were keyed in manually at the checkout productivity could fall, because this took longer than ringing up prices. This was less important to retailers who sold small numbers of high-value commodities.

In the majority of the major chains, most senior managements clearly saw the branch manager as a problem, and had been at pains to eliminate any local discretion to decide what stock his or her store should take. Head office controllers were convinced that they could optimise store performance at a distance. They could totally disaggregate sales data. Store managers often had low status and were not trusted to know best what their own store would be successful at selling. Nor in most cases were they going to be given access to the EPOS data which would enable them to experiment. Thus at one chain 'What the Board wants to do is to remove that discretion from the shops, to make the computer system so clever that the system would get [re-ordering] basically right every time.'

Problems arose in trying to integrate buyers into the system. The essence of the difficulty was that while a company could see what was selling, it had few ways of knowing from this data what lines not stocked could be selling *more* quickly. This depended in the last analysis on the central buyers' 'feel' and 'intuition' for what the market might demand. (Stories of famous buyers' hunches were legion.) Many were certain that they would wish to see the buyer's craft absorbed into the EPOS driven system, but they could not envisage how this could be done. Said a senior manager,

> I don't see that our system is clever enough to make deductions. It may be one day, but I think that there are so many things that you need to do just to handle the everyday routine of our business that I think that it will be a long time before it comes about, and may never come about.

What EPOS did was to speed up the feedback loop between buying and selling so that good and bad buying decisions showed up more quickly. To enhance this, stores tended to be classified into strictly standardised types.

EPOS systems often showed unexplained variations in sales patterns over the country. Buyers created 'forced orders' on to the stores so as to see the sales effect – whether or not the local manager wanted the new line. Some store managers complained that head office did not draw on their local knowledge to explain sales variations.

In the Taylorised ideal type, HQ managers believed that local buying or reordering discretion would merely generate incomprehensible idiosyncrasies in the branch network, and that central buyers would lose track of what was going on. The central buyers' decisions would soon become meaningless because it was said that they would not be able to tell how good or bad their hunches had been from a reading of the sales data. Centralised control was vital to centralised buying, even if buyers could only use EPOS data on a 'suck-it-and-see-basis'. Most companies in this category agreed that they had 'managed out' entrepreneural skill at the branch level – a process which older branch managers deeply regretted. Indeed, companies now aimed for marginal, incremental and safe improvements in sales performance. Entrepreneurs did 'not really fit in too well'. Control of data had been achieved at the expense of traditional retail skills.

However, the most extreme case of de-skilling was found on the warehousing side. Systems had been implemented which translated each store delivery note into a logical warehouse picking order for warehouse personnel. The objective had been to eliminate discrepancies between what stores were supposed to receive and what the warehouse actually sent but in pursuing this objective a new problem had occurred, due to a syndrome termed 'aisle blindness' or 'pickers' amnesia'.

The problem was that warehouse picking had been de-skilled to a point where workers had too little to think about to retain their attention to the job. For example, as one manager pointed out:

When it comes to the picking, the computer conveniently prints the branch invoice in the same sequence to the way the products are laid out [in the warehouse]. So far as our worker is concerned, he picks up the Sheffield shop and walks along taking three from this [location] four from the next and he's walking slowly down. This is logical. No need for memory. With the old [paper based system] there were so many bits of information that were lacking that they had to use their own skills and ability and memory to operate. It was the deliberate mental compensation which they had which gave them their satisfaction.

Now we're going to the system whereby all the effort, all the information is all at hand. And there's nothing left for the brain to do. So they're almost like pigeons in a pigeon hole you know. A battery hen type situation ...

Pickers amnesia – a psychological problem of people doing order picking because of the repetition. The information given to human beings is so simple and so we're into human errors. It is a problem because the quality of staff you get at the pay we offer means we're getting a [casualised] workforce.

Now they're not thinking about what they're doing, and this means they forget where they are. They may think that a line is out of stock because they're looking at the wrong picking location without knowing it – not the one where the stock really is. This means that stuff might not reach the store, though we can't be sure it's because of thieving or because of this aisle blindness.

From a psychological point of view I'd like to see a bit more human engineering – when you rearrange the work more to fit the aspirations and abilities of the individual, rather than getting the individual rearranged to suit the job.

Yet management could not decide whether a reversal in policy would increase productivity, by regaining the workers' attention.

At the moment there is too much pressure in society and in the economy to achieve short term results . . . In the meantime I think we just sort of use people and pick them up and drop them – use them like tools a little bit . . .

And so from a psychologist's point of view rather than an accountant's point of view it's probably getting worse. Eventually I think society will demand something better.

For a few, the quality of work had improved. Another manager argued that:

A few people get interesting jobs – like working out where to store products to reduce the backaches. Yes, certainly a supervisory level will certainly be more interesting. But for the ordinary shop-floor worker if you like, the work is more monotonous.

The main advantage of de-skilling has been an increase in job flexibility. With the replacement of skilled reach truck drivers by an automatic retrieval system the skill profile had become more uniform throughout the warehouse, and most workers could do most jobs, 'within about four days'. These contradictory observations support Wilkinson's claim (Wilkinson, 1983) that efficiency gains from the use of new technologies are difficult to evaluate conclusively. Deskilling technologies can have contradictory effects.

SUMMARY

EPOS systems can be used to reinforce a Taylorian division of labour in retailing. Much of the work is factory-like, and there is little to differentiate management roles in a large chain store HQ from centralised manaufacturing companies. Entrepreneural skills are eroded and the DP system is intended to enhance the marginal profit on the most profitable high volume lines.

This strategy compromises lower managerial discretion and can create de-skilling effects which compromise labour productivity. These negative aspects need not be due to deliberate obstructivism among shopfloor workers. Workers may simply lose some of their ability.

Among the fourteen retail companies which I looked at more closely, eight conformed to the centralising tendency which I have idealised here. They included national chains in DIY, household goods, electrical goods, petrol, food, chemist and related goods, books and stationery, and clothing. Of these eight, the electrical goods, chemist, household goods and food chains fitted the ideal type in all aspects while the remainder presented a good, to very good fit to type.

NEW TECHNOLOGY FOR CRAFT RETAILING

Six of the case studies did not fit the Taylorian mode; indeed five contrasted strongly with it. Instead of an intense division of labour, job responsibilities were quite wide on the shopfloor, and the career and training approaches were markedly different. With only a little hesitation, I will refer to this second group as craft retailers. This group was comprised of one national food supermarket chain, one national men's clothing chain and four prestige shops from the Bond Street and Regent Street area of London. The analysis indicates ideal-type tendencies found within these retailers. Here EPOS became an extension of, rather than replacement for, the art of retailing.

The essence of this different approach was that sales data was devolved to store managers, or in the case of department stores to the departmental heads. This decentralised decision-making in a clear way so that local managers had responsible autonomy for all the factors that their counterparts in the Taylorian model had lost. They decided what lines, how many of each, what layout (except for the food chain) what price (again discretion was more limited in the food chain) which promotions and which kind of displays.

The ability of practise craft retailing came from an apprenticeship based training system. Excepting the food chain, none of the rest had progressed very far towards multi-tier entry and divisional specialisation. Sideways promotions were commonly made for the sake of experience. Above all, the buying, selling and merchandising (stocking/display) functions were not rigidly separated. Buyers were promoted from sales personnel and women buyers were much more in evidence. When buyers were not away negotiating supplies, then they were usually expected to go on to the sales floor *to sell*. The belief was that only from a direct experience of customer reactions could a buyer truly judge what the market might demand. A close interaction with staff and customers gave buyers their 'feel'. The four London stores were most categorical that it was of paramount importance to preserve these skills because they *depended* on buyers 'getting it right'. These stores sold on the basis of the 'ambience', 'style' and 'special (X Co) look'. They would undermine this should they de-skill and regiment the retailing functions. Buyers' decisions were acts of faith not safe computer bets.

Unlike the mass-retailers, the craft retailers had not sought to justify EPOS on the basis of 'hard benefits' alone. I have the distinct sense that they were adopting the new technology in a rather similar way to the approach they took in all purchasing decisions. 'Mr Z just felt the time was right and EPOS was probably going to contribute a lot to the business'. They would feel their way forward in confidence.

The craft retailers were distinct from the first group in many other ways. One of the four London stores had lobbied the governement not to undermine the minimum wages legislation, nor to cut back on further education for retail staff. They felt worried that casualisation of retail employment was inadvisable and that it did not suit their business needs. They 'preferred quality to quantity' but felt that they had become isolated on the relevant policy-making bodies. One other like-minded retailer, it was said, had expressed major reservations on the employment policies of the CBI because of the Confederation's refusal to resist government policy on the wage and training issues. As a training manager explained 'Winston Churchill knew all about this you know ... you just can't go for cheap labour ... it's really a bit frightening.' Only with a great deal of reluctance had they taken on YTS trainees. Management were embarrassed because they sympathised with trade union demands that workers be paid to their value.

Staff were courteous and knowledgeable. They took an 'advisory' stance, and would discuss purchases in an informed way. Typical comments included the following remarks from a DP Manager:

> Let me reiterate, everyone, every level of management that is, has the dual responsibility for the buying and the selling operation, or the control or overseeing of it ... We have an extremely short management chain with only three levels operating under a Board of Directors, providing us, we believe, with the great strength of total involvement at all levels on all facets of the business.

The inventory reductions which Taylorised companies had looked for from the outset, came as accidental surprises to the craft retailers. For example a departmental manager recalled:

> The very presence of a computer produced a certain amount of disciplined thinking. Basic merchandise layouts, both in store and in warehouse improved dramatically both in terms of clarity and association. [Both are important] from the store's and the customer's point of view ... and better stock availability ... *Side benefits that had not been envisaged.*

Throughout he emphasised that he was discovering new ways of managing more effectively as he 'played' with the sales data. The last thing he aimed at was labour reductions. As far as he saw it EPOS was 'by definition labour intensive'.

Shopfloor staff in craft retailing were much more inclined to make positive assessments about their working lives. They particularly valued their own ability to make judgements about individual customers and to adjust their approach accordingly. They enjoyed making a sale and took pride in the tacit knowledge of the craft.

Store layouts often depended on a salesperson's ability to draw the customer's attention to 'comparison goods'. This presented a strong contrast to computer-optimised self-service layouts, where the 'sales staff' no longer engaged in any real selling. Recently a company takeover had led to the elimination of a sales-staff centred layout. It was reported that the new company refused to employ anybody who had worked under the old company for more than twelve months. It was felt that they could not be retrained into the more passive new role. They 'wouldn't be able to leave customers alone'.

Whereas 'craft' sales staff saw customer self-service as an expropriation of their skills, Taylorised staff were indifferent to the presence of customers. Moreover, younger customers, were embarrassed by 'service' and were 'put off by a sales approach'.

CONCLUSIONS

The second ideal type of retail organisation is an inversion of the first in several respects. In place of the relentless stress on specialisation, de-skilling and the centralisation of control which characterises the Taylorist approach, craft retailing broadly trusts the skills of store managers and shopfloor staff. The approach of each type of retailer is reflected in their approach to, and implementation of EPOS. Although market position, product market and geographical location help to define the two camps in retailing, they are not decisive. At least one food chain of supermarkets – which we might have expected to fit the Taylorist model – in fact displays much of the craft approach. Less detailed knowledge of two other national chains (not discussed here) suggests that they also fall quite clearly into the craft category.

What are the implications for discussions on the labour process? First, and rather obviously, Taylorism is the dominant organisational form found among larger retail companies. But it is by no means universal, nor is it the only management strategy which leads to profit or control maximisation.

Second, EPOS technology seems to be malleable, fitting either of the ideal types described here. In the Taylorist strategy branch managers become redundant *as managers*, while there are no more than a few actual redundancies. In craft retailing there is a distinct increase in the demand for 'analytical store managers'. And in all cases there is an increased demand for numerate senior managers.

Thirdly, although I can give no precise estimate of emotional commitment, it was clear enough that Taylorised retailers depended far less on emotional control over, and through their workforces, than did the craft retailers. For most retailers, that is, factory-like direct control strategies suffice. This strategy has its limits in so far as directly controlled workers will, for a number of complex reasons (deliberate or otherwise) not perform emotional labour, so long as they have minimal defences against the demands of managers and customers. However we should be forewarned by Hochschild's work, that in some market circumstances, even Taylorised retail enterprises begin to demand emotional labour.

Fourthly, and much more controversially, it is possible to suggest that emotionally committing employment is a far more profound managerial control strategy. Workers who fall under the spell of 'artistic' retailing become shop-workers at all times. Unlike Taylorised workers they are much less able to 'leave work behind', while managers everywhere face this personal experience of work too.

Emotional labourers – literally labourers in their own emotions – tend to adopt the mannerisms of the store in rather the same way as traditional bank workers are supposed to have adopted bank values concerning their private lives. However much more enjoyable their experience of work may be when compared with that of factory-like workforces, they are in this specific sense less free and more duty bound. I find myself led to a position which suggests that from this uncomfortable standpoint, direct control strategies may be preferable, and non-emotional labour less alienating than many jobs which we normally think of as 'better'.

Finally I think we can point to limits which will help to retard what amounts to an expansion of the service sector into the emotional realm. For example, where there is a conflict between labour productivity and emotional work – at the checkout, in the nursing ward – then the scope for emotional labour is fleeting and impersonal. The need for one defeats the other. In other areas such as the sale of life assurance, high value goods, theme parks, holidays, financial advice, where the work cycle may be longer, then the commercialisation of emotion is much more extendable. These areas deserve greater attention from labour process research, particularly as we now have a wider research vocabulary with which to describe them.

Notes

1. I wish to stress that throughout my research (which has variously covered local authorities, manufacture and banking, as well as retailing) I have found managers to be open and helpful towards research. I am almost never refused access, and this has caused me to doubt the traditional trajectory of qualitative social science research, particularly in relation to industrial sociology.
2. Hochschild's argument is *not* that factory work is devoid of emotions. It is simply that the emotions there are not directly drawn into commodity relations.

References

Braverman, H. (1974) *Labour and Monopoly Capital* (London: Monthly Review Press).
Burawoy, M. (1985) *The Politics of Production* (London: Verso).
Friedman, A. (1977) *Industry and Labour* (London: Macmillan).
Evans, M. K., Blase, J. J. (1984) 'The Moral Perspective, The Life Insurance Agent as Guardian of the Family Ethic'. Paper to the *1st Standing Conference on Organisational Symbolism and Corporate Culture* Lund, Sweden (Macmillan).
Golding, D. (1980) 'Establishing Blissful Clarity in Organisational Life; Managers' in *Sociological Review* 28 (4) pp. 763–82.
Hochschild, A. R. (1983) *The Managed Heart; the Commercialisation of Human Feeling* (London: University of California Press).
Howton, W. F., Rosenberg, B. (1965) 'The Salesman: Ideology and Self-Imagery in a Prototypic Occupation' in *Social Research*, 32, 277–98.
Knights, D., Willmott, H. (eds) (1986) *Managing the Labour Process* (Aldershot: Gower).
Mills, C. W. (1951) *White Collar* (London: Oxford University Press), Autumn, 277–98.
Reed, M. (1986) 'Labour Process Theory and the Sociology of Management'. Paper to the *4th Aston/UNIST Conference on the Organization and Control of the Labour Process,* Birmingham.
Knights, D. (1975) 'Drummers, Punters and Others' in *The Sociology of the Salesman* (Unpublished Masters, UMIST).
Smith, S. L. (1985) 'Work Organisation, Gender and Technical Change in Banking: The Social Limits of Scientific Management'. Paper to the *3rd Aston/UMIST Conference on the Organization and Control of the Labour Process* Manchester.
Smith, S. L., Wield, D. (1988) 'New Technology and Bank Work: Banking on IT as an "Organizational Technology"' in Harris, L. (ed.) *New Perspectives on the Financial System* (London: Croom Helm).

Storey, J. (1986) 'The Phoney War? New Office Technology: Organisation and Control' in Knights, D. and Willmott H., eds *Managing the Labour Press* (Aldershot: Gower).

Teulings, A. W. M. (1986) 'The Power of Corporate Management: the Powerlessness of the Manager' in Knights, D. and Willmott, H., ibid.

Wilkinson, B. (1983) *The Shop Floor Politics of New Technology* (London: Heinemann Educational).

8 Beyond Taylorism: Computerisation and QWL Programmes in the Production Process*

Lorraine Giordano

This chapter is part of research conducted for the author's doctoral dissertation. The dissertation is based on a case study of a plant which designs and manufactures computer systems and parts for both the US Department of Defence and as a commercial manufacturer. The dissertation examines changes in the technical and social organisation of the labour process as work is automated and Quality of Work Life programmes are implemented to address problems at the point of production. A central issue in this research is to study the extent to which these processes are linked and represent managerial attempts to address uncertainty and changes within the market. Within this overall framework, the impact of automation on occupations and the nature of job skills are analysed. The study of QWL will not emphasise the neo-human relations perspective of its role as a job enrichment programme, but will be analysed in terms of its role in the re-organisation of the labour process.

Empirical data was collected through in-depth interviews with workers whose occupations are interrelated in the production process – machinists, methods, drafters and design drafters and of Quality Circle participants in each of the representative occupations.

*I would like to thank David Knights and colleagues at the Conference on the Organisation and Control of the Labour Process held at Aston University, April 1986, Sophia Catsambis, Linda Cushman and Cherni Gillman, Wolf Heydebrand and Ruth Milkman. I owe a special debt of gratitude to Miriam Frank.

INTRODUCTION

The last two decades have seen rapid changes in the way work is per-formed, where this work is done, the kinds of work available for people, and even whether some will work at all. Part of the reason for this is the fact that industrial organisation is being re-shaped by two distinct, yet inter-related, processes – computerised automation and labour-management programmes. Popularly known as Quality of Work Life, or QWL, these programmes are organisational strategies designed to address production, motivation and control issues on the shop floor.[1]

Automation and QWL represent current industrial attempts to re-organise production methods. In the broadest sense, they are part of management's efforts to control uncertainty in production and secure profits by reducing labour costs and increasing predictability in production. Historically, management has always adopted techni-cal and social methods which would maintain, if not increase, control over production. As Nelson points out, the factory system that emerged in the US between 1880 and 1920 was not simply the product of mass production techniques but also of changes in management practices. Social welfare programmes and the develop-ment of a systematic supervisory system were part of this development.[2]

Automation and QWL will be examined in terms of current indus-trial and managerial changes and as interrelated processes within these changes. The extent of this relationship depends on how far:

1. industry can utilise fully automated systems in its production process;
2. automation is used to reorganise existing production methods;
3. the industry is decentralising operations and/or centralising aspects of its planning and decision-making;
4. top management is able to engage the co-operation of middle and lower level managers who may feel their jobs are in jeopardy;
5. upper level management will, in turn, support those decisions made on the local level;
6. management depends upon and can gain workers' co-operation in reorganising production;
7. workers resist these efforts, the strength of their organisation, and past history of labour relations.

All of these processes contribute to the form automation and QWL will assume within a given industry and, indeed, within a given plant. The diversity of corporate needs around these factors will subsequently mean a diversity in the implementation of QWL programs and the use of automated technology. This chapter will examine computerised automation as it affects the organisation of the work process and the nature of skills required. It will also address the role of QWL in the work process, labour relations and its importance for corporate reorganisation and decision-making.

AUTOMATION AND QWL PROGRAMMES: ISSUES IN THE LABOUR PROCESS DEBATE

This chapter will attempt to show the concrete ways automation and QWL interact and their effects on the labour process. The questions of skill, control and hierarchy will inform this work. However, the emphasis of the analyses of these processes will be on their relational aspects rather than traditional categories of efficiency, rationality and integration. It will also go beyond the radical critiques which focus on de-skilling[3] and methods of control.[4]

Analysis of skill changes brought about by automation has emphasised either the de-skilling thesis of Braverman[5] or the 'reliable employee' developed by Blauner's comparative study of technology, skill and autonomy.[6] However, recent work on job redesign[7] has challenged the narrow technological perspective which has formed the basis of much of the critiques of the labour process. Rather, attention is focused on the broader social relations of production, including market changes and the demand for the kinds of skills and work organisation these changes require – among them flexibility and team work.

There is no question that de-skilling remains as a factor in the reorganisation of the work process. The tendency toward displacement of labour, skills and fragmentation are, as Marx argues, part of the historical process of the subordination of labour under capitalism.[8] Proponents of Braverman's thesis[9] view the computerisation of the workplace as the ulimate form of Taylorism. The use of robotics to create the worker-less factory and the application of computerised automation to work which had successfully resisted Taylorist practices in the past represent the most far-reaching attempts at de-skilling labour. Central themes focus on the dissolution of craft skills and the fragmentation and rationalisation of scientific and technical skills. While these are existing trends in the labour process, some of the skills required in computerised production demand *qualitatively* different skills – more abstract in nature. A distinction needs to be drawn between those skills which are actually lost in the process and those which are, in fact, translated into new forms that continue to be based on conventional knowledge.

Therefore, if skill changes are carefully examined, the processes of de-skilling and the introduction of new skills and/or occupations are *concurrent processes*. At any given historical moment, the labour process embodies de-skilling, skill development, conflict and co-operation. As tendencies within production, Thompson identifies them as 'unfinished processes' which are historically determined.[10] A more inclusive analysis of the organisation of work would consist of:
1. existing technical and social divisions of labour;
2. the history of labour relations within a firm;
3. market conditions;
4. the competitive strength of the firm.[11]

Within this framework, is is important to consider the fact that computerisation affects both process *and* product, significantly impacting on what is to be produced, rapidly changing market needs, as well as the methods used to produce those goods and services. Kelly argues that the contemporary movement for flexible work groups represents managerial strategies for improving their competitive position within the market as well as to increase control over the labour process. Technology, therefore, represents one aspect of a multi-dimensional analysis of the study of skills and the organisation of work.[12]

Strategies for managing changes in work redesign includes gaining the co-operation of the workforce. QWL appears to be part of this reorganisation process and represents a form for introducing change into the organisation of work and soliciting ideas for increasing or maintaining a competitive edge within the market. Much of the attention given to this process has centred around motivation and/or job satisfaction.[13] As Knights and Collinson point out, although there is a recognition by neo-human relations theorists of the social relations of production, it is perceived 'as a resource from which workers extract what is necessary to satisfy their individual "needs" '.[14] They argue, however that to accept this premise as a basis for understanding co-operation leads to a distortion of conditions under which workers participate in this process. In addition, reliance on workers' co-operation suggests somewhat of a capitulation by management to workers' demands for increased participation as well as a recognition of their knowledge of the production process and the informal organisation on the shopfloor. It is, in actuality, part of the 'contested' terrain' of the workplace control. The use of informal work groups to both solve production problems and act as a mechanism for discipline and co-operation suggests workers' resistance to both the process and outcomes. Although QWLs remain embedded within the traditional bureaucratic hierarchy, they also operate, to a degree, *outside* of it in the context of an informal decision-making body. The existence of such an informal mechanism for decision-making at the point of production contradicts Edwards' thesis of separate and successive forms of control. Instead, it tends to support Thompson's notion of a 'combination of managerial structures'.[15]

QWL is designed to facilitate consensus. However, the democratic tendencies within this process are mitigated by management's right to define the parameters of the agenda. Its ideology and format of democratic, voluntary participation encourages both conformity to the process as well as a framework for challenging managerial prerogatives.

QWL and automation can, therefore, be examined as both forms of organisation and control of the labour process. The flexibility of computerised automation as a production tool and in the organisation of work encourages such use of informal (yet bureaucratically controlled) mechanisms (QWL) to meet corporate goals. As Child notes, 'the flexible nature of new technological hardware and particularly its software may in fact permit a range of alternative working arrangements'.[16] QWL operates to facilitate varied and flexible work patterns. Child's representations of managerial strategies[17] for organising the labour process can, therefore, be extended to include QWLs along with the implementation of technology. This model would indicate that both automation and QWL interact and affect the use and organisation of skills and the mechanisms and forms of control.

MICROPROCESSORS AND AUTOMATION

The microprocessor is the core electronic component in automated equipment. A child of the first computer, the ENIAC, a large, room-sized computer with numerous vacuum tubes, the microprocessor is based on the development of the micro 'chip' – a single piece of silicon which contains all of the computer's processing components. Its compact size, along with increased computing and memory capabilities, has expanded its use and the possibilities for application in areas that were previously impractical with the larger computers. Microcomputers in production technology, information gathering and information processing are used to reorganise both labor and decision-making. Referred to as the 'Third Industrial Revolution', computerisation is having profound structural effects on work performed in the public and private sectors, in production and service industries, and at all levels of the organisation – from the shop floor to the executive suite.

Two features distinguish computer automation from its predecessors:
1. the flexibility of its application to all phases of the production process;
2. the capacity to store and generate the different types of information gathered in that process.

Earlier forms of mechanisation and the mass production techniques introduced in the 1920s replaced some of the physical labour and increased the speed and improved the continuity of production. However, mass production also included the use of specialised tools and extended the division of labour. Manual work, therefore, always remained the central element in production.[18] In the 1950s, cybernetics and continuous process production introduced high speed processing to industries manufacturing liquid and gas products, in particular petroleum, chemical plants, and food processing. Manual and skilled labour were then replaced with technical processes and industry-specific skills. The nature of the technology at that time limited its application almost exclusively to these industries. However, continuous process production methods could not be applied to the metal working industries or to clerical operations. Nevertheless, it was (and is) an important part of the history of computerising production methods.

Like previous technological innovations, microcomputer-based automation has eliminated jobs as well as created new categories of work. However, this form of automation differs from past technologies in its unique ability to link each phase of production through the computer system. It is both multi-functional and re-programmable and can easily be adapted to changes in production needs.[19] For example, the current growth in the steel industry centres around those corporations who have developed specialty steel industry centres or who use innovative process technologies to produce standard goods.[20] Both strategies include the computerisation of production facilities. The most far-reaching changes will come with the flexible manufacturing system – FMS. Since 75 per cent of parts produced are done in small or medium batches, FMS is able to manufacture items as cheaply as most mass production systems. In addition, different products can be manufactured on the same line. According to *Fortune*,[21] General Electric uses flexible automation to make 2000 versions of its basic electric meter.

Computerised automation can also provide management with immediate access to production output as well as inventory and cost control within a plant. The 'global factory' has become a term applied to the way production and managerial linkages have been forged between domestic and international corporate facilities.[22] Ford's 'world car' – whose parts are designed, manufactured and assembled in Brazil, West Germany, Ireland and the United States, symbolises the extent to which operations can be centrally directed and co-ordinated for an increasingly competitive global market.

Computerisation of both production and management information systems has several major consequences.

First, it offers the means to eliminate whole series of operations by programming them into the computer, using robots, or re-combining operations. Skills that are programmed are no longer the province of one particular occupation. These automated skills instead become a part of the general body of knowledge available throughout the internal apparatus of an industry, and can under-mine workers' specific control of production – thus laying the groundwork for possible job elimination.

The situation faced by printers in the newspaper industry clearly illustrates this tendency. During the 1960s Local 6 of the International Typographical Union (ITU) successfully negotiated a contract with four major New York City daily newspapers[23] with substantial provisions on automation. The union won:
1. complete jurisdiction over jobs created by automation;
2. control over re-training;

3. union approval of the introduction of automated equipment;
4. shares in productivity savings as a result of automation;
5. no economic concessions in exchange for job security.[24]

However, the introduction of typesetting computers, video terminals, optical scanners and high speed phototypesetting machines still drastically reduced the number of employed printers in the United States and Canada. Between 1969 and 1976 this occupation declined by 24 per cent[25] with a likelihood of a continued downward turn through 1990.[26] As the Bureau of Labour statistics indicates, the growing development and use of these more technologically advanced printing methods eliminated many of the jobs printers had been re-trained to perform. In addition, the expanding industry output of the 1960s slowed down considerably. ITU estimates that an additional 25 per cent of composing room jobs were lost because of automation in printing.[27]

Second, a countervailing, but related, tendency is a 'shift in the lines of demarcation between jobs'.[28] Automated equipment's memory capabilities have been allowing workers to perform a wider range of operations. Computers can also simplify particular job functions which then makes it easier for workers in related occupations to perform them. For example, computerised numerical control machines reduce the necessity for using operation sheets that machinists follow when they produce a part. Experienced machinists can, with some training, programme these machines and eliminate the need for process engineers to methodise the job. As a process engineer working in a defence plant explained it:

> Right now the equipment I've seen – the lathes and the milling machines – are more or less getting so that if you have a man who is smart enough with a machining background, he can program the machine right there to do just about anything that I can do in the APT language [computer programming language] ... The technology has caught up to the point that now what they are really going to need is a good methods machinist.[29]

Machinists who have mastered computerised numerical control believe they have gained considerable freedom to plan and programme the machine's operations. Computerisation provides access to a wider range of information and brings together skills separated by training, the division of labour and job jurisdiction. Occupations, like machinists and process engineers (methods), which share a body of knowledge increasingly face the possibility of shifts in job skills. What once could be labelled a deliberate infringement on job classification becomes less obvious if information is available at the push of a button. Upgrading one occupation can threaten the survival – or a significant amount of the work – of another. Procedures which formerly required lengthy calculations and a knowledge of advanced math are now completed by the computer, simplifying some of the time-consuming detail work.

However, acquisition of computer skills does not always translate into job upgrading or pay increases. While programming clearly represents additional skill, it may not be seen as comparable to those replaced by automation. As a process engineer pointed out:

> One time an executive board member tried to get us an increase in pay because we require a new skill to program these NC machines and we had to acquire additional skills to run the CAD/CAM machine. The answer that he got was that we should be getting paid less since the programming makes it easier for us. We didn't even have to know math to program. And you really don't have to know how to do it because the machine will do it for you.[30]

A third and related consequence of computerisation is the possibility that some occupations will experience a radical downward shift in skills or qualifications necessary to perform a job, as in the case of telephone testers. According to Bob Hoffman, shop steward, Local 1101, Communications Workers of America (CWA),

> Testers were responsible for using whatever necessary equipment, skills, knowledge and experience to determine where the trouble occurred ... Now what you have is ... a clerk who sits at a terminal, and the clerk is almost always a minority female, while the tester was almost a white male ... She punches your phone number in and the computer is programmed to perform certain tests on the line and will kick out a code. She cross-references the number on a chart and dispatches an appropriate repair person.[31]

Automated test equipment has not only eliminated a skilled craft, it has replaced this well paid, autonomous occupation with a highly routinised clerical job – dominated by a female work force – whose pay scale is drastically below that of testers and whose promotional opportunities to any line of craft work are limited or non-existent.

A fourth consequence of automation is that it offers greater flexibility in management control over the decision-making and production process. According to Sanders, computerisation of information has allowed management to use the same information for different purposes. At the executive level, it furnishes data for planning purposes, while middle management uses it primarily as a mechanism for control.[32] The use of computerisation in the decision-making process has contributed to the development of an industrial organisation whose planning and financial decisions are centralised and whose operations are frequently decentralised and highly interdependent. Long-range planning for production and the co-ordination of interdependent operations are, increasingly, being centralised. With computerised production schedules, inventories, and product sales, decisions regarding on-site production issues become delegated as the primary responsibility of local management, including product quality and the use of skills. Decentralisation also includes design of a structure that will aid corporate planning strategies and insure maximum compliance with scheduling and the co-ordination of production.[33] This kind of industrial reorganisation requires the creation of new mechanisms for communication between corporate headquarters and its divisions. Among its goals are greater co-ordination of interdependent operations, and the commitment of workers and managers to participate in this reorganisation through their involvement in the set up and maintenance of such a mechanism. Toward this end, Stern and Kanter have identified the recent development of a permanent 'parallel (bureaucratic) structure' capable of dealing with risks and uncertainty within the decision-making and production process. This parallel structure requires a flexible work organisation, problem-solving techniques, and flexible labour-management relations. Common in these structures are QWL programmes. They affect non-routine production problems and channel information back to the traditional bureaucracy.[34]

LABOUR – MANAGEMENT COOPERATION

The QWL movement has been associated with two well-publicised, yet very different issues: 'Japanese style' management and workplace democracy. American industrial folklore credits Japanese business with a visionary approach which has re-directed adversarial labour-management relations toward a more co-operative accomplishment of goals.[35] It is not uncommon to hear American workers attribute Japan's competitive edge to its labour-management programmes (Quality Circles), saying that these programmes originated out of Japan's cultural practices, i.e., loyalty of the company to workers as expressed through guaranteed lifetime employment.[36] In addition, human relations proponents have used the issue of motivation to 'emphasize those aspects of work and reaction to work that *seem* amenable to manipulation in the interests of *both* employees and employers'.[37] Not only does motivation explain the 'devotion' of Japanese workers in terms of a cultural phenomenon, but it is also used as appropriate evidence for the place of worker 'participation' in Western democratic societies.

Within this context, workplace democracy is often cited as the only solution to job dissatisfaction and the 'right to dignity' on the job. What workers want, we are told, is more responsibility, more input and decision-making, more respect, and less authoritarian control.[38] As abstract qualities, they are, in themselves, admirable and, according to democratic ideals, desirable. Few would argue with the need for greater participation in and control over the work in which we are engaged. Yet the use of the term workplace democracy (or its equivalents – participative management, or work humanisation) is misleading. Workplace democracy is, as Vaughan[39] sees it, a 'catchword' implying consensus. It is, in effect, assumed to be a shared experience and, as such, requires neither justification nor definition.

Witte[40] questions the validity of the use of the term 'democracy' as it applies to work under capitalism. Accepted notions of meritocracy and corporate rights to profits, along with varying degrees of influence and rewards within the production process, undermine the very principle of democratic organisation. Nevertheless, there has been a profusion of books, articles, and seminars devoted to the topic and to the potential results of such a movement. These include: increased job satisfaction and a lessening of job stress, absenteeism, and drug and alcohol abuse.

There has been no lack of organisations to promote labour-management programmes. The US Department of Labor[41] lists over 200 centres, programmes and private organisations, including university programmes, regional area programmes within the public sector, and joint labour-management programmes in the private sector. The federal government, under the Department of Labor and the Labor-Management Services Administration, created the Division of Co-operative Labor-Management Programs in 1982 'to encourage and assist employers and unions to undertake joint efforts to improve productivity and enhance the quality of working life'.[42] Previously, this work was carried out by the National Center for Productivity and the Quality of Work Life (formerly the National Commission on Productivity and Work Quality and under Nixon-Ford, the Productivity Commission).[43]

Quality of Work Life, or QWL, is a generic term representing a wide range of labour-management programmes. Specific types of programmes have been developed under such titles as: Employee Involvement, Quality Circles, Job Enlargement, Job Enrichment, Work Humanisation, Participative Management, Group Problem Solving, and Autonomous Work Groups. Each type of programme is designed to encourage particular forms of work organisation and decision-making, depending upon the nature of the industry and technology. For example, job redesign is prevalent in service sector industries, whil autonomous work groups are often instituted in highly automated, continuous process plants.[44] However, as Wrenn notes, most writings on the subject do not make distinctions between the different programmes, and there is little, if any, clear definition of the terms and their meanings.[45]

QWL, however, was not 'made in Japan', nor is it a contemporary phenomenon born out of the frustrations of a dissatisfied and youthful workforce as some proponents claim.[46] History provides evidence of similar attempts at gaining workers' co-operation, inspiring company loyalty, and avoiding work stoppages. Such past industrial inducements include the formation of the Whitley Councils and Joint Production Committees in England during the First and Second World Wars respectively; the Labor-Management Committees under the War Production Board in the United States during both World Wars; and various profit-sharing plans and human relations projects and experiments during the early 1900s.[47]

Like earlier labour-management co-operation programmes, QWL emphasised productivity, motivation, and co-operation. What distinguishes QWL from its historical counterparts are:
1. the integration of QWL into the reorganisation process as corporations centralise control over planning and decentralise authority over local operations;

2. the emphasis on the development of skills which are consistent with the needs of automated work process – flexibility, independent judgment, initiative, and team work.

AUTOMATION, QWL AND THE WORK PROCESS

The technical and social divisions of labour, authority relations, the specific uses of skills, knowledge and technology are all part of the social relations of the production process. Consequently, changes in any aspect of production will, by the nature of its relationship to the others, effect changes in them as well. The forms and extent of these changes will depend on a number of factors, including the nature of the industry, worker resistance to these changes, level of production techniques, and the strength of the industry in the marketplace.

Historically, the struggle between labour and management over the right to determine and control the use of skills and the organisation of work have shaped the social relations of production. In this age of global capitalism, recentralisation of corporate planning and increased autonomy of local management is structuring the production process and represents a contemporary strategy to assert managerial control.

Although automation and QWL affect different aspects of the labour process, they are, in essence, *two sides of the same process* and, therefore, inextricably linked. The structure of work includes elements of planning and decision-making as well as the actual physical work. To examine one aspect without its relationship to the other is to miss the interconnectedness of these basic and essential features of production. Therefore, within this context, automation and QWL represent changes in the technical and social divisions of labour and, as such, are embedded in the existing social relations of an organisation.

QWL and automation significantly contribute to recentralisation of planning and the decentralisation of authority over production decisions insofar as both are information-gathering and transmitting processes. The capacity for automated equipment to be used as an information system depends, to a great extent, upon workers' abilities and willingness to generate and fully utilise available computerised data. QWL is a formal and systematic, yet flexible, means of accomplishing this goal. Data generated through computerised management information systems – known as MIS – provide local management with specific problems and goals concerning cost, scheduling and efficiency. The role of QWL is to use this computer-generated information as it relates to efficient use of skills, product quality and the co-ordination of automated processes within the plant.

Because automation simplifies segments of the work process, management has the opportunity to re-design production according to its short and long-term needs. Job re-classification and the development of work teams promote a wider and more flexible application of skills in the use of computerised equipment. Through the problem-solving format of QWL, management can promote and sustain changes in work organisation. It encourages workers to draw on their experience and understanding of the production process and to be flexible in the use of their skills to create innovative solutions for cost, quality, and efficiency problems at the point of production.

A classic example of work reform is the General Foods dog food plant in Topeka, Kansas – commonly known as the 'Topeka experiment'. Built in a suburban area, it was designed to be a 'model' facility – highly automated and operated by workers organised into loosely hierarchical work teams called autonomous work groups. General Foods' interest in this approach stemmed from labour troubles in its Kankakee, Illinois plant and, consequently, the plant's low productivity rates.

Staffed by non-union workers, and therefore uninhibited by union work rules and seniority rights, General Foods' Topeka management encouraged job rotation, job redesign and worker responsibility for supervision and discipline; at the same time management designed and maintained the organisational structure within the plant. this enabled a certain amount of decision-making to be decentralised while management could still maintain basic and traditional controls over the organisation of the entire process.

Supporters of work reform saw this programme as representing a movement toward workplace democracy and the future in work organisation. However, as Schrank points out, the appeal to worker control or work humanisation was somewhat misleading as work shifts competed to increase productivity rates. Intense peer pressure within work groups to maintain or surpass production rates were further results of the Topeka project.[48] Walton, a consultant on the project, raises several important factors often overlooked in the discussion of Topeka.

1. Workers were carefully screened for select attributes before being hired.

2. General Foods had created a 'new corporate-level unit' responsible for monitoring and co-ordinating the activities of the Topeka plant and developing similar organisational structures in other plants.

3. Management by objectives was the basis for production decisions made by the work teams. Workers were expected to create patterns of work organisation which would achieve managerial goals.[49]

The different production needs of industries determine both the kind and extent of automation installed in plants. There are two basic uses of computers in production. They can be applied to a range of operations to increase accuracy and versatility in the use of materials and methods without a major re-structuring of the production process. On the other hand, computers can be part of a larger automated system which, as Shaiken points out, directs production activities and 'will define, collect and control the processing of information throughout the factory'.[50] Both uses will increase the predictability of performance. However, fully automated industries tie together all of the production processes, often reorganising work in very dramatic ways. For example, General Electric has spent approximately $500 million automating its locomotive plant in Erie, Pennsylvania. Computers will store all the design and manufacturing data and information on production needs which will be transferred automatically from one machine to another. GE's dishwasher plant in Louisville, Kentucky, includes the use of robotics and an inventory monitoring system. As a part is used in the assembly process, another is simultaneously being produced.[51] Moreover, these computerised processes tend to be linked with management information systems, which monitor productivity, inventory and quality control.

On the local level, computers provide managers with detailed data and the ability to spot potential problems in production flow and defects in parts or assembly. On the corporate level, these data are analysed in relation to larger corporate goals and used to develop and assess strategies for increasing productivity, creating new products and co-ordinating production and delivery schedules. For example, General Motors has used data on productivity output in their Fisher Body plants to raise work quotas. Called 'whipsawing' by unions, plants were expected to compete with one another in increasing productivity with the threat of plant closures or outsourcing.[52] Computerised data have been provided to workers by local managers on their productivity status. 'At Fisher Body's Flint, Michigan hardware plant, management issues a weekly newsletter that includes a chart tracking labor costs at the plant compared with those at other divisional hardware plants. Quarterly, the newsletter also discloses how the plant's quality audit stacks up against the others.'[53]

Dramatic changes in world trade patterns and the uses of computerisation in both production and communications have forced corporations to adopt new mechanisms for responding to global market conditions. Kanter notes that in order to be successful, organisations 'will need to be able to bring particular resources together quickly, on the basis of short term recognition of new requirements and the necessary capacities to deal with them'.[54] Decisions on planning and resource allocation are increasingly being made on the corporate level which, Kanter indicates, 'shift the ways functions and units line up with respect to each other'.[55] Parallel structures have emerged which transgress traditional boundaries and create new patterns of managerial communication.

The implications of decentralisation have extended to the executive suite. Trends indicate substantial reductions in corporate staff. Tom Peters notes that major corporations such as US Steel, Ford and General Electric have been steadily cutting staff positions.[56] According to Peters, these reductions are part of the second wave of corporate decentralisation. The first occurred after the Second World War when industries expanded into different product lines and created separate divisions, each responsible for their own operations and markets. The second wave or 'radical' decentralisation reduced the large centralised reporting system built up to oversee and monitor each division. For example, GE has consolidated its businesses into three groups: one consists of its service businesses, another industrial automated products, and its third and largest, appliances.[57] Increasingly, GE's corporate planning has been focused on an economic analysis of the industry's position in the global market. Policies include: increased capital expenditures to automated existing facilities; the acquisition of a wide range of industries from CAD (computer-aided design) manufacturing to financial services; and the disinvestment of businesses which do not maintain a good share of the market.[58]

The shift toward local responsibility for specific production goals is part of this large movement to re-structure the corporation. Decentralisation allows decision-making flexibility which will complement and inform the corporation's long range financial and planning strategies and will respond to unanticipated market changes or crises. Traditional departmental lines of communication and decision-making are being abandoned and re-grouped, often according to product areas. Known as 'vertical linking', workers and management have two major responsibilities: to identify the problems and strengths of their operations; and to plan and implement the necessary changes in order to meet corporate goals.

Most noteworthy here is the growing importance of and reliance on line management to set up and maintain this system.[59] Their task is to create a mechanism for problem-solving and the motivation of their subordinates to participate in such a process. QWL is often the vehicle used to carry out this process. Because it involves delegation of responsibility to subordinates and the blurring of conventional lines of authority, it has not always been a welcome change. Several factors contribute to managerial reluctance. First, it pinpoints problems existing under a manager's or supervisor's domain. In traditional bureaucratic culture, this is viewed as a sign of ineffective leadership. Lower level management may feel vulnerable and may resist exposing those areas under their control which could be criticised as unproductive. Second, this process requires workers to participate actively in the identification of problems as well as to initiate suggestions for improvement and change. Again, within a traditional bureaucratic framework, subordinates have no input into managerial decisions. Engaging workers in the definition of work area problems and in the propositions of solutions further contributes to supervisors' feelings of expendability.[60]

In Gyllenhammer's analysis of work re-design at Volvo, he points out that 'foremen carry the heaviest responsibility in implementing changes'.[61] They are not only expected to change their own orientation to their jobs – from disciplinarian to co-ordinator – but to motivate workers to participate in this process as well.

Third, upper level management may not be willing to institute suggested changes even though there was an initial financial and organisational commitment to the programme. Uneasiness with changes in long-standing corporate policies and management practices could result in little actual support for concrete proposals. As one former participant remarked:

We spent months arguing over a suitable topic. When we finally agreed on one we surveyed the workers in our area and researched several possible ways of approaching the problem. We figured out the best one, worked out all the details of how it would be implemented and the cost saving to the company. Our supervisor loved it, his boss loved it and his boss's boss loved it. We presented it to upper management and they said they would get back to us and we never heard from them. That was six months ago. What's the use of doing all this work if they're going to ignore it?[62]

Ultimately, however, it is the anticipation of increased productivity and flexibility of the workforce that motivates management to establish new mechanisms of organisational decision-making and control. The countless uses of computerised information gathered from every facet of a company's operations can only be realised in an environment equipped to implement them. Management knows that operators can either perform the basic functions to get a job done or, by working with the information stored in the computer, find faster, less costly and improved production methods. As a machinist said: 'On the Hurko [a computerised numerical control machine] I am only limited [in the use of the machine] by my imagination and my skill as a machinist.'[63] No matter how sophisticated a computer system might be, its value as an information and production system remains limited if workers choose to restrict themselves to minimal use of the data.

Certainly, this is nothing new in labour-management relations. Managers have always known that worker co-operation is essential regardless of production methods. However, as Drucker states, there is a 'change from organizing production around the doing of things to things to organizing production around the flow of things and information'.[64]

QWL AND CORPORATE PLANNING

Efforts to increase control over production are reflected in current corporate planning strategies. General Motors is in the process of creating a decentralised yet highly structured organisation. QWL programme reflects a new commitment: GM wants more flexibility in production methods, in the use of skills, and in the implementation of new forms of data gathering and decision-making. According to William Duffy, Executive Consultant at GM, the overall plan is to foster the development of interdependent production and management methods within individual plants rather than duplicate traditional forms of work organisation.[65] In this way, plants will be able to organise work according to the needs of particular product lines, output goals, and prevailing management – labour relations.

However, GM plant design and operations are far from being autonomous. They are linked to the corporation through management teams. These teams must organise work so that it meets overall corporate goals and maintains a system that can manage these interdependent units. Duffy's outline of management personnel indicates constriction rather than elimination of the managerial hierarchy, with a considerable shift in organisational responsibilities. He states:

> Rethinking the numbers of levels of supervision is a result of more than an effort to improve communications. It is part of a larger concern with better integration of staff functions at all levels of the plant ... When designing plant 55, the Pontiac Motor Division set up a special sanction group of sub-staff heads. They worked together to integrate division staff decisions impacting on a plant's goals. In other words, the group is there to ensure that Engineering Staff and Personnel Staff at the division level do not set conflicting priorities for the plants. In the plant, meanwhile, the management team is also set up so that they can easily communicate with each other and thus coordinate resources in order to best meet plant goals.[66]

Attempts to control elements of production and limit uncertainties in the process are also exerted on the shopfloor. Automation, along with job re-design into 'work units', has eliminated workers and created new job categories which focus on monitoring production and maintaining product quality. 'For example, in "Job Design", many characteristics of an operator's job are designed into the manufacturing machinery, therefore, high operator commitment must be a goal in machine design to insure the machine's productivity.'[67] According to this plan, workers' *knowledge* continues to be an important factor in production. However, skills are now only *indirectly* exercised in the form of monitoring and maintenance of automated processes. This diffusion of skills limits workers' ability to perform specific operations, while it simultaneously requires a broad range of general purpose – and more abstract – functions.

To ensure commitment to overall corporate goals and to maintain co-ordination of activities within the plant, QWL programmes have been built into work units and management teams. They serve to:
1. transmit information to and from the shop floor concerning corporate goals, productivity, cost, and quality control;
2. encourage participation in planning and problem-solving within the unit, hopefully increasing the commitment toward these goals;
3. provide local management teams with information on production output from the shop. This will increase their ability to carry out corporate goals on the local level and will provide upper management with access to information on operations within the work unit.

On the surface, this strategy of work reorganisation and shop floor planning has the ring of 'worker participation'. Certainly, it stands in contrast to the assembly line with its singular speed and the limitations of movement for those tied to it. Nevertheless, the kinds of participation required and sought after in these and similar work re-design projects refer primarily to the system of production. It is less a format for workers' interests and concerns than for the systematic integration of such general needs as autonomy, control and creativity into the formal and informal operations of an organization. By focusing on the notion of participation, some of the underlying consequences of this process are ignored. Most importantly:
1. management has a mechanism for appropriating shop floor knowledge on a systematic basis;
2. workers' input is encouraged insofar as it contributes to corporate goals and continues to provide information to meet these goals. It engages workers to view efficiency and productivity as their responsibility and, along with various forms of profit-sharing schemes, creates a sense of commitment to profit-making proposals. The goal of securing workers' co-operation is masked by the appeal of decision-making, participation and economic incentive.

CONTEMPORARY INDUSTRIAL DEMOCRACY

Corporate ideology that explains the contemporary movement for worker participation draws on traditional notions of democracy, updated to reflect current social and economic conditions. Much in the same way that industrial democracy served as ideological support for works councils in the early 1900s, the social and political movements of the 1960s and 1970s – for self determination and community control among African Americans, Native Americans, women's groups and Hispanics and Asian Americans – became the backdrop for 'worker participation' in decision-making and QWL. Current proponents of industrial democracy combine the concern for dignity generated by the movement for civil rights and the need for 'relevance' and self expression extolled by the 1960s counterculture to create a generational interest in workplace democracy. Contemporary strategies in the pursuit of worker co-operation combine ideas promoted by human relations school of the 1920s, e.g., the emphasis on the importance of informal work groups, with the sophisticated techniques of psychological motivation that developed in the 1960s.

Contemporary workers are believed to represent a 'new breed'. Raised in 'post-war affluence', they are said to be no longer satisfied with simply having a job or with the routine nature of most work, as their parents might have been. They are identified as self-seekers who are more interested in intrinsic rewards. But this interest in self-satisfaction need not interfere with increased rates of productivity. In fact, as Yankelovich and Immerwahr suggest, 'expressive values can enhance the work ethic when the people who focus on personal growth see their jobs as an outlet for their own self-expressive development'. They note, however, that 'people are not working as hard as their belief in the work ethic indicates that they should be.'[68]

Faced with a workforce which appears ready, willing and able to increase productivity, American management has been urged by social scientists to stop inhibiting their workers' desire for self-fulfillment and to use this available resource to regain America's competitive edge in the international market.[69] Japan's rise from the devastation of the Second World War to its current position of economic power is usually pointed out as an example of its efficiency. Labour-management co-operation in general and Quality Circle programmes in particular are often cited as the backbone of Japan's economic success. QWL advocates also scrutinse American unions, suggesting that 'inflexibility' of work rules inhibit workers' opportunity to create meaningful changes in their work.

According to this position, work rules have simply become bureaucratic procedures – part of a previous era of labour-management relations based on management mistrust and their

Taylorist vision of the organisation of work. With an 'enlightened management' willing to forego adversarial styles of labour relations and co-operate with workers in humanising the workplace, unions' concern for contract protection appears to be a hindrance to what has been called an expanded role for labour in the decision-making process.

Issues of worker participation and quality of work life are often presented by industrial relations consultants within a market research model of job satisfaction. While recognising the predisposition in human nature toward rewarding and creative forms of work, the experience is essentially transformed into sets of attitudes and needs which can ultimately be satisfied within the context of a 'humanised' market. The social basis for human fulfilment in the work process has thus been shifted toward psychological gratification, leaving aside the context of social relations. In the psychological framework, issues of conflict and control are translated into 'variables' such as technology, management policy, or changing social values, and QWL becomes the answer to *symptoms* of prevailing labour problems – job dissatisfaction, fragmented work, and authoritarian rule.

Beyond workplace democracy and worker participation as ideological solutions to worker apathy and discontent is a more fundamental reason for promoting QWL. The growing interdependence of a global capitalist economy and the intense competition it engenders has forced corporations to reorganise production methods and internal communications and decision-making, as has been argued earlier. The divisional autonomy along with centralised decision-making and control that characterised industries from the 1920s to the 1960s has become increasingly unworkable as competition forces innovations in products, marketing strategies, and production techniques. Centralisation of management authority helped control production by increasing volume and standardising products and production methods; but now shifts in control to a decentralised, yet flexible, interdependent system of management reflect variability of production methods, market changes, and demands for more specialised products and services. As Reich states: 'the basic premises of high volume, standardized production – the once potent formula of scientific management – are simply inapplicable to flexible-system production.'[70]

QWL is a technique that encourages not simply co-operation

(although it is a critical aspect of flexible manufacturing), but co-ordination of complex tasks within these new production methods. It is first and foremost an *organisation* tool designed to integrate operations which will increasingly depend on skill, judgement, and initiative. The widespread application of computers and computerised equipment, including robotics, to all phases of production, office information, and communication systems integrates skills, occupations, and information demanding collective strategies for achieving production goals.

Industries in their concern over the role of middle and lower level management indicate how far they are willing to go in reorganising decision-making. The foreman, in particular, is identified as a pivotal representative of corporate management in the reorganisation process. With direct ties to the shop floor, the first-line supervisor is in the best position to:

1. discuss the introduction of changes in production and product – as a 'representative' of management;
2. gather and transmit information on production problems – particularly those concerning quality and scheduling – from production workers directly to plant managers;
3. heighten the interaction among those involved in related areas of production.

A report in *Iron Age* notes that the foreman's role is changing from task master to communicator between labour and top management. Increasingly foremen are learning skills assessment, human resource management, and problem-solving techniques.[71] With computerised equipment and information systems, access to productivity data is available to all levels of the organisation.

Decentralising such decisions as scheduling, production costs, and quality control allows – actually requires – information sharing on corporate goals and production development, on the one hand, and production problem-solving and the co-ordination of activities, on the other. QWL programmes are used to solve such problems because they serve as two-way communication systems. Information about corporate planning is disseminated with an expectation that reactions to these plans will be relayed back to management and that strategies for implementing these plans will be negotiated by workers and foremen. Because this process involved workers' ideas, it is mistakenly viewed as democratic participation. However, Dickson's study of participation concluded that:

participation is more likely when the organization has structured the framework for participation and retains management control. The decentralization of authority through participation occurs when the organization is able to structure its activities and establish rules and procedures which otherwise limit the exercise of authority through participation.[72]

Simmons and Mares, proponents of QWL, concede that 'no ultimate control has changed hands', citing the case of the programme sponsored by General Motors and the United Auto Workers.[73] In fact, GM has continued to develop strategies for reduction in its workforce while vigorously promoting QWL and joint problem-solving committees to improve productivity rates.[74] An in-depth study of two UAW plants on the extent of control exercised by Quality Circle participants concluded that the notion of workers' control remains largely illusory in that the *numbers* – not the *range* – of choices expanded. As communications devices, they appear to create more openness while, realistically, they 'do not alter the distribution of rewards or authority or the mechanisms through which power is exercised'.[75]

QWL AND THE UNIONS

The internationals of such unions as the United Auto Workers UAW), Communications Workers of America (CWA), and United Steel Workers of America (USWA) who have supported co-operation with management and committed resources to establishing QWL programmes represent workers in industries who have suffered, or are threatened with, massive layoffs. Where plants remain opened, automation – and a reduction in the workforce – appear likely. The American Telephone and Telegraph divestment and the automation of both product and process within the telecommunications industry raises some serious questions regarding jurisdiction rights over jobs created by computerisation and CWA's ability to continue national contract bargaining. For these unions, QWL represents a strategy for job security. The international policy of the United Electrical Workers (UE), and the International Association of Machinists (IAM) is one of non-participation in QWL. The IAM suggests the use of collective bargaining to address QWL issues. The International Union of Electrical Radio and Machine Workers (IUE) has voted to support the concept of participation and will assist locals who decide to participate in its set up. However, the IUE has not entered into the kinds of joint participation efforts which charaterise the policies of the UAW, CWA and USWA.[76]

The support for QWL appears to rest on the secondary outcomes of participation:
1. improved communication between workers and managers;
2. feelings of influence and control over aspects of the work process;
3. actual influence on select production issues.

To accept these outcomes as primary and legitimate means toward achieving workplace democracy obscures the fundamental role of QWL as a decentralised *management* decision-making process which addresses the issues of cost, efficiency, productivity and product quality at the point of production. Moreover, the terms of participation are circumscribed largely by management's production needs, i.e., improving productivity and efficiency. These are *primary* QWL objectives. Job satisfaction and a general improvement in the quality of work life are also important aspects of QWL. However, they are not pursued simply as ends in themselves, but as contributing to overall improvements in productivity.

Although internationals have agreed to back QWL (indeed, the AFL-CIO in its report, 'The Changing Situation of Workers and Their Unions',[77] sees 'non-adversarial' relationships as a 'goal' of the labour movement in general), resistance to co-operation remains both within the upper echelons of participating unions as well as among the rank and file. As Fraser points out, the formation and continued operation of QWL requires that the work group 'break up established centers of collective resistance and ... rebuild group solidarities around goals prescribed by management'.[78]

In QWL, collaboration is an essential part of the process. Yet union officials and QWL participants continually find themselves walking a very fine line between acting in their own self-interest and assuming managerial responsibility for increased productivity and efficiency. Such a challenge to union representation and workers' self interests are not easily resolved. Conflicts emerge at the shop level regarding QWL decisions and decision-making by consensus. Participants have stated that, for them, ultimately the decisions made are management decisions. Shop stewards, trained to represent union members and act on complaints and grievances, feel that QWL infringes on their rights as union officials. Several voiced a

desire for union-run circles under steward leadership dealing solely
with union and worker issues (as opposed to company circles and
company oriented issues).[79] At the level of contract negotiations,
unions are reluctant to drop traditional bargaining positions as corporations demand concessions of hard won benefits and work
rules.

CONCLUSIONS

Automation and QWL represent changes in the structure of industrial organisation as capitalism becomes an increasingly global,
more interdependent economic system. Computerised technology is
both an information gathering tool and a production technology,
and together these reorganise the production and decision-making
processes. QWLs are not designed simply to enrich jobs or the
'quality of work life'. These programmes are an integral part of the
information transmitting systems between the shop floor, plant
management, and corporate headquarters whose purpose is to plan
strategies to implement change, particularly in the areas of productivity, product quality, cost reduction, efficiency and labour
relations. Efforts at job re-design are outcomes of technological *and*
managerial changes aimed at making the use of workers' skills and
the production process, in general, more flexible. Increasingly, jobs
in automated industries will depend upon skills involving problem
solving and team decision-making and the exercise of independent
judgement, commonly called 'trouble shooting'. Not coincidentally,
they are core skills used in QWL progammes.

Confronted with the importance of strategic planning in the co-
ordination of production, distribution and product development,
management has also been faced with its own reorganisation.
Automated industries have re-structured managerial activities to
reflect a concern with long-range planning and, simultaneously, the
capability to be flexible in meeting short-term needs. Trends indicate
a recentralisation of decisions concerning interdependent operations
and an increase in the responsibilities of local management particularly in the development and maintenance of a decision-making
system including 'the motivation and training of their subordinates'.[80] The format of QWL appears to be particularly well suited
for this purpose. It is, at once, an informal fluid process around

problem-solving on the local level while firmly remaining embedded within the organisational hierarchy.

The human relations strategy has a very real place in decentralised decision-making. The involvement of workers in the process of re-designing operations may increase the likelihood of their co-operation in its implementation.[81] In fact, management consultants offer job satisfaction through 'job enrichment programmes' as solutions to the problem of reducing labour costs and increasing human resource utilisation.[82] Management consultants are the modern equivalent of the human relations expert and the industrial psychologist of the 1920s. The resurgence of human relations practitioners – who, according to Fischer, had been in decline through the 1960s[83] – comes at a critical point for labour. As industries begin their re-organisation, management consultants have become the architects for programmes to tighten control over production, ensure labour's co-operation and integration into the process, and create alternatives to collective bargaining and union organising. Strauss notes that many companies have expanded their human resource departments which are increasingly responsible for developing participative management programmes and strategic human resource planning, stressing cost effective evaluation of performance.[84]

As Parker and Hansen show, the potential for divisiveness and a weakening of labour solidarity are also all too real outcomes of QWL. For example, they point out that 'older workers are now [considered] "slow", and employees who didn't mind "carrying" them in the past now see them as a drag on productivity'.[85] Moreover, contract issues inevitably surface in QWLs. Quoted in *Fortune*, Robert Cole, Director of the Centre for Japanese Studies at the University of Michigan, states that it is almost impossible to avoid contractual matters if QWLs are to seriously approach production problems.[86] Work rules and job classifications, typically insurance against job loss and erosion of skilled work, eventually come to be viewed as 'inefficient' and 'cumbersome' when productivity issues emerge under the guise of simplifying work.

Nelson[87] and Harris[88] document the historical consolidation of production processes, the centralisation of managerial control and the development of collective bargaining as the pattern for stabilising labour – management relations within a maturing economic system. They locate these changes not simply in the emergence of the

Beyond Taylorism

factory or mass production techniques, but rooted in the development of monopoly capitalism and its demand for high volume production. In much the same way, contemporary strategies for
collective bargaining and negotiated settlements reflect the shift
toward a global, interdependent economy. The agreement signed by
the UAW and GM for its production of the Saturn car is an
especially significant example of the hoped-for future of collective
bargaining. Saturn will be a new GM corporation – 'the ultimate
corporate laboratory, and opportunity to introduce new systems in
everything ranging from supplier relations to distribution to
labor'.[89] The union contract will be treated as what has been called a
' "living document" subject to continuous modifications'.[85] The pre-
dictable traditional collective bargaining agreements negotiated
under more stable economic conditions impede management's
ability to respond to fluctuations in the market.

Contracts which can be re-negotiated at any time removes a major
barrier to more effective long-range planning and quick response to
crises in the industry. Automation and QWL are a central part of
Saturn's future. In its highly automated plant, workers will be
members of 'work units' composed of between 6 and 15 members.
Among their responsibilities are: 'producing to schedule, performing
to budget ... job assignment ... absenteeism, accepting new members
and provisions of breaks.'[91] There is one job classification for production workers, and units are responsible for organising their
assigned work. Traditional union responsibility for union representation, i.e., filing grievances, will instead be handled by a 'conflict
resolution procedure', also conducted by consensus.[92]

Over the last few years, concession bargaining has won corporations changes in work rules, job classifications, two-tier wage
scales and profit sharing plans in lieu of wage increases. The flexibility of the Saturn contract effectively diminishes the argument
that these kinds of changes are concessions and eliminate
management's commitment to honour its agreement. They merely
become contractual 'modifications'.

In the legal arena, the National Labor Relations Board has
awarded corporations the right to transfer work from one plant to
another as part of its policy of corporate re-structuring, as in the case
of Otis Elevator Company,[93] and to lower its labour costs, as in the
case of Milwaukee Spring,[94] transferring whole or parts of a
manufacturing operation in mid-contract.

While management continues to re-shape the work process

around computerised production methods, unions have developed some strategies of their own to deal with its effects on jobs and collective bargaining. The International Metalworkers Federation (IMF) appealed to unions around the world to 'notify [them] of any "extraordinary activity" in their plants' indicating that work has been re-located from striking German plants.[95] The technology which allows work to be electronically transferred from one plant to another also increases the potential for a movement toward international labour solidarity. Domestically, unions have used the concept of QWL to fight plant shutdowns and increase participation in production. The United Electrical Workers enlisted the aid of the community and local government in New Bedford, Massachusetts in fighting the closure of Morse Cutting Tools. The prospect of job loss and social dislocation within the community prompted the city to threaten Gulf and Western (the parent company) with a declaration of the right of 'eminent domain' if Morse was to be closed. In another case, to attract new buyers, workers at a GE steam-turbine plant scheduled to close developed a list of environmental products which could be successfully produced.[96]

The use of computerised automation and the institution of QWL in the labour process are part of the historical continuation to control production, enlist labour co-operation, and reduce uncertainty within the marketplace. However, as much as they represent the ongoing struggle for control, they are also part of the current shift in capitalist development and reflect both the historical continuation of struggle between labour and capital, and the specificity of this struggle as it relates to the emergence of a new global economic order.

Notes

1. Quality of Work Life (QWL) is an 'umbrella' term covering a wide range of management-instituted programmes. Although the types of programmes differ in structure and style, they are all primarily concerned with increasing productivity, product quality and co-operation of the workforce in production. The distinctions between these programmes are important in that each is designed to address particular problems within different types of production and service sector industries. However, for the purposes of this paper, QWL will be discussed in general terms and in its relationship to other industrial changes.

2. Daniel Nelson (1975) *Managers and Workers: Origins of the New Factory System in the U.S. 1880–1920* (Madison, Wis.: University of Wisconsin Press) p. 25.

3. Harry Braverman (1974) *Labor and Monopoly Capital* (New York: Monthly Review Press).

4. Richard Edwards (1979) *Contested Terrain: Transformation of the Workplace in the 20th Century* (New York: Basic Books).

5. David Noble (1977) *America By Design*, (New York: Alfred Knopf); Harley Shaiken (1984) *Work Transformed: Automation and Labor in the Computer Age* (New York: Holt, Rinehart and Winston).

6. Robert Blauner (1964) *Alienation and Freedom* (Chicago, University of Chicago Press); Martin Meissner (1969) *Technology and the Worker: Technical Demands and Social Processes in Industry* (San Francisco: Chandler Pub. Co.).

7. John Kelly (1985) 'Managements' Redesign of Work: Labour Process, Labour Markets and Product Markets' in *Job Redesign*, David Knights, Hugh Willmott and David Collinson (eds) (Brookfield, Vt.: Gower Pub.) pp. 30–51; Craig R. Littler, 'Taylorism, Fordism and Job Design' in *Job Redesign*, D. Knights, H. Willmott and D. Collinson (eds), pp. 10–29.

8. Karl Marx (1975) *Capital, Vol. 1* (New York: International Publishers).

9. Philip Kraft (1979) 'The Industrialization of Computer Programming: From Programming to "Software Production"' in *Case Studies on the Labor Process*, Andrew Zimbalist (ed.) (New York: Monthly Review Press) pp. 1–17; David Noble, 'Social Choice in Machine Design: The Case of Automatically Controlled Machine Tools' in *Case Studies on the Labor Process*, Andrew Zimbalist, (ed.), pp. 18–50; Harley Shaiken, *Work Transformed*.

10. Paul Thompson (1983) *The Nature of Work: An Introduction to Debates on the Labour Process* (London: Macmillan Press).

11. P. Goldman, D. Van Houten (1977) 'Managerial Strategies and the Worker', *Organizational Analysis: Critique and Innovation*, K. Benson (ed.) (New York: Sage) pp. 110–27.

12. John Kelly, 'Management's Redesign of Work: Labour Process, Labour Markets and Product Markets' in *Job Redesign*, D. Knights, H. Willmott and D. Collinson (eds), pp. 30–51.

13. Frederick Herzberg (1973) *Work and the Nature of Man* (New York: Mentor Books); John Simmons and William Mares (1983) *Working Together* (New York: Knopf); William Ouchi (1981) *Theory Z: How American Business Can Meet the Japanese Challenge* (Reading, Mass.: Addison-Wesley).

14. D. Knights, D. Collinson, 'Redesigning Work on the Shopfloor: A Question of Control or Consent?' in *Job Redesign*, D. Knights, H. Willmott, and D. Collinson (eds), p. 200.

15. Paul Thompson, *The Nature of Work*, p. 152.

16. F. Child, 'Managerial Strategies, New Technology and the Labour Process' in *Job Redesign*, D. Knights, H. Willmott and D. Collinson (eds), p. 112.

17. *Ibid.*, p. 113.

18. Daniel Nelson, *Managers and Workers*.
19. Carol Haddad (1984) 'Technological Change and Reindustrialization: Implications for Organized Labor' in *Labor and Reindustrialization: Workers and Corporate Change* (ed.) Donald Kennedy (Dept. of Labor Studies: Pennsylvania State University) pp. 137–66.
20. Charles Sabel (1982) *Work and Politics: The Division of Labor in Industry* (Cambridge: Cambridge Univesity Press).
21. Gene Bilinsky (1983) 'The Race to the Automatic Factory', *Fortune*, 21 Feb. pp. 52–64.
22. Harley Shaiken, *Work Transformed*.
23. These papers include the *New York Times*, *New York Daily News*, *New York Post* and the *World Journal Tribune*, the latter a merger of the *New York Herald Tribune*, *New York Journal American* and the *New York World Telegram and Sun*. Harry Kelber and Carl Schlesinger (1967) *Union Printers and Controlled Automation* (New York: The Free Press).
24. Ibid., pp. 267–69.
25. T. Rogers, N. S. Friedman (1980) *Printers Face Automation* (Lexington, Mass.: Lexington Books, D. C. Heath and Co).
26. Bureau of Labor Statistics (1982) 'The Impact of Technology on Labor in Five Industries', Bulletin 2137 (Washington, D.C.) p. 11.
27. Ibid., pp. 12–13.
28. In a phone conversation about the effects of automation on skill and collective bargaining, Pete Kelly, President of Local 160, United Auto Workers, Detroit, used this phrase to describe the changes in the content of jobs affected by automation. He indicated, however, that the effects of automation on his members were more in terms of de-skilling rather than upgrading.
29. Interview with process engineer working in a New York area defence plant, 25 January 1985.
30. Interview with process engineer working in a New York area defence plant, 10 January 1985.
31. Labor Notes Conference, Detroit, Michigan, 17 June 1984.
32. Donald H. Sanders (1970) *Computers and Management* (New York: McGraw-Hill) pp. 124–5.
33. Herbert A. Simon (1977) *The New Science of Management Decision*, revised edition (New Jersey: Prentice Hall).
34. Barry Stein and Rosabeth Moss Kanter (1980) 'Building the Parallel Organization: Creating Mechanisms for Permanent Quality of Work Life', *Journal of Applied Behavioral Science*, vol. 16, no. 3.
35. Raymond Dreyfack (1982) *Making It In Management – The Japanese Way*, (Rockville Center, N.Y.: Farnsworth); John Simmons and William Mares (1983) *Working Together* (New York: Knopf); William Ouchi (1981) *Theory Z: How American Business Can Meet the Japanese Challenge* (Reading, Mass.: Addison-Wesley).
36. Ths author is currently researching the effects of automation and QWL on the organisation of the labour process. In the course of interviewing QWL participants on their experiences, they invariably comment on the foresight of Japanese management on labour-relations, their respect for employees ideas and experiences. They are convinced that QWL is a

194   *Beyond Taylorism*

uniquely Japanese 'product'. Training manuals provided by management consultants to the corporations participating in QWL programmes
cite Japan's development of the QWL philosophy and application to
industry. At the same time, however, they are generally unaware of the
problems Japanese workers face in sectors of some of these industries.
The concept of 'just-in-time' production goals in based on a large
supply of temporary, non-union workers hired to meet production
quotas and laid off when it has been accomplished. This is in contrast
to most suppliers in the US (particularly in the auto industry) whose
workers are unionised.

37. Ivar Berg, Marcia Freedman and Michael Freeman (1978) *Managers
    and Work Reform: A Limited Engagement* (New York: The Free
    Press).
38. *Business Week*. 11 May 1981; Delmar L. Landen, 'The Real Issue:
    Human Dignity', *The Work Life Review*, Nov. 1982; Richard E. Walton,
    'How To Counter Alienation in the Plant', *Harvard Business Review*,
    Nov./Dec., 1972, pp. 70–81.
39. Edward Vaughan, 'Industrial Democracy: Consensus and Confusion',
    Industrial Relations Journal, Mar./Apr. 1980, vol. 11, no. 1, pp. 50–56.
40. John F. Witte (1980) *Democracy, Authority and Alienation in Work:
    Workers' Participation in an American Corporation* (Chicago: University
    of Chicago Press).
41. US Department of Labor, Labor-Management Services Administra-
    tion, 'Starting Labor-Management Quality of Work Life Programs',
    (Superintendent of Documents, US Government Printing Office:
    Washington, D.C., Sep. 1982).
42. Ibid.
43. Irving Siegel, Edgar Weinberg (1982) *Labor-Management Cooperation:
    The Amercian Experience* (Kalamazoo, Michigan: W. E. Upjohn
    Institute for Employment Research).
44. Charles Hecksher (1980) 'Worker Participation and Management
    Control', *Journal of Social Reconstruction*, Jan./Mar.
45. Robert Wrenn (1982) 'Management and Work Humanization', *The
    Insurgent Sociologist*, vol. X1, no.3, Fall, pp. 23–38.
46. Daniel Yankelovich, John Immerwahr (1984) 'Putting the Work Ethic
    to Work', *Society*, Jan./Feb. pp. 58–76.
47. Mick Marchington (1980) *Responses to Participation at Work* (Westmead,
    England: Gower Pub. Co.); Harvie Ramsey, "Cycles of Control: Worker
    Participation in Sociological and Historical Perspective", *Sociology*, vol.
    11, no. 3, Sep. 1977, pp. 481–506.
48. Robert Schrank, "On Ending Worker Alienation: The Gaines Pet Food
    Plant", in *Humanizing the Workplace*, Roy P. Fairfield (ed.), (Buffalo,
    N.Y.: Prometheus Books, 1974), pp. 119–140.
49. Richard Walton, 'How to Counter Alienation in the Plant',
50. Harley Shaiken, *Work Transformed: Automation and Labor in the
    Computer Age*.
51. *Fortune*, 28 May 1984, p. 21.
52. Outsourcing refers to the process of transferring production to non-
    union shops in the US and abroad, for example, to Mexico.

53. *Wall Street Journal*, 7 Nov. 1983, p. 6.
54. Rosabeth Moss Kanter (1983) *The Change Masters* (New York: Simon and Schuster) p. 41.
55. Ibid., pp. 52–53.
56. *The New York Times*, 21 April 1985.
57. Ibid, 5 May 1985.
58. Ibid.
59. The foreman's role, in particular, has increased in importance as corporations decentralise authority. This point will be discussed further in the section, QWL and Corporate Planning.
60. This applies to relationships within levels of management as well, particularly in view of the fact that horizontal decision-making increases within a parallel decision-making structure.
61. Pehr G. Gyllenhammer, 'How Volvo Adapts Work to People', *Harvard Business Review*, July/Aug., 1977, p. 112.
62. Interview with former Quality Circle participant, 5 Feb. 1985.
63. Interview with machinist working in a New York area defence plant, 10 Apr. 1985.
64. Peter Drucker, *Technology, Management and Society* (New York: Harper and Row, 1970), p. 47.
65. William Duffy, 'Participative Plant Design and Redesign: The STS Approach', *The Work Life Review*, vol. 11, issue 1, Mar. 1983, pp. 12–16.
66. Ibid., p. 16.
67. Ibid., p. 14.
68. Daniel Yankelovich, John Immerwahr, 'Putting the Work Ethic to Work', pp. 66–7.
69. *The New York Times*, Week In Review, 11 Sep. 1983, p. 3.
70. Robert Reich (1983) *The Next American Frontier* (New York: Times Books) p. 40.
71. Paul Cathey, 'Industry's Man in the Middle', *Iron Age*, 2 Jan. 1983, pp. 36–9.
72. John Dickson, 'Participation as a Means of Organizational Control', *Journal of Management Studies*, vol. 18, no. 2, 1981, p. 170.
73. John Simmons and William Mares, *Working Together*.
74. Joseph Espo, 'GM Seeking to Cut 80 000?' *The Flint Journal*, 18 Feb. 1984, p. 1. In an internal document by Alfred W. Warren, Jr., General Motors Vice President for Industrial Relations, stated that company goals for increased productivity included: cutting its workforce by 80 000 by 1986, changes in local seniority work rules, the introduction of new technology, replacing national contract bargaining with a 'continuous problem-solving process' at the local level and competitive bids to obtain parts within the corporation and from outside suppliers. Alfred Warren has been a major figure in the GM/UAW Quality of Work Life Program.
75. Robert J. Thomas, 'Participation and Control: New Trends in Labor Relations in the Auto Industry' Center for Research on Social Organization, University of Michigan, Ann Arbor, Working Paper #315.

76. Internal memo to all IAM District and Local Lodges, 26 May 1982; UE Policy Book 1981–82; IUE 16th Constitutional Convention, Resolution on Worker Alienation, 1974.
77. AFL-CIO Report, 'The Changing Situation of Workers and Their Unions', 1985.
78. Steve Fraser, 'Industrial Democracy in the 1980's', *Socialist Review*, vol. 13, no. 6, Nov./Dec. 1983, p. 111.
79. Based on interviews with shop stewards and Quality Circle and former Quality Circle participants.
80. Herbert Simon, *The New Science of Management Decision*, p. 123.
81. Paul Goldman and Donald Van Houten, 'Uncertainty, Conflict and Labor Relations in the Modern Firm 1: Productivity and Capitalism's "Human Face"', *Economic and Industrial Democracy*, vol. 1, 1980, pp. 63–98.
82. David A. Whitsett (1971) 'Job Enrichment, Human Resources and Profitability', *New Perspectives in Job Enrichment* (ed.) John R. Maher (New York: Van Nostran Reinhold Co.).
83. Frank Fischer (1984) 'Ideology and Organization Theory', in *Critical Studies In Organization and Bureaucracy* (eds) Frank Fischer, Carmen Sirianni, (Philadelphia: Temple University Press) pp. 172–90.
84. George Strauss (1984) 'Industrial Relations: Time of Change', *Industrial Relations*, vol. 23, no. 1, Winter, p. 4.
85. Mike Parker, Dwight Hansen (1983) 'The Circle Game', *The Progressive*, Jan., pp. 32–5.
86. *Fortune*, 2 Apr. 1984.
87. Daniel Nelson, *Managers and Workers*.
88. John Howell Harris (1982) *The Right To Manage: Industrial Relations Policies of American Business in the 1940s*, (Madison, Wis.: University of Wisconsin Press).
89. Cary Reich, 'The Innovator', *The New York Times Magazine*, 21 Apr. 1985, p. 80.
90. *The New York Times*, 'GM Contract Aims to Foster Union-Management Cooperation', 28 July 1985.
91. Jane Slaughter (1985) 'UAW-Saturn Pact – "Total Cooperation"', *Labor Notes*, Aug. p. 15.
92. Ibid., p. 15.
93. *The New York Times*, 'The N.L.R.B. Has a New Lineup and Line', 15 Apr. 1984.
94. Bureau of National Affairs, *Employee Relations Weekly*, 'Unions Face New Hurdles, Threats after "Milwaukee Spring" Ruling', 6 Feb. 1984, p. 131.
95. Ibid., 'Metalworkers Federation Acts to Help Striking West German Auto Workers', 4 June 1984, p. 691.
96. *The New York Times*. 'Unions are Shifting Gears But Not Goals', 31 Mar. 1985.

9 Computer Redesign and 'Labour Process' Theory: Towards a Critical Appraisal

Martin Beirne and Harvie Ramsay*

In recent years, management strategies and techniques for redesigning jobs along 'participative' and 'enriched' lines, which previously went acclaimed with little or no critical comment, have come under closer scrutiny. That scrutiny has exposed the often thinly disguised efforts at intensifying work and inducing docile acquiescence which underlie many such company initiatives. It has also revealed in many cases a rather poorer success rate, even for management, than is found or hinted at in the orthodox celebrations of job reorganisation.

One element of many critical (predominantly 'labour process') examinations of job reform is a link between the pace of technological developments and applications in the last decade or so and the need to redesign work tasks and enhance employee commitment. Given this, it is perhaps surprising, and certainly disconcerting, that relatively little of this work has sought to investigate the locus of the most radical applications of computing technology and the site of the most sweeping potential and consequent changes, namely the office. Moreover, any survey of orthodox magazines and journals on the organisational aspects of computer-based information handling (the core task of most offices) will reveal a proliferating enthusiasm for a translated form of participation/enrichment, usually termed 'user-involvement'. In an effort to assess this vitally important but relatively neglected area of changing work organisation we have

*The authors wish to thank the publishers of the *Computer Users' Yearbook* for granting access to their (1985) directory of computer installations and for allowing their Scottish listings to be used for mailing purposes.

sought to begin gathering information on the practice of user-involvement. This chapter sets out our observations on the literature and the findings of the first stage of our fieldwork in order to identify the questions requiring careful, critical investigation.

JOB REDESIGN IN THE OFFICE: SOME PRELIMINARY OBSERVATIONS

Valuable studies of the office from a broadly labour process perspective do exist, not surprisingly given Braverman's own emphasis thereon (e.g. Kraft, 1979a; Crompton and Jones, 1984; Cooley, 1980, 1981). Recent research has confirmed, moreover, that the new technology is having a far more extensive impact on white-collar employees across the gamut of 'office' workplaces (in manufacturing itself, in finance and other service sectors, or in government administration for instance) than on most shopfloors. This is not surprising since microprocessors are not primarily components designed to make robots, but to handle information, hence the parallel term 'information technology'. The potential impact on office organisation is far more radical, too, than that on the shopfloor where technological change has been steady. In the office, apart from the typewriter in the eighteenth century and the photocopier in the nineteenth, technical gadgetry has always been at the margins of a highly labour-intensive labour process. The appearance of a new technology, the computer, capable of transforming the processing of the substance of office work – the generation, storage, retrieval and presentation of information – thus has enormous promise to management. As a major proportion of total labour costs even in manufacturing has come to be centred in the administrative system, so the attraction of seeking savings there has expanded apace (Baldry and Connolly, 1986).

Insofar as job redesign is indeed a response to pressures for reorganising the labour process for competitive purposes, then it might be expected to be as prevalent in the office as on the shopfloor. The fact that the best-known and most-discussed redesign programmes still concern the factory floor may be taken to imply for one thing that enrichment programmes and the like in the office are less easily explained in this way. None the less, many redesign programmes have been located in offices – and there is some evidence that these are more successful for management than many shopfloor schemes

(Kelly, 1982). One reason for this is probably that a greater unionateness, organisation, and general awareness of conflicts on the shopfloor is likely to ensure a degree of suspicion and resistance to schemes there.

Another, related but distinct, factor here concerns the gender relations of the office. A number of recent studies have shown the important relation between labour process changes and the shifting gender ascription of jobs. The changing gender definition of office jobs accompanying the shifting gradation of work over this century has been delineated, particularly that associated with the spread of such mechanisation as had already occurred prior to computerisation (Barker and Downing, 1980; Crompton and Jones, 1984). By 1981, census figures show that 37 per cent of women in the British labour force were located in routine non-manual work, and they constituted 71 per cent of all employees in those grades. This confirms an extension of the trend to such occupational segregation common to both the USA and the UK (Dex, 1985).

Little work has been done on the specific interaction between job redesign programmes and the gendered division of labour. Yet is has been observed that a number of the classic human relations experiments were actually carried out on women, including office workers, and that this may not be unrelated to the success of these experiments (Brown, 1976). Moreover, other fragments of studies suggest that in some circumstances women may be less resistant to management blandishments (notably where they are marginalised by a male-dominated labour movement) and may thus respond less hesitantly to manipulative devices installed in a paternalistic manner by management (Pollert, 1981). Of course, the danger of stereotyping a 'female acquiescence' must be guarded against, but the dynamics of gender are clearly potentially central to any proper evaluation of job redesign in the office. There is a danger, otherwise, that our caricature of the redesigned job concerns a glamourised picture of the draughts*man*, and that the struggle for control in the process of computerisation is depicted merely in terms of the re-skilling or de-skilling effects of CAD.

Insofar as the argument concerning 'participative' redesign with new technology extends to the office context, then most post-Braverman labour process theory would predict a potential for management reliance on such schemes to achieve flexible and effective operation of computerised systems. True to this prediction, a substantial body of 'mainstream' literature has grown up advocating a participative social organisation of work around computer-based information systems (CBISs). We shall give a brief exposition of the main strands in this literature, and in particular of its most developed and influential variant in the form of the work of Enid Mumford and a number of associated writers, before returning to a commentary on these approaches (and on the absence of any critical assessment in the labour process literature or within the labour movement) in the final sections of the paper.

MANAGEMENT THEORY AND 'SYSTEMS' RESEARCH

The management behavioural science tradition has found purchase on the question of the organisation of CBISs courtesy of a persistent and often spectacular failure of such systems to match or even approach their technically specified performance levels. While some of the problems could be traced to the cumbersome mechanics and physical tetchiness particularly of the early 'batch' systems (based on a core mainframe to which information was fed or from which it issued in large and physically daunting loads), or to the crudity of much software, in practice the main 'bugs' were human. Distrust, resistance, or just a refusal to adapt to the new system saw immense new inefficiencies emerge, with parallel information systems being maintained, poor quality data undermining the credibility of the computer in line with the GIGO principle (Garbage In, Garbage Out), and sometimes even more manifest forms of sabotage.

The obvious response was to seek to enlist the help and involvement of the opposition. As one recent survey of the literature observes:'It is almost an axiom of the MIS [Management Information Systems] literature that user-involvement is a necessary condition for successful development of computer-based information systems.' (Ives and Olson, 1984, p. 586.) The technological advance of computing is seen not as making this inevitable, but certainly as rendering user-involvement a far more viable option. The new on-line, networked systems potentially provide direct user access to CBISs to supply or draw information from them. Hence, a choice is available for management in their construction of the social organisation to operate the developing systems.

There is no single pattern of research or prescription on this avenue of management choice, however. Indeed, the existing literature is marked by a polarisation of views based on contending ideologies of organisational development. On one side, thinly disguised mutations of Taylorism attempt to plug gaps in conventional technically-dominated design approaches with strategies aimed specifically at acquiring information or generating consent (and in some cases compliance) among employees in work areas targeted for technological innovation. Approaches in this mould tend to rely on relatively uniform presentations of standard scientific management themes – hierarchy, division of labour and in particular the severance of conception from execution – advanced from a general perspective on *systems rationalisation* that accentuates the purity of the scientific method and the dominance of managerial prerogatives. By contrast, *computer redesign* formulations are fundamentally opposed to technology-driven systems. On this line, the heirs to the Tavistock tradition promote the participative design of computing systems as a legitimate end in itself, allowing users an opportunity for self-expression and trust. Rather than advocating the best 'expert' design, adherents insist that participation is a means to ensure that proposed systems are acceptable and beneficial to all concerned. From this standpoint they question the legitimacy of the traditional hierarchy of authority in the systems design process, and develop their 'solutions' on the assumption that it is possible to construct systems to meet the 'needs' of organisations and their employees simultaneously. This is expressed in pure form in methodologies geared not merely for participation but for user-design of entire systems.

PARADIGMS AND PERSPECTIVES ON PARTICIPATIVE DESIGN

Systems rationalisation and computer redesign provide the dominant common frames of reference in terms of which permissible options are formulated and theoretical disputes conducted in respect of participative systems design. However, the approaches within these perspectives are still more diverse than this simple characterisation suggests. Various shades of opinion exist within the respective paradigms, together with different angles on and arguments for participative design. None the less, three broad categories can be delineated in each case, as outlined in Table 9.1. These strategies are distinguished by their particular focus on

distinct threads within each perspective leading to (at least potentially) different practical implications for the form and content of
employee participation and for the precise meaning of user-
involvement.

Technocentric design   strategies replicate the essential features of
Taylorism as a result of their adherence to the conventions of the
'pure systems' models that have dominated the world of computer
design and implementation in recent years. In this regard, and
through the more fundamental parity of their underlying values and
theoretical presuppositions, they provide a benchmark for assessing
the theoretical and practical significance of user-involvement and
participative design schemes. At the most obvious level, these
approaches accept Taylor's definition of 'one best way' of organising
the labour process. The principle of 'full specification' enshrined in
these conventions imposes a definite discipline on the systems
building process to the extent that operating procedures are reduced
to their constituent sub-functions which are analysed, 'optimised'
and implemented in a step-wise fashion. The 'logical' sequence of
these processing events is determined in advance and solely by
technical data narrowly conceived as the basic building blocks of
functional systems. This process of structuring the intellectual
exercise of determining systems requirements has the additional
effect of advancing the separation of conception and execution. The
'systems' model implies that design is the sole responsibility of
computer professionals, and, since complete specification requires a
monopoly of knowledge, the first task for the expert is to render the
labour process independent of the local knowledge and expertise of
the human operator. Of course, the reality of the situation is that
brainwork can never be confined to the hallowed halls of computer
services departments, planning centres or to the 'lay-out' departments
in classic scientific management formulations. None the less, the
intricate logic of this 'pure' computer science arguably incorporates
a broader and yet more sophisticated attempt: 'to dissolve the labour
process as a process conducted by the worker and reconstitute it as a
process conducted by management' (Braverman, 1974, p. 170).

Passive user-involvement   strategies are frequently advanced by less
belligerent systems thinkers to combat systems 'noise'. From a complementary starting position in respect of ideological assumptions,
and accepting that technocentric methods are valuable for the

generation of ideal-typical conventions, approaches in this vein contrive certain concessions for labour to counteract problems of data capture and resistance to implementation. Implicitly, these problems require more than financial incentives and reward schemes for their resolution. Hence, a modicum of well regulated involvement is prescribed, with a range of conditional variables to determine the appropriateness of participation in given situations. Relevant procedures relating to this aspect include:

1. *Status assessment* Target user groups are rated according to their degree of influence over the process of systems development (based on their crucial knowledge, operational or formal hierarchical power resources) or, ultimately, in the use of the system (cf. Edstrom, 1977).

2. *Vetting of likely candidates* Systems designers commonly shoulder the discretion to appoint participants selectively on the basis of their estimation of a user's predisposition to divulge information or to promulgate the chosen message for systems acceptance and effective use on the shopfloor (cf. Edstrom, 1977).

3. *Determining the scope for involvement* Participation by top level management or high status groups is typically endorsed for the initiation stage to establish the extent and direction of organisational change. Direct user or shopfloor involvement is prescribed for the systems design study (conceptualisation) and for the installation phase. Conversely, systems professionals are granted autonomy for systems analysis – programming and procedures design (cf. Edstrom, 1977; DeBrabander and Edstrom, 1977; DeBrabander and Thiers, 1984).

4. *Defining appropriate tactics* Partisans of passive involvement have prescribed a specific range of tactics for use by computer professionals in 'user-involvement' situations. Interview and questionnaire schedules are frequently included here in contradistinction to the free involvement of 'selected' participants at the 'appropriate' stage of the development process.

By these methods of involvement and through the values, vocabulary and orientations of systematic rationalism, the principles and precepts of scientific management are sustained.

The approaches to user-involvement subsumed in the category *ergonomic systems design* have abstracted aspects of advanced research in hardware construction and software mechanics for use in placating user hostility at the so-called 'man-machine interface'. Recent ideas and methods relating to the creation of user-orientated

Table 9.1 Theoretical perspectives on participative systems design

	Systems Rationalisation			Computer Redesign		
	Technocentric design	Passive user-involvement	Ergonomic systems design	Socio-technical design	Organisational design	Organisational politics
Organising concept	Centralised (specialist) design	Selective user-involvement	Selective user-involvment – Human factors engineering	Participative systems design	Participative systems design	Participative systems design
Design strategy	Generic systems design – complete specification of technical features prior to implementation	Specific systems design – in organisational context of systems use	'User-features' incorporated in design	Systems customisation	Systems customisation	Systems customisation

Strategic objectives	Technical operating efficiency	User-acceptance knowledge - acquisition	User-acceptance	Organisational effectiveness Job satisfaction Motivation Self-determination	Organisational flexibility	Conflict resolution
Systems building procedures	Systems analysis Division of labour Cost-benefit analysis	Classification of conditional variables for user-involvement - Necessary participants - Stage of developments - Status of users	User measurement - questionnaires - interviews Product features design	ETHICS Method - Job satisfaction analysis - Variance analysis - Steering committees Participative by 'consultation', 'representation', 'consensus'	Progressive decentralisation with increasing levels of 'turbulence' in organisational environments	Compensation /Reward /Incentive schemes
Ideology	Scientific management	Scientific management	Scientific management	Human relations	Human relations	Several contending ideo-logies in wider debate. In abstracted form: Human relations

high level programming languages, conversational procedures and query languages have been particularly influential in this regard. While these techniques in themselves are of potentially great significance for the co-operative design of computer systems, their narrow use in human factors engineering is designed only to elicit user acceptance and expedite the productive use of pre-specified systems. This is especially true in the case of approaches geared to the incorporation of standard and often additional, optional design characteristics in the popular range of off-the-shelf business systems. These strategies seem to harbour the notion that user-involvement can be secured by fiat. Marketing policies based on ergonomic ideas and equations confront potential buyers with the idea that the advertised package will seduce users and facilitate effective use with harmonious interaction at the user–computer interface. Of course user participation is, once again, passive. Manufacturers rely, at best, upon the tactics categorised in approaches to passive user-involvement, namely, restricted interview schedules and questionnaires. Moreover, under the rubrics of 'end-user' and 'user-led' computing much effort is expended in co-ordinating the development of management control techniques and software products and matching various permutations of these with particular staff groups, types of application and sets of circumstances at large in host organisations. The tactics and procedures employed towards this vision of a well-managed process bear more than a passing resemblance to the other measures outlined above in the discussion of passive involvement (cf. Rockart and Flannery, 1983).

Socio-technical design   strategies incorporate important prosocial as well as technical 'operating' objectives in the application of the latest computer and communications technologies. In fact, the proponents of this line believe that recent innovations in networking and the provision of on-line services provide both the spark for a renaissance in conceptions and applications of job reform and catalysts for ameliorating the conditons of labour and advancing democratic rights at work (Mumford, 1979a). Building on the major concepts of orthodox theory – joint optimisation and responsible autonomy – and drawing heavily on established critiques of purely technical approaches to the mechanisation of production lines (Davis *et al.,* 1955), these approaches incorporate what purports to be a tool-kit for engaging meaningful user-involvement and effective design.

Ostensibly, traditional 'structured' design methodologies have failed to achieve an appropriate 'fit' between the characteristics of computer technologies and the social and psychological needs and desires of users. At one level, arguments suggest that the problem stems from the dominance of 'instrumental reason' in the analytical framework for systems analysis and design. That is to say, the process of analytical reasoning whereby designers confront their problems and contrive their solutions is circumscribed by the exclusive use of technical criteria for defining problems and developing solutions (Weizenbaum, 1976, Bjorn-Andersen and Eason, 1980). On another level, theoretical and empirical studies suggest that concrete design procedures are infused with the ideological trappings of scientific management. Put simply, Taylorist principles are manifest in 'compliance models of men' that tend to reinforce the efforts of computer professionals to 'optimise' the technical sub-systems of organisational operations at the expense of social sub-systems (Hedberg and Mumford, 1975, Taylor, 1979, Dagwell and Weber, 1983). From the socio-technical point of view, the solution to the resultant problem of synchronisation lies in making systems design a joint venture in which users and professionals co-operate throughout the development process. To this end, the various programmes and strategies that have been advanced incorporate permutations of the keynote methodologies devised by Mumford and Weir (1979) and Pava (1983). These strategies comprise the same basic techniques, although Mumford and Weir's ETHICS method (an acronym for Effective Technical and Human Implementation of Computer Systems) is geared mainly to production systems and routine events, while Pava's approach is addressed to design in non-routine (office) environments. The precise mechanics of these methodologies derive from the practical innovations associated with earlier generations of job-centred socio-technical theory, including job satisfaction analysis and variance analysis of technical procedures. Moreover, in recent practical experiments these techniques have been linked to three different levels of user-involvement corresponding with Mumford's (1976) classification of consultative, representative and consensus design. On each of these dimensions and without exception, the instigators of the relevant projects have proclaimed that participative design is beneficial for both employees and their organisations. Given these claims, and in light of their genealogy, socio-technical strategies will provide the main focus for discussion in this paper.

Organisational design strategies place socio-technical and job redesign theories at the centre of broader and marginally more sophisticated analyses of organisational operations. Adhering to established moral (human relations) conventions, advocates of this line argue that job design cannot be isolated from organisational design and that task composition is dependent upon organisational interactions at a higher level than basic socio-technical theory suggests (Davis, 1976, 1977; Davis and Taylor, 1979). While socio-technical approaches are cognisant of the importance of environmental fluctuations, they deal mainly with questions of human-technical interactions, usually under specific environmental circumstances. By contrast, organisational design concentrates on uncertainty and 'turbulence' in modern international markets and the need for 'human activity systems' (systems with a high degree of interdependence and low separability of man from machine) to ensure continued organisational effectiveness. The methodological procedures developed on this argument relate levels of 'uncertainty', 'complexity' and 'illiberality' in organisational environments to the 'adaptive' capabilities of modern computing technologies (Wainwright and Francis, 1984). This basically means that on a scale of unpredictability the responsibility for design can be forced down the organisational hierarchy until appropriate levels of expertise are reached.

Organisational politics approaches to systems design draw on wider debates and broader analyses of the political implications of computing technologies. Emphasis is placed on technology as a tool that can be turned towards the aggrandizment of power in environments characterised by continuous battles for power, influence and prestige between groups with conflicting interests. At the broader level, analysts focus on inter and intra organisational relations and disputes, differing in their analyses and conclusions according to an array of contrasting value assumptions and notions of power and conflict. Pluralist analyses are probably the most common in this widely construed political perspective, although various species can be identified – institutional, unitary, committed, macro-political pluralists and so on. By contrast, computer redesign variants concentrate on intra organisational distributions of power conceptualised within the confines of existing human relations perspectives (Markus, 1983, 1984). The task of analysing the full range of organisational politics approaches lies beyond the scope of the present paper and we intend to do little more than indicate their existence.

THE ENTHUSIASM FOR PARTICIPATIVE DESIGN

There is no questioning the appeal of the arguments and proposals associated with the participative computer redesign perspective to anyone critical of the processes of degradation and advancing management control depicted by Braverman and others. There is a strong potential for alliance with the participative proponents' concern for people having the chance to develop and use their creative abilities, and with their scorn for the narrow instrumental rationalism that suffuses orthodox top management and systems engineer/analyst approaches to information systems design and associated task redefinition. This can be seen in any comparison between the writings of, say, Cooley or Hales from the left of the labour movement, and of Rosenbrock, Land, Mumford or Bjorn-Andersen from the ranks of critical systems engineering or managerial social science. All are agreed on the flawed nature of the rationality which treats people as if they were robots – or, more likely, as if they were of less importance still (cf. Rosenbrock, 1981). All argue that there is a choice of how an MIS or CAD system is formulated and that its operation can be designed to accommodate differing conceptions of user roles, i.e. there is no fixed, single (and de-skilling, fragmenting, routinising) option. All suggest that given the impact of people on the working of systems in pactice (however degraded their official task definition), a more participative system will also surely prove to be a more effective system.

Because of this appeal, the ideas of participative design theorists are often accepted enthusiastically, in much the same way as (and perhaps even more so than) the wider rubric of Quality of Working Life which represents the popularised presentation of other job redesign proposals. It is certainly to be celebrated that some unions are coming out of their traditional reactive and defensive posture, and a narrow preoccupation with the immediate terms and conditions of the employment contract, to take a positive interest and initiating role in campaigning on job content and work satisfaction.We have seen clear evidence of this in the results of our survey of trade unions, which also shows not only the already well-documented growth of union activity seeking to regulate new technology in general (Baldry and Connolly, 1986; Williams and Steward, 1985; Gill, 1985) but also an emerging awareness and formulation of official policy and guidelines on user-involvement specifically. Several unions claimed to have agreements covering user-involvement or participative design, in some cases a large number being reported. In four cases, unions reported the involvement of national officials in participative design exercises. No industrial action on this issue was reported by any union, though some indicated that the wider question (as they saw it) of new technology agreements had required occasional action.

Interestingly, unions were fairly divided in their views of user-involvement schemes. They split evenly on whether they were typically genuine efforts to involve employees in decision-making, though only two felt it made the unions' job of representing members harder. Most felt it both increased efficiency and job satisfaction, but also that it would cost jobs in the long run and that it was a device to induce employee acceptance of prior management decisions. None the less, none thought its extension would decrease union bargaining power, and half thought it would increase it.

JUSTIFIABLE AMBIVALENCE

Our own assessment to date of participative design would be that this ambivalent and often seemingly contradictory union view has justification. In fact we would go further: we believe that available evidence requires a far more critical appraisal and cautious engagement with future projects than is currently provided in the labour movement or academic literature. The basis for this view is already implied in the earlier sections of this paper, namely that the redesign process and results in the computerising office need to be looked at through the same critical prism invoked for assessments of job redesign initiatives in production (and orthodox office) contexts. The starting point for such an analysis is that a management decision to initiate job redesign is unlikely to be born of a humanistic altruism. On the contrary, management objectives will focus around increasing efficiency and management control, whether this is explicitly articulated or an implicitly constrained goal.

In order to pursue this line of reasoning we will now work through some aspects of this critical perspective – or rather set of perspectives, since the basic premises of a radical or Marxist certainly do not lead to any single, straightforward judgement (cf. Ramsay, 1985; Kelly, 1985) – for computer redesign schemes as will be clarified below.

As a prologue to this, one thing should be made clear. We are not suggesting that the proponents of participative design are con-spirators seeking to deceive white-collar employees into delivering themselves into the hands of those who would exploit them. We claim no definitive insight, but personally view their proposals as liberal idealism, and as such insensitive to hidden agendas, contradictions, power relations and the enhancement of manage-ment control to which their perhaps genuinely radical intentions may open a path. In this they recall the uncritical vulnerability of Blumberg (1968), whose much-quoted case for industrial democracy as a solution for 'alienation' drew on an array of human relations experiments notable for the strictly passive and manipulated role they assigned to their subjects, or of Pateman (1970), whose criticism of pluralist abstentionism seemed more effective than her apprecia-tion of the dangers of unitarist incorporation (see Ramsay, 1987).

More directly, the faith in the 'joint optimisation' of efficiency and satisfaction, the equation of the latter with democracy, and the belief in the 'organisational validity' of their solution, documents the line of descent of computer redesign from the socio-technical school of the Tavistock Institute. In this tradition, whatever the principles announced in the publications of socio-technical theorists, the role of the researcher is typically that of 'facilitator' with a dependence not on the subjects of schemes but on management. In effect, they are consultants, with all the dual role compromises this entails (Brown, 1967). As such, they are constrained first and foremost to make the machinery work, and so to adapt a recalcitrant or poten-tially troublesome workforce to the technical system in ways which are 'organisationally valid' – which amounts to their being accept-able to the management figures able to determine their fate (cf. Kelly, 1978; Hyman, 1972). If this characterisation proves accurate, the risks of non-vigilant enthusiasm for the rhetoric of the computer redesign apostles will be evident.

'LABOUR PROCESS' APPROACHES

In trying to ascertain the real dynamic of job redesign, a number of approaches have emerged within the 'labour process' tradition

(Ramsay, 1985). In a strict adherence to Braverman's views it could only be seen as an insignificant gloss on a continuing process of fragmentation, de-skilling and management acquisition of greater control of clerical tasks. By defining 'Taylorism' (or its side-kick Fordism) in broader terms to cover all strategies aimed at increasing management control over labour, the specific fragmentation of tasks may be presented as less crucial, and modern technologies which seem to call for individual job enrichment or flexible group working may then be seen as instigating a new phase of 'neo-Taylorism' or 'neo-Fordism' (Montmollin, 1974; Palloix, 1976; Aglietta, 1979).

Other writers in this broad tradition cannot accept this stretching of Taylor*ism* so far from the original ideas of Taylor (or at least their usual expression nowadays) and prefer to see redesign strategies as a possible choice presented to management, in particular by technological change. Friedman's (1977) term 'responsible autonomy' has been widely adopted to characterise this approach. It is usually accompanied by arguments that Braverman has underrated the capacity of labour to resist or evade management controls, which renders company policies that much more vulnerable in some circumstances. New technology may be used to try and suppress resistance, but in some cases this may not be a viable option for management (e.g. tight labour markets, or a need for extensive employee support to make new systems work), and again the attraction of real concessions of control to workers may come to the fore. Although most of these writers recognise that 'responsible autonomy' may lead to successful incorporation of worker initiatives, at once taming them for management and overcoming resistance to change, they generally incline to a somewhat optimistic view of the potential for labour advances (Kelly, 1985). In this'voluntarist'perspective some writers drift to a 'positive-sum' view which ends up not far removed from joint optimisation.

In the view of one further variant, this last perspective is correct to recognise the indeterminate, contradictory and struggle-suffused texture of management–labour control relations. However, this is not regarded as justifying a drift to a joint optimisation position, since there remain severe structural limits and constraints on the potential for worker gains, and since control remains a matter of contested exploitation by capital rather than potential consensus. The dangers of incorporation or other severe costs to labour are felt to be underrated. At the same time, the focus of 'labour process'

approaches in general on production or even product market conditions was argued to overlook the influence of other, wider social
relations of power on impulses for management to concoct and try
out 'participative' experiments which were often ineffectual in
practice (Ramsay, 1985).

It is possible to apply these different perspectives to read-off
parallel accounts of user-involvement in computer systems design
and implementation with striking facility. Thus the Bravermanesque
view would see all such developments as superficial, ergonomic
exercises at most, doing little to conceal a progressive degradation of
office work by appropriating user skills into the computing system.
Such an approach is not without considerable backing from empirical
studies on the use of computing systems (Crompton and Jones, 1984;
Cooley, 1980, 1981), an observation to which we shall return.

The neo-Fordist variant might view the emergence of networked
systems in place of the earlier batch computers as requiring a well-
packaged user-involvement programme but one still well within the
systems rationalisation paradigm in practice. As such, in practice
new working methods would be introduced, but entailing passive
involvement only, and so continuing management's extension of
control. Mumford-type programmes would be seen as reducing to
this in applied content.

The voluntarist approach could take a far more positive view of
participative design and of the subsequent proposals for multi-skill,
flexible team working in the programme of Mumford and others.
Although potentially more critical of real management motives and
of the substance of user-involvement, this school of thought is
broadly compatible in tenor with the relatively favourable reaction
to the ideas of the computer redesign paradigm which prevails.

Finally, the sceptical variant (for want of a better label) would
accept the need to ascertain the real-world practice of computer
redesign, including acceptance of the possibility that it may provide
a gateway to genuine employee benefits and control, rather than
writing it off by *a priori* assertion. None the less, there would be a
disinclination to trust the claims of a commitment to effective participation or of positive results for user-involvement programmes
without solid evidence. The emphasis on structural constraint leads
to an alternative reading of findings, noted above, that most
computer systems lead predominantly to de-skilling, since most of
the studies identified earlier as confirming this adhere to a 'social

choice' view of the ambivalent potential for modern computing systems. The concept of constraint becomes an important one in the criticism of bullish participative theory as naive and idealist. Moreover, this approach seems better attuned than the voluntarist alternative to analyses of the persistent structures of hierarchy in white-collar work, and of sustained and extended gender segregation and role ascription which we have already noted as central to any meaningful comprehension of social relations in the office[1].

In what follows we shall try to outline some answers to the key questions which we think should be asked of computer redesign theory and practice. In evaluating these, the voluntarist and sceptical perspectives are treated as the most viable, since both embody the non-determined, contested view of management–labour relations which seems to accord with the most plausible discussions both of the technology involved and of acceptable epistemology more generally.

WHERE DOES COMPUTER REDESIGN FIT?

In his elaboration of how management may seek to use new technology to increase productivity, flexibility and control, Child (1985) distills four strategies: *direct labour displacement*; *contracting systems*; *job degradation*; and *'polyvalence'*. Only the last of these fits any idea of job redesign, involving as it does the breakdown of task demarcations and the horizontal enlargement of the scope of jobs. Such a change offers no participation as such, however, and does not fit the kind of involvement proposed by Mumford which goes beyond task extension and flexibility (though a passive user-involvement scheme might entail such changes).

This suggests that Child's list needs extension to consider other possible strategies which are variants on participation/job redesign. Kelly (1982), in what constitutes by far the most detailed and extensive review of this area, identifies three forms of job redesign. *Flowline reorganisation* involves changes close to those described by Child. *Flexible group working,* which Kelly suggests is more likely in process technologies or their equivalent, involves arrangements which allow for greater employee interaction and co-operation on a team basis, probably assuming some lower-level management functions. The degree of work group autonomy can vary markedly, but a potential for a 'responsible autonomy' strategy exists theoretically at least.

Kelly argues that such innovations may constitute a break from Taylorist individualism, but in practice are none the less often very similar in their origins as means of tackling competitive labour cost crises. Finally, *vertical role integration* entails the acceptance of greater exercise of responsibility by employees through job enrichment – in other words, the assumption of (low level) management functions by individuals.

To complete the list of strategies we would need to add the wider, consultative or other representative forms of participative strategy which management may adopt. However, the task at hand is not to complete the list of options, but to consider computer redesign approaches in light of these strategies. Kelly observes that vertical role integration in particular has characterised white-collar experiments within job redesign in general. He also finds, as was noted earlier, that such schemes have a markedly superior success rate in the office to that recorded on the shopfloor. This he attributes to a rise in intrinsic motivation among white-collar workers, in accordance with the standard job enrichment theory of motivation but not often reproduced among blue-collar workers. While Kelly seems unsure of how to explain this phenomenon, his account implies that white-collar workers are more responsive to management efforts to secure their co-operation than their shopfloor counterparts.

Although only a few cases of white-collar flexible group working are reported by Kelly (1982), it is this approach which is at the leading edge of the proposals advanced by Mumford *et al.* for modern computerised offices. This seems to enhance the prospects for 'responsible autonomy' as an option at least. Moreover, if the greater success in general with job redesign in the office could be carried over, the prospects for management (and at least possibly for employees) of significant gains must be recognised.

In this and subsequent discussion we will pass comment on two studies published by Mumford to exemplify her work – one in Rolls-Royce (Mumford and Henshall, 1979), the other in ICI (Mumford, 1983a). The latter study is of a group of five secretaries, whose self-reported account makes it clear that their position and outlook gave them a measure of responsibility which they also accepted as tying them wholeheartedly to the objective of efficiency (cf. Barker and Downing, 1980). It is hard to see the outcome as involving more coherent group ties than previously, although the reported solution did involve integrated tasks to some extent. These tasks involved the displacement of typewriters by a word-processing system rather than any major computer networking. The Rolls-Royce study, on the other hand, took place in the Purchase Invoice Department which was introducing a new computing system. Here the option of a full multiple-skill group system was rejected, and after some pressure salesmanship by management, a dilute alternative was accepted. In the ICI case and (given the grading structure) for many of the Rolls-Royce employees it seems women were the subjects. In each case the managers being 'serviced' were apparently men – in Rolls-Royce one of these taking a leading role that led to him co-authoring the book on the experiment. It is not made clear where the resistance to management preferences for a fully flexible working group came from, but as it was 'senior' clerks who were noted as the least supportive (p. 60) one could speculate that loss of gendered status just might have been involved.

Our other main empirical referent is a survey of Scottish companies with computing systems. This survey was conducted between January and May 1986 and yielded a response rate of 48 per cent, with 121 returns (38 per cent) useable for analysis. It is to be emphasised that these results tell us only what data processing managers report, and while this is of considerable importance given the dearth of information on user-involvement schemes, it can cast only some light on a few of the questions raised here. It cannot, for example, substitute for case study work.

Notwithstanding these limitations, the survey does give us some useful information on the profile of user-involvement. Although a bias towards replies from companies operating (or claiming to operate) user-involvement policies may be expected, it is still remarkable that 84 per cent of managers reported such a general policy in their companies. 73 per cent claimed users were always consulted (and another 17 per cent 'frequently' consulted) on changes or modifications in computer-based systems, although when asked about involvement in actual design the figure fell to 40 per cent 'always' (plus 21 per cent 'frequently').

Mumford stresses the role of external consultants as facilitators (and implicitly in setting a radical programme), but 79 per cent of companies reporting user-involvement said they had sought no outside advice. Managers in 71 per cent of these organisations also reported that no pre-project training courses for users or their representatives to gain competence had been sponsored. Only 1 per cent felt a lower priority would be assigned to user-involvement in future,

52 per cent foresaw no change, and 41 per cent a higher priority. 76 per cent saw user-involvement as 'crucial' or 'very important' in computer design generally in the future.

PARTICIPATIVE DESIGN – OR JUST USER-INVOLVEMENT?

Given the above mixed observations on the possible significance of user-involvement, the crucial question to be addressed concerns the extent to which genuine participation in design and implementation decisions is really a feature of user-involvement programmes. Clearly participation may take place to differing degrees and at various stages of computing systems conception and implementation. In crude outline, the stages may be defined as goal-setting (in which the objectives and parameters for the planned system are conceived), design of means (which involves several layers of systems analysis and adjustment), and the implementation and evaluation/fine tuning of those means. The further into the process one gets, the more time, money and solidifying thought have already gone into rigidifying the system, and the more residual any participative influences must become.

But of course it is also necessary to decide whether a presence at meetings at any particular stage allows significant influence to be exerted. As Hirschheim (1982) observes, user-involvement at some level is almost inevitable, and this 'obviousness' or triviality was expressed in numerous comments accompanying returns to our survey, which may be taken as devaluing somewhat the prevalence of user-involvement noted above. Participation is a different matter. There is no reason to presume that full participation in design will accompany user-involvement in implementation.

To these issues must be added the question of 'who are the users being involved ?'. Again the meaning is quite different if it refers to a manager or senior group in, say, a stock control department working with DP staff to produce a useful system, as compared with a full-team participative design exercise with the whole department. Hierarchy and gender return to the fore where only subsets of departments are involved.

Turning to the Mumford studies first, the degree of involvement of the five secretaries in the ICI case seems *prima facie* quite impressive (only the aftermath, discussed later, weakening the case as presented). One would like to interview those involved and observe the actual process oneself to be convinced (or at least *we* would given our past experience of checking consultants' reports!), but barring this the example stands. Whether its participants were simply incorporated into the management values they served, and acted as their own worst enemies, is not possible to judge one way or the other from the text.

More serious problems arise with the rather more extensive Rolls-Royce case. To summarise, the design objectives and the kind of work system desired, seem to be clearly predefined by management. The 'internal consultant' was the co-author, and Systems Manager of the Accounting Department, and the Design Team consisted of users selected by management rather than elected representatives. Resistance and suspicion are reported intermittently, but passed off as due to unsuccessful communication in a manner straight out of the classic Jaques study of the Glacier Metal Company in the early Tavistock days (Jaques, 1951). Yet the solution agreed in this fashion proves to be a dilute compromise which Henshall hopes will lead to his own preferred alternative in good time (p. 73). One critical assessment (from a 'labour process' theorist) describes it more acerbically as a 'reprehensible exercise in deception' where 'crude manipulation pervades every page' (Kraft, 1979b). Again the need for a cross-check seems urgent.

If these cases leave the optimistic observer with a sense of concern, then this must be reinforced by some other findings of the Scottish survey. As might be expected for those researching on participation in any context, almost all the initiative for participative design was reported as coming from some management source. When the composition of user groups is considered, there is a predictably strong tendency to involve middle and senior management, a lesser inclination to include lower management and clerical workers (only 37 per cent of schemes including the latter), and almost none to bring in secretarial staff (reported in only 4 per cent of schemes). Moreover, very few design teams (less than one in ten) involve the entire user population, with almost three-quarters following the Rolls-Royce model with management appointing user representatives. Predictably, non-managerial white-collar users are predominantly involved, if at all, in implementation and operational adjustment phases of any system's introduction (47 per cent of cases); they are asked to help identify problems initially in 27 per cent of cases, but that this is a superficial involvement seems to be indicated by the fact that they are reported to take part in the decision to innovate in only 3 per cent of cases, and in the goal setting process following this in just 6 per cent. Steering committees, almost invariably with veto powers, are staffed almost exclusively by middle and senior management, including DP management. This hardly seems likely to be a basis for resisting instrumental rationality in the systems analyst's outlook.

Finally, in only 8 per cent of cases did even our management respondents claim any success for participative design in 'advancing democratic rights', although Mumford and others state this as a pivotal element (and justification) of their approach. Almost as many respondents wrote across this part of the questionnaire something to the effect that this issue was irrelevant to the entire subject of participative design – including a return from one major manufacturer of computing equipment.

SOME 'LABOUR PROCESS' QUESTIONS

Given the question-marks which we have placed against a face-value reading of computer redesign theory as concerned with genuine advances in the democratic rights of employees in practice, there are now strong grounds for mounting a far more critical and wary evaluation. As a result, the need to address a number of questions already asked of mainstream socio-technical approaches in some quarters comes to the fore. Because of the orientation of research on the participative design of computing systems to date, all we can do at this stage is mark out some areas for future investigation, offering a few comments from our survey findings where appropriate. These questions can only be properly approached through case study research with any conviction.

Increasing work intensity has been found to be associated with job redesign in general (Kelly, 1978, 1982), although measurement of this may be problematical in all but routine white-collar work. The impact of new technology in this area has sometimes been considerable, although it is again hard to judge the experiential aspects given the impact on productivity of the technology itself (Baldry and Connolly, 1986). In our survey, only one union predicted adverse effects in this area arising from user-involvement, and a majority expected some improvements – though most paradoxically saw it as an effect of such schemes to date. On the other hand, management respondents for the most part felt that participative design fostered a flexible approach to systems use (20 per cent very successfully, 51 per cent moderately successfully). They also felt that it motivated staff and encouraged higher productivity (11 per cent and 55 per cent respectively). These may well be unsupported (and perhaps 'public relations') claims, but if they were accurate they would imply at least some labour intensification.

Job losses are, of course, implied by increased work intensity or any other source of increased productivity, unless there is at least an offsetting increase in the work undertaken. It is often claimed on this score that one consequence of computerisation is an increase in the extent and quality of services provided by many departments, so that job loss is prevented by a generated demand for greatly increased information flows. On the other hand, in white-collar work which is being computerised in particular, there is a great danger in assessing employee reductions only at the point of redesign, since they may take place (often surreptitiously) in quite different locations in the organisation (Baldry and Connolly, 1986). In his study of job redesign, Kelly (1982) reports that where information is provided, there is an average job loss of 25 per cent, so the importance of scrutinising changes on this front is clearly of major importance. In line with their contradictory views on work intensity, trade unions split fairly evenly on whether user-involvement would cost jobs or not, despite their unanimously neutral-to-optimistic view of the impact on their bargaining power for instance.

Health and safety has become a particularly salient area for union-management relations over the issue of new technology in the office, although the slow realisation of some of the issues concerned stemmed from a lack of good independent research on the effects of VDUs and so forth. Past experience suggests that this may be an important area of joint regulation, although it is easily restricted to an involvement in ergonomics only by management. Company respondents in our survey tended not to see this as a significant issue (again a familiar finding on this topic), with only 7 per cent perceiving a positive impact, 24 per cent seeing the effect as uncertain, and 69 per cent seeing no great impact (or dismissing the question as irrelevant). The unions were more optimistic, with almost all expecting at least some improvements to arise from participative design.

Payment systems have repeatedly emerged as a submerged 'interference' within the orthodox, enthusiastic literature on various forms of job redesign and participation, often discrediting claims of increased productivity, employee satisfaction and so forth attributed by researchers to involvement (Carey, 1967, 1979; Kelly, 1978, 1982). Any claims concerning computer redesign will then need to be assessed with full knowledge of any accompanying changes of this sort. For the record, only 6 per cent of the companies in our survey said they had offered any additional remuneration along with a participative design exercise. Only one union foresaw substantial benefits in payment from such schemes, and a large majority expected little or no impact.

De-skilling/re-skilling is one of the more obviously important areas for examing the consequences of user-involvement. The orthodoxy effectively presumes that any impact must be in the direction of re-skilling, but there are obvious reasons for questioning this. Firstly, the potential for a pseudo-democratic form of involvement implies that overcoming resistance to change and finding inducements to persuade employees to accept what may actually be less varied or influential work may be a consequence of user-involvement in practice. Secondly, even if we accept the view that there is a choice on this score in the introduction of new, computer-based systems, there is plenty of evidence not only from sceptics (e.g. Crompton and Jones, 1984) but also from redesign enthusiasts themselves (e.g. Buchanan and Boddy, 1983) that in practice the de-skilling option is adopted by most managements. Indeed, this 'unfortunate' state of affairs is precisely that which the writings of the gurus of the field such as Mumford, Davis, Taylor or Bjorn-Andersen, rail against. The only question that needs to be raised to open this area up is whether this is indeed simply a matter of short-sightedness and misfortune, or whether it has more to do with the deliberate management strategies described for shop floor forms of new technology by earlier research (Noble, 1975; Shaiken, 1979a).

The first indicator of skill impact used in much of the literature often involves expressed job 'satisfaction'. In fact, this is a dubious measure which also assumes a highly vulnerable motivational and attitudinal model in most cases. Notwithstanding these methodological problems, we can report that in our company survey no response admitted negative effects on satisfaction, while 10 per cent felt schemes had been very successful in promoting it, and 61 per cent that they had been moderately successful. A majority of unions also saw it as increasing satisfaction. On operating skills directly, most unions perceived minor or negligible benefits, but one expected adverse effects. One further area concerns work autonomy and control, and here the union expectations were much the same as on skills, although two expected substantial gains in this area while one expected adverse effects. The ground clearly remains wide open for investigation, although the existing research noted above makes us far more doubtful about any likely benefits for labour than many in the labour movement appear to believe at present. Further, we would posit that it is important to distinguish short and long run effects of introducing computing systems. Existing research suggests that the transition to operating a new system often leans heavily on employee knowledge of old and new, but that the long term impact on employee control may be quite different.

Before leaving this topic, one further possible impact of computer systems in general, enhanced in likely importance by some of our findings on the actual nature of user-involvement described earlier, requires brief further attention. This concerns the impact of schemes on the internal segmentation and structure of the workforce. It is clear that computer redesign has every potential to provide a few enhanced or responsible tasks and a high proportion of routinised work, this being expressed through the participative exercise itself (e.g. by who gets represented in what way at what stage). Insofar as this differential impact occurs, it renders of limited value general questions as to the impact of schemes; indeed experience would lead one to expect that gender-differentiated impacts in particular would all too readily be overlooked.

The locus of control is the issue most obviously and directly related to the proclaimed democratic benefits of participative design. There are a number of ways in which computer redesign schemes could produce results which have been observed in other areas of participation and job redesign. Such exercises may expose employees to the expert power of management (Mulder, 1971), give them a sense of involvement without ceding any power, or induce greater acceptance of responsibility, increased effort or visibility to control checks (Pignon and Querzola, 1976; Kelly 1982). Voluntarists may none the less emphasise the potential for employees to find space to assert their own control (Wood and Kelly, 1982), but there may be good reason to suspect that the scope for such gains is nothing like symmetrical with the potential for management advantage (Ramsay, 1985). None the less, this remains an empirical question, and one in urgent need of evidence. In our own survey (which again is only of value in the absence of a fund of more direct information on this matter), trade unions were very much divided over whether user-involvement was a genuine effort to involve employees in decision-making; a majority agreed, though, that it was a device to persuade employees to accept prior management decisions (though again a significant minority disagreed). On the management side, 95 per cent claimed that participative design successfully overcame user resistance to change, and 89 per cent that it enhanced user understanding and ability to operate computer systems. This last finding, together with its companion that 71 per cent claimed success in fostering a flexible approach to systems use, may be taken to imply a possible reskilling within a flexible work task arrangement, yet also seems consistent with a greater management grip. In any case, joint optimisation remains only one reading of this. Again the ambivalence of such data indicate problems of research as much as anything else.

IS COMPUTER REDESIGN IMPORTANT?

One final question remains to be raised. The uncertainty surrounding interpretations of computer redesign highlighted in this chapter raises the possibility that for all the clamour surrounding the topic, it is in fact of little significance either way for the future of labour-management relations in the office. This has already been argued as a possibility for other forms of participation (Ramsay, 1980, 1985, 1987). It has been suggested that management often lacks any clear strategy to make the best use of such techniques, operating rather on a somewhat *ad hoc* and poorly thought out basis (see e.g. Rose and Jones, 1985), and there is no particular reason to suppose that computer redesign schemes will have been more carefully constructed. On the other hand, it has been suggested that implicit strategies may be built in by management's orientation without having to be fully articulated to bring some success (Child, 1985). Again, there is no substitute for empirical material.

A few fragments of information may be mustered here, and they do give at least some credence to the possibility of marginality of computer redesign. In our survey, for example, although 76 per cent of respondents rated user-involvement in systems design in the future as crucial or very important, only 41 per cent expected their organisation to give it higher priority in that future. Moreover, only 40 per cent felt that their organisation's DP or computer management problems had diminished as a result of user-involvement (12 per cent feeling they had increased). On the other hand, only one union felt user-involvement was of little significance in the final analysis. Interesting though these results are, however, they are not very discerning as far as judging between some of the above-described perspectives goes.

Another source of data is the existing literature on user-involvement, which contains a number of broadly critical assessments. These are of limited value for much of the ground we argue has to be covered, since their orientation is basically a sceptical managerial one. But from this position, they do interrogate the issue of whether such schemes can be shown to increase employee satisfaction, motivation, effort and efficiency (Hirschheim, 1982; Ives and Olson, 1984; Markus, 1984 among others). They find that on all scores the evidence is unconvincing or contradictory, despite the widespread and undiluted praise for such innovations. It is found that management rarely conducts proper evaluation exercises of such projects, and that so far the signs are that a scheme is a one-off and unsustained exercise (Hirschheim, 1982).

A reconsideration of the two Mumford studies referred to earlier actually gives a similar impression to the sceptical reader. In the Rolls-Royce case, we saw that management were unsuccessful in overcoming all hostility or in getting acceptance of their preferred option. In addition Kraft reports that no hard evidence is provided on satisfaction or efficiency, and that his own efforts to obtain such evidence by enquiries to Professor Mumford failed to yield any substance (Kraft, 1979b). In the ICI study, an afternote by Mumford herself reports that the secretarial group undertaking the exercise found their influence declining with her withdrawal and a loss of commitment on the management side (Mumford, 1983). She herself notes the implication that without active interest on the part of management, employees are unable to sustain influence – an observation which takes on rather different significance to that which she attaches to it in the context of the analysis advanced here.

Suggestive though this information is, it would be disingenuous to cite it as proof that user-involvement is a paper tiger, considered from whichever angle. Voluntarists may well draw their own encouragement from the apparent inchoate nature of management objectives, for instance. Moreover, an approach which sets out hoping to find 'the' typical outcome of user-involvement is committing an error all too common in the participation literature (and beyond it). Rather, it seems reasonable that the results will vary with various contingencies and chance events. After all, we have already argued that user-involvement is a far from homogeneous phenomenon, and the same applies to computing systems, managements, office workforces and numerous other factors. This search for a definitive outcome is another fault of much of the literature mounting criticism-from-within for example. More realistic would be a search for a contextualised pattern of outcomes, seeking to discover where (from the point of view of labour) participation tends to yield genuine influence, employees are likely to find opportunities to advance or dangers of facing unforeseen costs, and so forth. Naturally, this makes the research task another order greater in difficulty.

Our own reading of the evidence does not incline us to abandon our scepticism about the benefits of participative design exercises from the employee viewpoint. A critical awareness of the limitations of that evidence commits us to keeping an open mind, however. What we do think is clearly indicated by the information available to us is, firstly, a need for a far more independently critical approach to the proposals of even outwardly radical computer redesign perspectives in the context of the employment relationship which prevails in the real world. Secondly, it follows that there is an urgent need to ask the detailed questions of the practice of computer redesign and user-involvement more generally which have been asked of its intellectual forebears to striking effect.

Notes

1. At this point in our research, we are unable to do more than highlight the dynamics of gender as an area for close attention in proposed case study work. However, we should note that the existence of segmentation and gendered hierarchy may weaken the extent to which white-collar 'successes' for job enrichment constitute real challenges to the separation of conception and execution as voluntarists seem to think (cf. Kelly, 1982).

226   *Computer Redesign and 'Labour Process' Theory*

References

Aglietta, M. (1979), *A Theory of Capitalist Regulation* (New Left Books).
Baldry, C. and Connolly, A. (1986), 'Drawing the Line: Computer Aided Design and the Organisation of the Drawing Office', *New Technology, Work and Employment*, vol. 1, no. 1.
Barker, J. and Downing, H. (1980), 'Word Processing and the Transformation of the Patriarchal Relations of Control in the Office', *Capital and Class*, no. 10.
Bjorn-Andersen, N. and Eason, K. (1980), 'Myths and Realities of Information Systems Contributing to Organisational Rationality', in Mowshowitz, A. (ed.) *Human Choice and Computers 2* (North Holland).
Blackler, F. and Brown, C. (1975), 'The Impending Crisis in Job Design', *Journal of Occupational Psychology*, vol. 48, no. 3.
Blackler, F. and Brown, C. (1985), 'Evaluation and the Impact of Information Technologies on People in Organisations', *Human Relations*, vol. 38, no. 3.
Blumberg, P. (1968), *Industrial Democracy: The Sociology of Participation* (Constable).
Braverman, H. (1974), *Labour and Monopoly Capital* (Monthly Review Press).
Brown, R. (1967), 'Research and Consultancy in Industrial Enterprises', *Sociology*, vol. 1, no. 1.
Brown, R. (1976), 'Women as Employees: Some Comments on Research in Industrial Sociology' in Barker, D. and Allen, S. (eds) *Dependence and Exploitation in Work and Marriage*.
Buchanan, D. and Boddy, D. (1983), *Organisations in the Computer Age* (Gower).
Carey, A. (1967), 'The Hawthorne Studies: A Radical Criticism', *American Sociological Review*, vol. 32, no. 3.
Carey, A. (1979), 'The Norwegian Experiments in Democracy at Work: A Critique and a Contribution to Reflexive Sociology', *Australia and New Zealand Journal of Sociology*, vol. 15, no. 1.
Child, J. (1985), 'Managerial Strategies, New Technology and the Labour Process', in Knights, D. *et al.*, *Job Redesign*.
Cooley, M. (1980), *Architect or Bee?* (Langley Technical Services).
Cooley, M. (1981), 'The Taylorisation of Intellectual Work' in Levidow, L. and Young, B. *Science, Technology and the Labour Process*, vol. 1 (CSE Books).
Crompton, R. and Jones, G. (1984), *White-Collar Proletariat: Deskilling and Gender in Clerical Work* (Macmillan).
Dagwell, R. and Weber, R. (1983), 'Systems Designers User Models: A Comparative Study and Methodological Critique', *Communications of the ACM*, vol. 26, no. 11.
Davis, L. E. (1976) 'Developments in Job Design' in Warr, P. (ed.) *Personal Goals and Work Design* (Wiley).
Davis, L. E. (1977), 'Job Design: Overview and Future Directions', *Journal of Contemporary Business*, vol. 6, no. 2.
Davis, L. E. (1980), 'Changes in Work Environments: The Next 20 Years', in Duncan, K. *et al.*, *Changes in Working Life* (Wiley).

Davis, L. E., Canter, R. and Hoffman, J. (1955), 'Current Job Design Criteria', *Journal of Industrial Engineering*, vol. 6, no. 2.

Davis, L. E. and Taylor, J. (eds) (1979), *The Design of Jobs*, Second edition (Goodyear).

DeBrabander, B. and Edstrom, A. (1977), 'Successful Information Systems Development *Management Science*, vol. 24, no. 2.

DeBrabander, B. and Thiers, G. (1984), 'Successful Information Systems Development in Relation to Situational Factors Which Affect Effective Communication Between MIS-Users and EDP-Specialists', *Management Science*, vol. 30, no. 2.

Dex, S. (1985), *The Sexual Division of Work* (Wheatsheaf).

Edstrom, A. (1977), 'User Influence and the Success of MIS Projects: A Contingency Approach', *Human Relations*, vol. 30, no. 7.

Friedman, A. (1977), *Industry and Labour: Class Struggle at Work and Monopoly Capitalism* (Macmillan).

Gill, C. (1985), *Work, Unemployment and the New Technology* (Blackwell).

Hales, M. (1980), *Living Thinkwork: Where do Labour Processes Come From* (CSE Books).

Hedberg, B. (1975), 'Computer Systems to Support Industrial Democracy' in Mumford, E. and Sackman, H. (eds) *Human Choice and Computers* (North Holland).

Hedberg, B. and Mumford, E. (1975), 'The Design of Computer Systems: Man's Vision of Man as an Integral Part of the Systems Design Process' in Mumford, E. and Sackman, H. (eds) *op. cit.*

Hirschheim, R. A. (1982), 'Assessing Participative Systems Design: Some Conclusions from an Exploratory Study', *LSE Working Paper*.

Hyman, R. (1972), *Strikes* (Fontana).

Ives, B. and Olson, M. (1984), 'User Involvement and MIS Success: A Review of Research', *Management Science*, vol. 30, no. 5.

Jaques, E. (1951), *The Changing Culture of a Factory* (Tavistock).

Kelly, J. E. (1978), 'A Reappraisal of Socio-technical Systems Theory', *Human Relations* vol. 31, no. 12.

Kelly, J. E. (1982), *Scientific Management, Job Redesign and Work Performance* (Academic Press).

Kelly, J. E. (1985), 'Management's Redesign of Work: Labour Process, Labour Markets and Product Markets', in Knights, D. *et al.*, *op. cit.*

Kraft, P. (1979a), 'The Industrialisation of Computer Programming: From Programming to "Software Production"' in Zimbalist, A. (ed.) *Case Studies on the Labour Process* (Monthly Review Press).

Kraft, P. (1979b), 'Challenging the Mumford Democrats at Derby Works', *Computing*, 2 Aug.

Land, F. and Hirschheim, R. (1983), 'Participative Systems Design: Rationale, Tools and Techniques', *Journal of Applied Systems Analysis*, vol. 10.

Land, F. (1984), 'The Impact of Information Technology on the Workplace', in Piercy, W. (ed.) *The Management Implications of New Information Technology* (Croom Helm).

Littler, C. (1985), 'Taylorism, Fordism and Job Design', in Knights, D. *et al.*, *op. cit.*

228   *Computer Redesign and 'Labour Process' Theory*

Locke, E. A. and Schweiger, D. M. (1979), 'Participation in Decision Making: One More Look', *Res. Organisational Behaviour*, vol. 1.
Markus, M. L. (1983), 'Power Politics and MIS Implementation', *Communications of the ACM*, vol. 26, no. 6.
Markus, M. L. (1984), *Systems in Organisations: Bugs and Features* (Pitman).
Markus, M. L. and Robey, D. (1983), 'The Organisational Validity of Management Information Systems', *Human Relations*, vol. 36, no. 3.
Montmollin, M. (1974), 'Taylorisme et anti-Taylorisme', *Sociologie du Travail*, vol. 16, no. 4.
Mulder, M. (1971), 'Power Equalisation Through Participation?', *Administrative Science Quarterly*, vol. 16, no. 1.
Mumford, E. (1976), 'Towards the Democratic Design of Work Systems', *Personnel Management*, vol. 8, no. 9.
Mumford, E. (1979a), 'The Design of Work: New Approaches and New Needs', in Rijnsdorp, J. E. (ed.) *Case Studies in Automation Related to the Humanisation of Work* (Pergamon).
Mumford, E. (1979b), 'Consensus Systems Design: An Evaluation of This Approach', in Szyperski, N. and Grochla, E. (eds) *Design and Implementation of Computer Based Information Systems* (Sijthoff and Noordoff).
Mumford, E. (1981), *Values, Technology and Work* (Martinus Nijhoff).
Mumford, E. (1983a), *Designing Secretaries* (Manchester Business School).
Mumford, E. (1983b), 'Successful Systems Design', in Otway, H. and Peltu, M. (eds) *New Office Technology: Human and Organisational Aspects* (Pinter).
Mumford, E. (1985), 'Defining Systems Requirements to Meet Business Needs: A Case Study Example', *The Computer Journal*, vol. 28.
Mumford, E. and Henshall, D. (1979), *A Participative Approach to Computer Systems Design* (Associated Business Press).
Mumford, E. and Weir, M. (1979), *Computer Systems in Work Design – The ETHICS Method* (Associated Business Press).
Murray, F. (1983), 'The Decentralisation of Production – The Decline of the Mass-Collective Worker?', *Capital and Class*, no. 19.
Murray, R. (1985), 'Benetton Britain: the New Economic Order', *Marxism Today*, vol. 29, no. 11.
Noble, D. (1987), 'Social Choice in Machine Design', *Politics and Society*, vol. 8.
Palloix, C. (1976), 'The Labour Process: From Fordism to Neo-Fordism', in CSE Pamphlet No. 1, *The Labour Process and Class Strategies*, Stage 1.
Pateman, C. (1970), *Participation and Democratic Theory* (CUP).
Pava, C. (1983), *Managing New Office Technology* (Free Press).
Pollert, A. (1981), *Girls, Wives, Factory Lives* (Macmillan).
Pignon, D. and Querzola, J. (1976), 'Dictatorship and Democracy in Production', in Gorz, A. (ed.) *The Division of Labour* (Harvester).
Ramsay, H. (1980), 'Phantom Participation: Patterns of Power and Conflict', *Industrial Relations Journal*, vol. 11, no. 3.
Ramsay, H. (1985), 'What is Participation For?: A Critical Evaluation of "Labour Process" Analyses of Job Reform', in Knights, D. *et al. op. cit.*

Ramsay, H. (forthcoming), *The Myths of Participation* (Macmillan)

Rockart, J. F. and Flannery, L. S. (1983), 'The Management of End User Computing', *Communications of the ACM*, vol. 26, no. 10.

Rose, M. and Jones, B. (1985), 'Managerial Strategy and Trade Union Responses in Work Reorganisation Schemes at Establishment Level', in Knights, D. *et al. op. cit.*

Rosenbrock, H. (1981), 'Engineers and the Work that People Do', *IEEE Control Systems Magazine*, vol. 1, no. 3.

Shaiken, H. (1979a), 'Numerical Control of Work: Workers and Automation in the Computer Age', *Radical America*, vol. 13. no. 6.

Shaiken, H. (1979b), 'Impact of New Technology on Employees and their Organisations', *International Institute for Comparative Social Research*, Berlin.

SPRU Women and Technology Studies (1982), *Microelectronics and Women's Employment in Britain* (University of Sussex, Science Policy Research Unit).

Tapscott, D. (1982), *Office Automation: A User-Driven Method* (Plenum Press).

Taylor, J. C. (1975), 'The Socio-technical Approach to Work Design', *Personnel Review*, vol. 4, no. 3.

Taylor, J. C. (1979), 'Job Design Criteria Twenty Years Later' in Davis, L. E. and Taylor, J. C. (eds) *The Design of Jobs*, Second edition (Goodyear).

Wainwright, J. and Francis, A. (1984), 'Office Automation – Its Design, Implementation and Impact', *Personnel Review*, vol. 13, no. 1.

Weizenbaum, J. (1976), *Computer Power and Human Reason: From Judgement to Calculation* (Freeman).

Williams, R. and Steward, F. (1985), 'New Technology Agreements: An Assessment', *Industrial Relations Journal*, vol. 16, no. 3.

Wood, S. and Kelly, J. E. (1982), 'Taylorism, Responsible Autonomy and Management Strategy', in Wood, S. (ed.) *The Degradation of Work* (Hutchinson).

10 The Use of Technology and the Development of Qualifications: How the Debate about the Labour Process is Viewed in German Industrial Sociology

Lothar Lappe

THE DIFFICULTIES WITH ANGLO-GERMAN COMPARISONS

In this chapter I discuss statements made in the debate about the labour process, particularly Braverman's views on the development of qualifications, and relate them to results of research conducted in German industrial sociology. In so doing, however, I have encountered two difficulties of which I first really became aware in 1986 during many interesting discussions at the Birmingham conference on 'Organisation and Control of the Labour Process'. They result from the systematic differences in the organisation of work, training, and industrial relations, as well as from the different research strategies pursued by industrial sociology in Great Britain and the Federal Republic of Germany.

There are vast differences in the vocational training offered in the two countries. Each year in the Federal Republic approximately 600 000 persons complete a training period of two and a half or three and a half years in what is known as the 'dual training system'. These skilled workers represent human capital from which businesses profit. Four fifths of the training takes place in the company, one fifth of it in state schools. Of the approximately 600 000 apprentices who passed their final examinations in 1984, approximately 270 000 were in manufacturing, including 103 000 fitters, mechanics, and the like, and about 293 000 tradesmen in service occupations. Approximately 250 000 of these 600 000 apprentices were women. About 50 000 apprentices were not able to find a job after completing their training and were registered as unemployed. Despite annual appeals by the unions to government and business to provide enough training places for young people who have completed their formal schooling and to hire the apprentices after their training, too little is being done.

Some of the aspects closely linked to this training system need to be looked at more closely. On the positive side, the broad qualifications that workers acquire in the course of their training make it easier for them to deal professionally with new technologies. On the negative side, however, outdated knowledge and techniques continue to hamper training programmes, and many apprentices – especially those in small and medium-sized companies, where training often does not take place in apprentice workshops – are frequently exploited and assigned to do unqualified work. Lastly, the fact that the qualification of young people through the system of vocational training is such a significant factor on the labour market explains the high level of interest that industrial sociologists and labour market researchers have in qualification profiles and the acquisition of qualifactions. Apparently, a similar system of occupational training is not as developed in the United States and Great Britain; it does not bestow a certified right to a qualified job.

Another interesting point that repeatedly came up in the Birmingham discussion was the difference between the British and West German systems of industrial relations. It was often pointed out that the introduction of new technologies in companies often leads to conflicts between the individual craft unions if it is unclear which occupational group – the elctricians, the machine workers, the lathe operators, or the fitters – will be operating the new production system. There is no such conflict in the German labour relations system because workers are often organised in unions spanning several occupational fields. For example, all industrial workers in machine building, electronics, automobile manufacturing, the base metals industry, precision engineering, and other areas belong to the same union, the Industrial Metalworkers' Union (Industriegewerkschaft Metall, IGM).

A particularly important aspect that must be taken into consideration when comparing Great Britain and the Federal Republic of

Germany is the fact that the research strategies in the two countries are diverging. One of the reasons for this difference in Germany stems from the elimination of the unions in the 1930s, fascism's repression of all enlightened social science, and the emigration of important researchers. In effect, both the personnel and the focus of German industrial sociology had to be re-established after the Second World War. The resulting lack of continuity is still evident.

In my view, the Anglo-Saxon research tradition is more oriented to industrial conflicts than is the case in Germany, particularly when it comes to the issue of control over working conditions and the accentuation of political dimensions in industrial relations. Such interests have found their expression in various types of research, especially intercultural studies on the system of industrial relations, the use of technology, labour mobility, and class consciousness (see, for example, Turner *et al.*, 1967; Dore, 1973; Gallie, 1978; Form, 1976; Cole, 1979). These studies may be credited with having helped prevent the narrow concept of technological determinism from gaining more than limited acceptance in the Anglo-Saxon context. By contrast, the notion that technology and work organisation vary with the type of company and business strategy in question, that they can be influenced by union control, and that they are largely dependent on cultural and social factors has received little attention in German industrial sociology.

Furthermore, the Anglo-Saxon research tradition set the trend for research on the life worlds of workers and the 'shop-floor culture' (Kornblum, 1974; Beynon, 1973; and Nichols and Armstrong, 1976, to mention just a few). One fascinating thing is that many historical studies by industrial soiologists ultimately tie into current empirical research or link *both* perspectives (for instance, see Penn, 1985; and Friedman, 1977).

German industrial sociology, on the other hand, is dominated by research programmes affiliated with and shaped by specific institutes and partially supported by public funds. German research does have something in common with Anglo-Saxon work in the area of industrial relations, however. The control over working conditions, a subject discussed so intensely in Great Britain and the United States, is only gradually becoming the subject of research in the Federal Republic (Jürgens and Naschold, 1984). The complete absence of historical analyses in the area of industrial sociology is a serious deficiency. Exceptions are studies by Schmiede and

Schudlich (1976) and Deutschman (1985). A major focus of research in Germany, which is represented primarily by the work of the Institute for Social Science Research in Munich, is the study of internal and external labour-market structures, the analysis of regional labour markets, and studies of the mechanisms and strategies of labour deployment.

The real strength of German industrial sociology, however, lies in technology research on specific sectors and production processes and in the elaboration and application of in-depth qualitative analyses of the qualifications, stress, and other aspects that a given job entails. This research interest is closely linked with systematic case studies of companies or sectors.

The large number of such studies, with their often very detailed analyses of job requirements, probably explains why Braverman has had so little impact on German industrial sociology. The extraordinary variety of the questions and themes, the thoroughness with which almost all branches and production sectors have been considered from different perspectives (special technologies and ways of organising work, different labour groups and labour maker strategies, for example) have never allowed the global types of questions posed by Braverman to be asked in the first place. It therefore seems particularly important to examine whether Braverman's ideas agree with recent findings of German industrial sociology on the devlopment and use of new technologies.

DIFFERENT CONDITIONS GOVERNING THE EMERGENCE OF PRODUCTION TECHNOLOGIES

According to Braverman, the capitalist work process represents capital's increasing control over the act of work. He argues the central Marxist position by stressing the trend towards the homogenisation of work and uniformisation of the workforce. He describes the process and the means by which capital forces the working class to submit to its control.

The focal point of the debate about the labour process is that the control strategies of capital eventually de-skill workers and downgrade work. Braverman (1977), Stone (1975), Marglin (1974), Zimbalist (1979), the Brighton Labour Process Group (1977), and others assert that these effects are inherent in the capitalist work process and that they permeate all work processes in all branches (including the service sector). The symptoms are (a) the replacement of skilled workers by machines or machine operators and (b) the division or subdivision of jobs, with the remaining qualified work being assigned to a few specialists and the few residual semiskilled or unskilled tasks being split up completely.

Braverman's study sparked a long standing debate about the validity of his theses. The discussion, however, is still restricted almost exclusively to Anglo-Saxon circles. While supporters such as Zimbalist and Montgomery believe that historical analyses essentially confirm the theses put forward by Braverman, critics such as Friedman, Wood, Littler, Thompson, Edwards and Penn not only doubt his theory's fidelity to reality, but also find serious faults in his methodology.

It is generally agreed that the various strands of development in the capitalist work process need elaboration so that questions about downgrading and de-skilling can be answered for specific, definable, empirical areas and manageable time periods rather than continuously being treated in a general fashion. This task requires an appropriate classification of industrial sectors (Littler, 1982) according to their production technologies or production areas. This should permit one to deal somewhat adequately with the non-simultaneities entailed by the introduction of new technologies and, hence, by the multifaceted nature of skill development.

Quite apart from the debate on the labour process, the analysis of downgrading and de-skilling was the central idea of the study by Kern and Schumann (1974) and other empirical research projects by the Sociological Research Institute (Soziologisches Forschungsinstitut, SOFI) in Goettingen (Mickler *et al.*, 1976, 1977; Lappe, 1981; Mickler, 1981). The underlying concept of my present research is the concept formulated by Kern and Schumann (1974), according to whom the conditions of human work and the way it tends to change are determined by the sophistication of the technical systems and the nature and scope of the potential for mechanisation. The speed of technological development, the range and level of the different technological leaps, and, therefore, the form of human work are also tied to the specific design of the production process in production areas bridging various sectors. Only when specific production areas are taken into consideration can one really understand and interpret the forms of human labour linked to the varied technological levels of the production process.

Beginning with a total absence of mechanisation processes, pure manual labour, the four essential elements of human labour can be identified (Kern and Schumann, 1974):
- feeding in and unloading the object being worked on;
- designing (planning and executing) the work sequence:
- controlling the work sequence;
- correcting the work sequence (planning and carrying out corrective measures).

The mechanisation that results from the development of production technology can then be seen as a process whereby these human labour functions are progressively subsumed in the technical apparatus. Simultaneously, the framework for the residual functions to be performed by humans is redefined and the scope and character of production work is largely determined. A further key assumption in defining the work, however, is that possibilities for designing the organisation of work exist at each technological level and that they determine how far the division of labour goes and exactly what the actual type of industrial labour is to be.

According to Kern and Schumann, the lowest level of the mechanisation process is *premechanised production work*, in which the design, control and correction of the work process and the feeding in and unloading of the objects being worked on is characterised by human toil assisted by nothing more than simple tools. Premechanised production includes craftwork, pure manual work, and both motoric and sensory conveyor-belt production. Levels of mechanisation and types of work are categorised in Table 10. 1. It is not possible to provide further details within the scope of this article.

One can speak of *mechanisation* when the execution of work and corrective operations takes place through mechanical power rather than by human muscle power. In such cases, the human functions involved are mainly those of planning work and corrective measures and of controlling the work process. It is, in other words, a matter of functions requiring the use of human senses and human intelligence (Kern and Schumann, 1974). Depending on the level of mechanisation, the types of work in this category entail the operation and monitoring of machines and apparatuses, control, electric switching, and control engineering.

Automatic elements become a part of the production process when technological instruments assume those functions that had still been

Table 10.1   Types of industrial work in Kern and Schumann (1974, vol. 2)

	Level of mechanisation	*Type of work*
Work in premechanised production	Pure manual operation (Level 1)	*Type 1*: Manual labour
		Type 2: Simply manual labour
	Production-line technique (Level 2) *Type 4*: Sensory conveyor belt work	*Type 3*: Motoric conveyor belt work
Work in mechanised production	Unifunctional single-aggregates necessitating permanent manual work (special machines, for example (Level 3)	*Type 5*: Operation of machines
		Type 6: Operation of apparatuses
	Single aggregates necessitating permanent correction by means of control instruments (Level 4)	*Type 7*: Control work
		Type 8: Electric switching power
	Multifunctional single-aggregates not necessitating permanent constant correction by humans (Level 5)	*Type 9*: Machine monitoring
		Type 10: Apparatus monitoring
	Aggregate systems (for example; linked individual machines; simple transfer lines) (Level 6)	*Type 11*: Systems monitoring
Work in automated production	Semiautomated single aggregates (Level 7)	*Type 12*: Automatic monitoring
		Type 13: Automatic control

ıble 10.1 (contd.)

	Level of mechanisation	Type of work
	Semiautomated aggregate systems (transfer lines, for example) (Level 8)	*Type 14*: Systems control
		Type 15: Control-room activity
	Fully automated manufacturing (Level 9)	

fulfilled by human muscle power in the mechanisation stage, in other words, as soon as the areas of process control and correction are at least partially mechanised (Kern and Schumann, 1974). The types of work falling into the category of automated production processes are robot programming and control, control engineering, and control room activity.

The authors were able to show that the course of technological development and the respective level of mechanisation varied with their respective types of work according to the specific form of the production process. This specific design and the different goals and conditions of the production process determine which existing or potential technical procedures are profitable and which are therefore likely to be in use. Such preconditions governing the technical structuring of individual production processes have specific characteristics:

- The nature of the inputs (raw materials or semi-finished products). As a rule, technical structuring of processes is more cost-efficient with fluid of gaseous inputs than with solid ones. The same is true for inputs that can be processed *en masse* without major changes (semi-finished products, for example).
- The nature of the products. The technical structuring of manufacturing processes involving homogeneous, standardised, finished products is generally more cost-efficient than those involving complex products that vary greatly.
- The nature of the production sequence. The more complex and varied the steps required to manufacture a product, the more

expensive it usually is to increase the level of mechanisation. By contrast, the mechanisation of simple, standardised work processes is relatively cost-effective as a rule.

It is striking, but not surprising, that there is a parallel to the ideas of Bryn Jones, who, like Kern and Schumann, draws on Bright (1958):

A second constraining influence on the allocation of task skills to new production technology might clearly be the market for a firm's or industry's product, and, allied to this, the physical characteristics of that product. Bright (1958), for example, compared levels of mechanisation in the electric light bulb industry, which achieved 'higher' levels of automation than the shoe industry. Light bulbs were saleable as standardized products made of materials which lent themselves to a high degree of automatic machining. Footwear designs changed frequently as a result of fashion changes, and production was variegated in terms of sizes and composed of materials that were difficult to adapt to automatic or semiautomatic machining operations. (Jones, 1982, p. 180)

Depending on how these production features are combined in more or less cost-effective moves to ensure the technical structuring of work, one can identify typical domains of industrial production that are roughly classifiable according to the criterion of unified production goals and that in general cut across all branches of industry. Such typical domains are the procurement, processing, conversion, and deformation of the work materials; assembly; packing; and transport.

In the following pages I discuss the production areas of mechanised manufacturing (machining), the welding process, and assembly, each area having its framework for technical structuring. At the same time, I would like to demonstrate that the use of technology can run in different directions and that the development of qualifications need not be linear. Examples will be drawn from machine-building; electronics, precision engineering, and automobile manufacturing; construction with steel and light metals; and the base metals industry.

NEW PRODUCTION TECHNOLOGIES AND THEIR IMPACTS ON THE DEVELOPMENT OF SKILLS IN THE GERMAN METAL INDUSTRY

Mechanised Manufacturing: The Advance of Computer-Assisted Manufacturing Processes Alongside Traditional Technologies

The answer to the question of whether technological development in mechanised manufacturing has led to permanent de-skilling caused by the introduction of CNC machines and flexible manufacturing systems depends on what the frame of reference is and on how reliable the operationalisation of the qualification concept is.

Thesis: The development of qualifications is variously assessed according to whether the skills required by CNC machines are compared with those required by the use of manually controlled machine tools or with those needed to use NC technologies. The level of qualification required by CNC aggregates is higher than that for the simpler NC machines or automatic machine tools but is not nearly as high as that required of a centre lathe operator using a manual machine tool. It is worth noting that the proportion of numerically controlled automatic machine tools among all machines tools is vastly overestimated; it is presently 6 per cent at the most.

The potential for mechanising machining processes is relatively great because techniques based on rotation are quite common. With correspondingly high financial expenditures, they can be used both for complex forms of the initial and the final product and for short production runs.

Mechanised manufacturing in the automobile industry, electronics, precision engineering and optics, machine-building, and the base metals industry is based on an almost bewildering variety of cutting and non-cutting machine tools. Depending on their level of mechanisation, these machines can be categorised as monofunctional single aggregates (specialised machine tools), multifunctional machine tools, and linked machine systems (transfer lines). Depending on the type of control involved, they can be categorised as mechanical, hydraulic, pneumatic, electrical, numeric, and guide and programme control machines.

The development of movable tool carriers permitted the simultaneous machining of several pieces and/or their loading/

mounting and removal during the machining phase. Total mechanisation was achieved by removing the workpieces mechanically. The transition from analogously controlled machine tools (curves, templates) to equipment that is digitally, i.e., numerically, controlled at last made the flexible use of this technology profitable for single and small production runs.

Conventional Machine Tools

A classic sphere of work for skilled metal workers is the use of traditional machining tools, which require the manual control of all complicated maneuvers. These machines permit a relatively wide range of choice regarding, for example, the specific cutting tools to be used, the setting of the tension and mounting of the workpieces, the selection of the cutting speed, and the procedure. Working with these machines and at these jobs, the conventional machine worker (such as the central lathe operator and the horizontal boring-mill operator) therefore summons all his patience, precision, acumen, and feel for the materials (Mickler *et al.*, 1977). Formal training for such work is correspondingly long – three to three-and-a-half years – in addition to subsequent on-the-job learning. Such jobs are gradually becoming less important because the work traditionally done by the conventional machine worker is being supplanted by two developments: the various types of non-numeric rotary automatic machine tools in mass production and the development of NC and CNC machines.

Nonnumeric Automatic Machine Tools in Mass Production

Mono- or multifunctional aggregates with guidance control or programmed control developed very early from conventional machine tools for the mass production of small components. The single and multispindle automatic machine tools of different makes in their almost overwhelming variety are usually placed in the 'automatic-tool hall'. Because the loading of these machines is now fully automatic, they no longer need to be tipped by hand, and because such machines are not prone to breakdowns, people with jobs involving them are there primarily to monitor a number of machines, a task structurally different from the using of a single machine. Typically, monitoring machines entails the indirectly productive functions (regulating, controlling, indexing, shifting gears, throwing switches) and the control functions. With stationary manufacturing processes having very high lot sizes, installation work is seldom required, particularly when single-purpose automatic machines are being used.

On the whole, the highly repetitive nature of the time structure does not directly affect the structure of actions performed when using the machines. The structure of *skills* that such work requires, however, is being restricted more and more to simple, routine work. The high sensorimotor proficiency that conventional machine operators used to have is being lost, and the need for planning has all but vanished. Furthermore, the amount of knowledge about materials and procedures that is needed for stationary jobs with long production runs is being significantly reduced, meaning that previously high levels of skill have been eroded by the developments in technology and work organisation.

Numerically Controlled Machine Tools

The transition to numerically controlled levels of production has caused an ever greater division and splintering of labour. The variety of skills required of conventional machine tool workers are being distributed among different functional groups (tool presetters, programmers, and NC-machine operators). The NC and CNC machine tools originally used primarily in the manufacturing processes of medium and short production runs but now used increasingly for high lot sizes as well are digitally controlled (by punched card, perforated tape, or magnetic tape). In addition, CNC machine tools have built-in microcomputers and can therefore be programmed freely. NC and, to an even greater extent, CNC machine tools are the development of an extremely flexible machine system, many varieties of which are being produced with different combinations of loading, number of spindles, and carriers for workpieces and tools. It is supplanting the traditional aggregates described above particularly in medium- and short-run production.

For the tool presetter the unity of setting up, planning, and machining functions is destroyed. Although a certain amount of sensorimotor skill and feel for the materials is still expected of such workers, their expertise is being limited to purely administrative knowledge about functions, measuring, and features of the various types of tools.

By contrast, the skills demanded of the programmer are both more complex and not totally distinct from those needed in machining.

The planning and preparatory character of the work bring aspects of strategic behaviour into the structure of the programmer's necessary skills. A new element is the need to identify errors and programming discrepancies when communicating with the NC machine operator and to take responsibility for deciding on the steps to be taken to correct the machine's programme.

It is the machine operators, however, upon whom the introduction of the NC machine has the greatest impact. Their functions are reduced to those of loading and unloading the machine, changing tools, and adjusting the machine's programmed work sequence when setting up and conducting the test run with the passage of the first workpiece. Monitoring and checking the sequence of automatic operations is becoming the central part of the job. Whereas the main part of the conventional machine operator's job used to be the machining of the workpiece, the main part of the job for the NC machine operator has shifted to the activity of observing the process.

None the less, it is important to point out that the variety of skills required of the NC machine operator is greater than what this simplified presentation would lead one to believe. The range depends on the size of the production run, the way work is organised in the particular plant, the strategy of labour deployment, and other factors (see Sorge *et al.*, 1982).

The more developed CNC machining centres represent flexible, easily convertible manufacturing systems for medium-sized production runs. More and more of the peripheral functions (the transfer of tools and workpieces) are increasingly being mechanised as well. In this area, too, ever greater numbers of individual machines are being linked as microprocessors continue to be developed. At the same time it is becoming possible to improve the programmer's work by technical means and aids and thereby deprofessionalise it to a job requiring little more than auxiliary skills. Programming can therefore be re-utilised for the machining job, the result being that it is reintegrated into the automatic tool, for it permits programming while machining is taking place.

Even so, Kern and Schumann (1984) are a bit overoptimistic about the possibilities of combining all production-related functions – from programming, supplying tools and workpieces, setting up, operating, and monitoring all the way to preventive maintenance and initial servicing – as the job of the machine operator. Whereas Mickler (1977) sees the work at CNC machining centres as only a somewhat more skilled form of operating a machine, Sorge *et al.* (1982) arrive at optimistic conclusions echoing those of Kern and Schumann (1984). From Sorge *et al.* (1982), one gathers that the increasing development and use of CNC machines is more likely counteracting the polarisation of qualifications and strict divisions of labour. This trend is expected to lead to a 'renaissance of skilled work' supported by CNC technologies that would permit workshops and users to make and change programmes more easily.

The number of NC machines, CNC machines, and flexible manufacturing systems in use is much lower than is generally believed and far below that forecast in the 1960s. According to a study conducted by the Association of German Machine Tool Manufacturers, only 6 per cent of West German machine tools were equipped with numerical control in 1985. The percentage was, however, significantly higher for specific types of machines and in small and medium-sized companies (Dostal and Koestner, 1982). The introduction of these machines has been slowed because of their tendency to breakdown, the organisational adjustments necessary to accommodate them, training problems, and difficulties in mastering of the software. Recently, this has been particularly true of the linked and extensive flexible manufacturing systems, where breakdowns paralyse preceding and subsequent phases of production and therefore risk being counterproductive (Moldaschl & Weber, 1985). As can be seen from the figures in Table 10.2, the production of CNC machines is increasing in both absolute and relative terms, while the number of NC machines has remained unchanged. Of the 5 803 NC machine tools produced in 1982, 5 580 (over 96 per cent) were CNC machines.

Welding Robots in Chassis Carcassing: Humanising the Workplace through Automation?

Thesis: The interaction between electronic control, sensory, and linking technologies in the form of operational systems and industrial robots has led to a significant technological breakthrough in the welding process over the past few years. This often evokes notions of production halls void of human workers, places in which robots perform the unpleasant jobs This is misleading, however. As with lacquering, welding entails a high proportion of unskilled manual – and highly stressful – residual tasks.

Table 10.2   The production and export of numerically controlled machine tools in the Federal Republic of Germany (including West Berlin), 1970–84

Year	Production	
	Total	Number of CNC machines within total
1974	985	...
1975	1085	...
1976	1289	...
1977	1979	651
1987	2451	1809
1979	3258	2848
1980	4743	4133
1981	5672	5351
1982	5803	5580

Source: Unpublished statistics from the Verband Deutscher Maschinen- und Anlagenbauer, e.V. (VDMA), 26 November 1985.

By contrast, the process of finishing the chassis is still at a relatively low level of mechanisation and entails many manual tasks. Many studies on the potential for automating chassis carcassing have come to the conclusion that the machining, not the loading, is the only aspect to have been automated thus far. Interestingly enough, industrial robots are not expected to be able to contribute much to the loading and the transfer of parts in the future because these tasks involve complex functions of perception, a variety of joining operations, the insertion of complicated parts and subsequent tasks, all of which are difficult to mechanise. A far greater potential for the use of industrial robots is seen to be the actual machining, particularly, it would seem, in spot welding.

Despite the highly mechanised state of some operations in this field, manual repetitive tasks dominate machining and assembly in chassis carcassing. One third of all jobs are residual, with the workers bridging the gaps between the steps that are mechanised. The fact that just under half of all jobs are those at a moving belt or a workplace linked to some other station gives one a general idea of the low level of qualification and the high level of stress that these residual jobs involve (Kalmbach *et al.*, 1980, p. 378; Benz-Overhage, 1983, pp. 119–25).

A closer analysis of repetitive tasks[1] shows that the working situation of those people bridging the gaps between mechanised operations are typically associated with great stress (such as blinding, noise, fumes, and tasks that must be performed above head level). Usually the addition of small parts on transfer lines and the operation of machines are strictly paced, low-skilled undemanding tasks requiring strength.

In the group of production-related activities,[2] there are more complex activities to be learned by the monitors, reworkers, and quality control personnel. The low proportion of workers who do the setting up can be explained by the advent of single-purpose transfer lines, which require little preparation. This might well change if more industrial robots are introduced.

The very small number of service personnel is also a good indication of whether the level of mechanisation is heterogeneous or low. [3] In the little mechanised chassis-finishing process at Volkswagen in Wolfsburg, the ratio of workers on piecework wages to maintenance personnel was 100 : 1.4. In the highly mechanised process of making the cages of automobiles from large modules, the ratio is 100 : 54, which is a further indication that increasing mechanisation (including the use of industrial robots) expands the proportion of more skilled maintenance workers within a firm's total workforce (Kalmbach *et al.*, 1980).

The future development of production work in this manufacturing area of the automobile industry, too, is seen very optimistically by Kern and Schumann (1984). While admitting that the firms they studied still followed the principle of fragmenting extreme functions (insertion of parts, maintenance, and quality control) and turning them into operations in their own right, the two researchers argue that the key functions between those operations (functions like controlling a machine or monitoring the installation) have been greatly enhanced. In keeping with the principle of task integration, everything from correcting control programmes, putting the installations into operation, securing the supply system, and overseeing the process all the way to carrying out routine maintenance and repair work is combined into one task, the result being that production activities will regain the calibre of skilled work (Kern and Schumann, 1984). Whether these optimistic views on the development of production-related tasks actually come to pass remains a question for further study.

Assembly: Can Industrial Robots Cope with Complex Tasks As Well?

Aside from mechanised manufacturing, assembly is the most important area of production in the automotive industry, the electronics industry, and precision engineering and undoubtedly the one requiring the greatest number of people in these fields. It still has a very low level of mechanisation, high labour intensity, a great deal of repetitive work, and a very small number of qualified monitoring and maintenance activities.[4] Many products in this area are complex in their design and construction. They are composed of numerous discrete parts of different shapes, sizes, and materials that must be successively joined with a variety of techniques, including welding, soldering, pasting, inserting, screwing, clamping and sewing. In addition, the products manufactured in electrical engineering, precision engineering, and optics require a great deal of visual and electronic inspection, calibration and adjustment.

Thesis: The variety of processing techniques and assembly parts complicates the construction and use of mechanical assembly equipment, making it possible to speak of specific obstacles to mechanisation (Lappe, 1981). But if these obstacles can be overcome – in conjunction with other streamlining efforts (aimed at the product, organisation of work, and procurement of materials – then the issue concerning the development of qualifications will not arise. Instead, the focus would shift to the problem that massive numbers of low-skilled jobs would be eliminated without the newly created, higher-skilled jobs (maintenance and testing) offsetting the loss.

The Current Level of Automation in Assembly Processes

Abele *et al.* (1984) state that manual assembly processes still dominate assembly techniques in a wide variety of structures: unsorted material in containers, simple linked installations (receding and rotary tables, belts, and storage units), and simple assembly devices like presses, jigs and special tools).

Between the manual assembly lines and groups are a number of *semi-automated assembly systems*, at which screwing, checking and adjustment activities are carried out. However, new technological possibilities have been opened up by the screwing system introduced in the 'Rabbit' assembly line in Volkswagen's Wolfsburg plant, where screws are pneumatically transferred over a distance of up to thirty metres, automatically measured for the precision of their fit, and screwed on accordingly.

The *fully automated assembly systems* usually involve unflexible single-purpose installations designed for a specific product. These systems must be completely rebuilt when the product is changed. However, short and medium production runs, small firms, subcontractors, and the like must be distinguished from long production runs and from large firms, which can apply their financial resources to sometimes excessive, but cost-effective, automation.

Flexible automation of assembly becomes possible through the use of microelectronic components in the manufacture of parts, monitoring, and process control (with sensors, for example), through the development of industrial robots, and the improvement of resources allowing flexible linking (inductive industrial vehicles, for instance).

The manual insertion of printed circuit boards is reduced in mass production and in the use of small homogeneous parts when insertion and subsequent inspection is automated (Benz-Overhage *et al.*, 1983).

As a result of the consumers' many specialised wishes, the variety of functions and, hence, of the discrete parts involved in the assembly of standard builder components appears to have increased in electronics, electrical engineering, precision engineering, and optics, making it seem extremely difficult to introduce systems for handling the assembly of these parts (Heinrich *et al.*, 1982).

In the *assembly of aggregates* in the automotive industry, the assembly of universal joints is fully automated with robots, and the assembly of cylinder heads is fully automated with linked assembly lines (as in the VW plant in Salzgitter) or with assembly lines for the completion of the drive units (as in the VW plant in Wolfsburg), work in which the possibilities offered by freely programmable robots are being increasingly exploited. In the industry as a whole, however, the assembly of engines, transmissions, and similar aggregates is done largely by hand, with the work being facilitated by screwing mounting and power jigs or with the attempt being made to make the work processes more flexible through measures like group work.

In *final assembly* all joining operations contributing to the end products in the automotive industry, electrical engineering, precision engineering, optics, machine-building, and other industries are combined. The discrete parts of the final product are transferred in the proper sequence by chain conveyors to workers stationed at conveyor belts, buffered stationary push tracks, and group work areas or are simply made available in containers or on shelves located next to the assembly line. The interlocking of automated systems for transferring parts and the flexible capacity of industrial robots in final assembly of the Rabbit in VW's plant in Wolfsburg shows the direction in which mass assembly can develop, at least in the large manufacturing plants of the automotive industry and electrical engineering. Even such complicated procedures as the assembly of rear axles, brakes and fuel lines and the installation of complete drive units with front axles can be altered according to the model of the vehicle being worked on. According to experts within the plants, the degree of automotation was increased from 5 per cent to 25 per cent when the transition was made from the first generation of the Rabbit to the second.

Despite the undoubtedly spectacular pilot projects for automated assembly, of which 'illustrious' Halle 54 of the Volkswagen plant in Wolfsburg is an outstanding example, assembly processes are still a very labour-intensive area dominated by highly repetitive manual activities. They call for uncomplicated, stereotyped movements at the lowest cognitive level of sensorimotor skills and at various levels of habituation. More complex sensorimotor activities involving great accuracy of movement, hand-arm-foot co-ordination, visual, audio, or tactile control of the motions required to execute a task, and intellectual demands going beyond the level of sensorimotor skills are performed only by the few individuals doing complex manual work (adjustment) and at a few control stations (Lappe, 1981; Benz-Overhage *et al.*, 1983).

Along with their low qualifications, industrial assembly-line jobs are characterised by an almost universal, strict division of labour that dissects the work process into simply structured, repetitive sub-operations, a situation that subjects the work to the pressure of wage systems designed to increase output. This is only one reason that assembly-line workers are exposed to very specific physical and increasingly serious psychic types of stress within the fields of work in which they are typically deployed.

The future Development of Automation in Assembly Work

As appropriate as they may be for assembly operations, industrial robots capable of being programmed along any axis of movement still founder on the still underdeveloped state of sensory technology (see Brodbeck *et al.,* 1981; Kalmbach *et al.,* 1980, for example). For the deployment of industrial robots in the flexible assembly of consumer products, it would, for example, be essential to improve sensory technology to enable machines to recognise the specific attitudes and orientations of component parts and to develop reliable tactile sensors. According to Abele *et al.* (1984), current product design is a serious obstacle to the automation of the assembly line in part because of the unwieldiness of the discrete components, the great amount of adjustment and adaptation involved, the visual inspection that is required during the assembly operation, and the lack of precision in the manufacturing.

We are on the threshold of sweeping change in assembly operations in the automotive manufacturing and electrical engineering, for plant investment in the coming years will be concentrated on measures to streamline such operations. The automation of assembly work is not the only area that can be rationalised in the near future, however. Others include product design appropriate for automated assembly (which is seen to be an even higher priority than attempts at mechanisation and automation), an inspection and change of assembly procedures, and a review of the organisation and structuring of work, with attention being given to actual mechanisation or automation and to the introduction of new manufacturing and joining technologies.

Amazingly, the greatest potential for savings are expected in the sphere of product design, not in mechanisation or automation. In the sector of machine-building, the chief effort at rationalisation will tend to be directed at optimising the organisation and structure of work because the components are so complicated and many. By contrast, the primary focus in electrical engineering will clearly be on mechanisation and automation. Within the areas that *can* be automated, the main thrust of automation in the next ten years will be in the field of modular assembly and final modules having fewer than thirty discrete parts. The development of single-purpose assembly robots will tend to increase only slightly if at all, whereas the number of automatic flexible modular assembly machines and assembly robots will increase dramatically as the expected fall in prices sets in.

The number of industrial robots installed in the Federal Republic of Germany since 1974 has grown by leaps and bounds (see Table

10.3). In view of fluctuating growth rates, which are based on rapid technological growth prevalent today, forecasts are very unsure. A projection from a sample survey conducted by Abele *et al.* (1984) indicates that between 5000 and 12 000 assembly robots will be installed in the Federal Republic by 1992. Forecasts for 1990 vary between 12 000 robots (Kuka and Becker in Otto, 1983) and 70 000 robots (VDMA in Otto, 1983).

Table 10.3   Number of industrial robots installed in the Federal Republic of Germany, 1974–85

1974	1975	1976	1977	1978	1979	1980	1981	1982	1983	1984	1985
133	243	399	571	620	1255	2301	3500	4800	6600	8500*	

*Estimate.

Source: Verband Deutscher Maschinen- und Anlagenbauer, e.V. (VDMA), cited in M. Kittner (ed.), *Gewerkschaftsjahrbuch 1985* (Cologne: Bund Verlag, 1985), p.

Changes in the organisation of work will be directed mainly at decoupling manual jobs from assembly operations and creating parallel systems or jobs. In this sense, then, work-structuring measures can be seen as
- alternatives to flexible automation in areas where the small size of the production runs precludes flexible automation in the foreseeable future;
- preparation for flexible automation in areas where the organisational conditions necessary for flexible automation must first be created; and
- a concomitant strategy aimed at creating the type of work that is worthwhile for humans and appropriate for machines when flexible automation is introduced.

The most interesting statements in the study by Abele *et al.* (1984) are undoubtedly those relating to the developments to be expected in skills. (These developments exist only in the forecasts of experts at this time.) Because of the advances expected in automation, most of the industrial experts who were surveyed assume that the proportion of skilled and qualified semiskilled workers in the labour force will remain stable or increase and that the proportion of the labour force's unskilled or marginally qualified semiskilled workers will shrink considerably, whereby firms putting a relatively high proportion of their automation-related investments into assembly operations predict more drastic reductions of unskilled and semiskilled assembly-line workers than all other firms do.

Industrial experts, however, said that they expect to find themselves confronted with many problems ensuing from flexible automation because of the demand it breeds for higher qualifications. Skilled and qualified semiskilled workers will benefit from this development; unskilled and marginally qualified semiskilled workers will not. But problems will arise for the skilled and qualified semiskilled workers in that the use of robots entails new servicing, maintenance, and programming qualifications not normally possessed even by skilled workers.

Risks of Automation: Layoffs

One could presume that the use of new technologies or a greater degree of automation leads to the replacement of unqualified, repetitive work with qualified maintenance and monitoring activities. According to this viewpoint, the workers relieved of their work by automation can be redeployed to other, more challenging, jobs.

This assumption appears to be too optimistic in that production by robots in itself creates few new, qualified jobs. For another thing, these new electronic technologies require less retooling and maintenance than conventional technologies because they are less prone to breakdown. Even a rather generous accounting of the jobs eliminated and the jobs created demonstrates the adverse effects on employment. For every labourer needed after industrial robots are introduced, five assembly jobs are dispensed with (Wobbe-Ohlenburg, 1982). This would mean impending disaster for workers holding assembly-line jobs. According to Abele *et al.* (1984), 250 000 assembly-line workers could be laid off. By 1992, between 32 per cent and 70 per cent of this potential impact will have been absorbed, meaning that between 80 000 and 170 000 jobs will be jeopardised by 1992. (On the whole, the authors assume that the lower number is the more realistic one.) Of the jobs directly affected, 70 per cent are in the field of electrical engineering, about 10 per cent in automotive manufacturing. Between 110 000 and 200 000 industrial assembly-line jobs will be eliminated by the year 2000, of which only a small part (15 per cent to 25 per cent of all jobs) can be blamed directly on the use of industrial robots.A much larger share (30 per cent) of all jobs will be endangered by measures taken in the area of product design alone (primarily resulting from the replacement of mechanical components by electronic ones and from new joining processes).

Nor is this all. It is often suggested in the discussion of new technologies that personnel would be transferred to different jobs or that qualifications would be upgraded. But the process of technological change 'in no way' affects employment 'in such a way that the person who performed repetitive work yesterday will tomorrow service the industrial robot that took his original job. Rather, it is obvious that adequate matching of the workers with the jobs they are qualified to perform involves two separate groups of people' (Wobbe-Ohlenburg, 1982, p. 161) This is especially true for the fields of work occupied mostly by women, fields in which experience has shown that technological change has polarised work into unqualified female and qualified male activities. Abele *et al.* (1984), too, state that women workers would be the ones hardest hit by lay-offs. With firms calculating that an increase in the level of automation in assembly work would eliminate unqualified activities and raise the qualificational requirements of the assembly personnel, it will be the unskilled and semiskilled workers – women – who will be affected by lay-offs because more women than men in the labour force are unskilled or semiskilled.

SUMMARISING APPRAISAL

Upon analysis of the research results, can one definitively refute Braverman's hypothesis of dequalification and downgrading in the West German metal industry? It is not all that simple. Admittedly, research on a small segment of the manufacturing processes leads one to avoid pat acceptance of his generalisations. In my opinion, though, Braverman has helped to pose discriminating questions about the various trends in the application of technology and in the work process, and these questions could become fruitful for empirical research.

We are now confronted with a large number of studies dealing with typical technological developments in the fields of computer assisted production processes, particularly with advances in the CNC technologies used in industry, the introduction of industrial robots and other systems for handling components, and specific microelectronic product innovations like the introduction of electronic monitors for machines, the possibilities for using microprocessors and microcomputers, and the impact they have on jobs. There is also more and more scientific research being done on recent developments in the area of mechanical manufacturing like flexible manufacturing systems and the changes that CAD/CAM is causing in vocational qualifications. These studies are providing an increasingly detailed picture of developments in qualification. It does not confirm the assumptions made in the hypothesis of general dequalification, but it also dampens nascent hopes that computer-guided production technologies will upgrade qualifications, that there will be a renaissance of skilled labour, and that labour's production intelligence will be rediscovered.

To conclude, I once again highlight the developmental trend of automation and the differences between the structure of qualification in the areas discussed in the preceding pages by juxtaposing the levels of mechanisation (see Table 10.1) with the qualification groups (repetitive, production-related, and maintenance – see notes 1–3).

Basically, a great amount of repetitive activities in a given area – as is the case in assembly – points to a low level of mechanisation and a high level of labour intensity. Vice versa, a great amount of maintenance and monitoring activities – as is the case in deformation – indicates highly mechanised, capital-intensive production operations.

MECHANICAL MANUFACTURING

For mechanical manufacturing, the treatment in the section on Mechanised Manufacturing (p. 280) is confirmed by the information on the levels of mechanisation and the degree of automation presented in Table 10.4. Kern and Schumann (1984) found that monofunctional single agregates (Level 3: operation of lathes, milling machines, power drills, etc.) coexisted with semiautomatic aggregate systems (Level 8: control of equipment on transfer lines) from 1966 to 1983. This advance of mechanisation in the automotive industry is expressed in the fact that the level of automation has increased from 40 per cent to 75 per cent of all activities. Basing their views on in-depth discussion with experts and observations in automotive

Table 10.4   Levels of mechanical manufacturing and automation in the Federal Republic of Germany

Year	Level of mechanisation[1]	Level of automation[2]
1966	3, 6/8	40%
1983	3, 8	75%
1990	8	80%

1. Level 1: Pure manual operation
   Level 2: Production-line technique
   Level 3: Unificational single-aggregates necessitating permanent manual work (special machines, for example)
   Level 4: Single aggregates necessitating permanent correction by means of control instruments
   Level 5: Multifunctional single-aggregates not necessitating permanent constant correction by humans
   Level 6: Aggregate systems (for example; linked individual machines; simple transfer lines)
   Level 7: Semi-automated single aggregates
   Level 8: Semi-automated aggregate systems (transfer lines, for example)
   Level 9: Fully automated manufacturing

2. The level of automation is indexed here in the terms commonly used by engineers: The share of mechanised or automated functions in a system's total number of functions is expressed in percentages.

manufacturing plants, the authors estimate that the next period, that from 1983 to 1990, will be marked by the disappearance of mono-functional single aggregates (Level 3) – which I consider to be very doubtful – and the increase in semi-automatic aggregate systems as the level of automation continues to climb to 80 per cent.

A different study (Kalmbach *et al.,* 1980) provides information on the corresponding structure of qualification at the beginning of the eighties (see Fig.10.1). The activity structure of highly mechanised, capital-intensive manufacturing (as it exists in the Volkswagen plant in Wolfsburg) is characterised by its minimal amount of repetitive work.

Most of the jobs are the so-called production-related activities, primarily those performed by the people who watch over the machines and by the quality-control personnel. It has already been pointed out that the qualification level of the CNC operator no

255

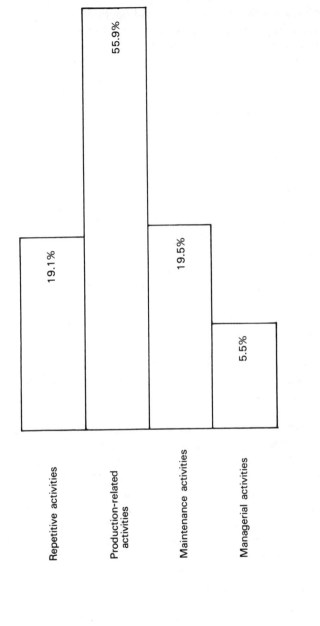

Figure 10.1 Activity structure in mechanical manufacturing

SOURCE Kalmbach, P. *et al.* (1980): *Bedingungen und soziale Folgen des Einsatzes von Industrierobotern* (Bremen: Universität) p. 539

longer matches that required by hand-operated automatic screwing machines. Moreover, the concept of combining various different tasks into a single, complex, qualified job (including shop programming) is questionable because it greatly depends on the organisational goals of the firms. There are few relatively qualified setup activities in these areas as far as single-purpose manufacturing is concerned. The number of setup men entailed in production runs of varying size and in flexible manufacturing will be much higher. Because of the very high level of mechanisation, 20 per cent of the work in this area of production involves mechanical and electrical maintenance.

Chassis carcassing

Automation in this area has always been slight and very heterogeneous, a fact one gathers from the range in the level of automation: from 10 per cent to 60 per cent in 1960 and from 40 per cent to 70 per cent in 1963 (see Table 10.5). Accordingly, it is typical for this area of production that traditional conveyor-belt manufacturing (Level 2: motory and sensory moving-belt work, i.e. manual welding) coexists with aggregate systems and semi-automatic aggregate systems (Level 8: misfeed detectors at linked, flexible welding robots on transfer lines). These two forms of production, with their respective kinds of activity, are likely to continue coexisting in the future as well. It is presumed, however, that homogeneity rather than the degree of automation will be increased in the long run.

A glance at activity structure (of the Volkswagen plant in Wolfsburg once again) shows that the qualificational profile of chassis construction, with its enormous amount of repetitive activities and the minimal amount of maintenance and monitoring work, clearly differs from the high mechanised areas of mechanical manufacturing but bears a striking resemblance to the area of assembly, which is not highly mechanised (see Fig. 10.2). In these areas of production, familiar patterns already described by Braverman come to light again: the activities bridging mechanised or automated parts of the production process, the jobs that take care of the residual and waste work created by the new technologies in welding and lacquering in automotive manufacturing and in the assembly area of the automotive and electronics industries. High-stress, low-qualified jobs are not completely eliminated by humanizing the workplace; indeed, they are recreated.

Table 10.5 Levels of mechanisation and automation in
chassis carcassing

Year	Level of mechanisation[1]	Level of automation[2]
1966	2, (6/8)	10–60%
1983	2, 8	40–70%
1990	(2), 8	70%

1. Level 1: Pure manual operation
   Level 2: Production-line technique
   Level 3: Unificational single-aggregates necessitating permanent manual work (special machines, for example)
   Level 4: Single aggregates necessitating permanent correction by means of control instruments
   Level 5: Multifunctional single-aggregates not necessitating permanent constant correction by humans
   Level 6: Aggregate systems (for example; linked individual machines; simple transfer lines)
   Level 7: Semi-automated single aggregates
   Level 8: Semi-automated aggregate systems (transfer lines, for example)
   Level 9: Fully automated manufacturing

2. The level of automation is indexed here in the terms commonly used by engineers: The share of mechanised or automated functions in a system's total number of functions is expressed in percentages.

Assembly

In the assembly of aggregates, particularly in final assembly (of cars and electrical appliances, for example), the degree of automation will remain relatively low. From 1966 to 1983, it increased from 5 per cent to 25 per cent in aggregate assembly and from 0 per cent to only 10 per cent in final assembly (see Tables 10.6 and 10.7). Contrary to popular expectation, the future will not offer many opportunities to change the picture in this area. Because of the product structure, assembly has always entailed conveyor-belt production (Level 2: motory and sensory conveyor-belt work). I doubt that semi-automatic single-aggregates (Level 7: monitoring of automatic machines) or even semi-automatic aggregate systems (Level 8: transfer lines with systems control) will prevail.

258

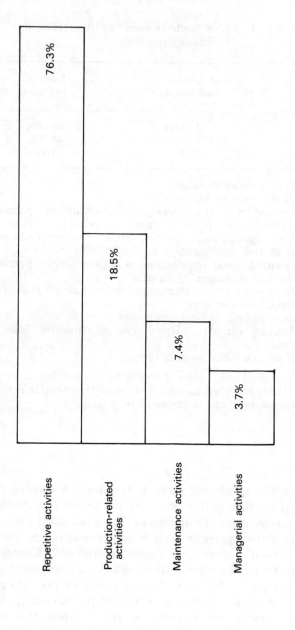

Figure 10.2 Activity structure in carcassing
SOURCE Kalmbach *et al.*, 1980, p. 380

Table 10.6 Levels of mechanisation and automation in
aggregate assembly

Year	Level of mechanisation[1]	Level of automation[2]
1966	2,	5%
1983	2, (7)	25%
1990	2, 7, 8	45%

1. Level 1: Pure manual operation
   Level 2: Production-line technique
   Level 3: Unificational single-aggregates necessitating permanent manual work (special machines, for example)
   Level 4: Single aggregates necessitating permanent correction by means of control instruments
   Level 5: Multifunctional single-aggregates not necessitating permanent constant correction by humans
   Level 6: Aggregate systems (for example; linked individual machines; simple transfer lines)
   Level 7: Semi-automated single aggregates
   Level 8: Semi-automated aggregate systems (transfer lines, for example)
   Level 9: Fully automated manufacturing

2. The level of automation is indexed here in the terms commonly used by engineers: The share of mechanised or automated functions in a system's total number of functions is expressed in percentages.

At an extremely low technological level, 84 per cent of the jobs involve repetitive activities, which in mass production can be considered unqualified work that anyone can do (see Fig. 10.3). Particularly in these labor-intensive areas, further mechanization and automation will confront us with ever greater problems that Braverman, too, has pointed out: unemployment brought about by the increased use of new technologies.

Table 10.7   Levels of mechanisation and automation in
final assembly

Year	Level of mechanisation[1]	Level of automation[2]
1966	2	. . .
1983	2, 7	10%
1990	2, 7, 8	20%

1. Level 1: Pure manual operation
   Level 2: Production-line technique
   Level 3: Unificational single-aggregates necessitating permanent manual work (special machines, for example)
   Level 4: Single aggregates necessitating permanent correction by means of control instruments
   Level 5: Multifunctional single-aggregates not necessitating permanent constant correction by humans
   Level 6: Aggregate systems (for example; linked individual machines; simple transfer lines)
   Level 7: Semi-automated single aggregates
   Level 8: Semi-automated aggregate systems (transfer lines, for example)
   Level 9: Fully automated manufacturing
2. The level of automation is indexed here in the terms commonly used by engineers: The share of mechanised or automated functions in a system's total number of functions is expressed in percentages.

Notes

1. Repetitive activities are connected directly to the flow of production, with every execution of the worker's primary function being a necessary contribution to the production of *each* workpiece. Most of these activities are brief and require little skill.
2. Production-related activities affect the flow of production indirectly. They ensure continuous production of standardised workpieces. As secondary production work, these activities are not directly coupled with the rate of the production. Some of these activities involve an intermediate level of qualification (for quality-control personnel and machine monitors); others require a high level of qualification (for systems controllers, transfer-line monitors, and setup personnel).
3. Maintenance activities are largely decoupled from the flow of production and affect it only when sources of interference must be eliminated. All such activities require highly qualified personnel (Wobbe-Ohlenburg, 1982, p. 34).
4. See notes 1 to 3.

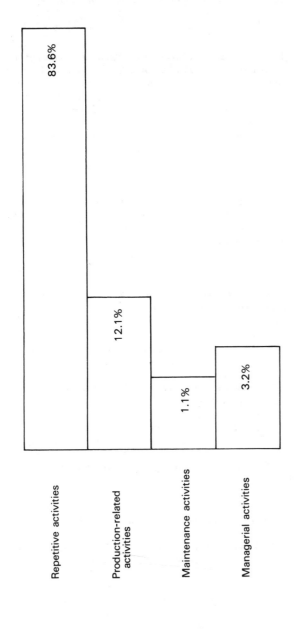

Figure 10.3 Activity structure for assembly operations
SOURCE Kalmbach *et al.*, 1980, p. 581

References

Abele, E. *et al.* (1984) *Einsatzmöglichkeiten von flexibel automatisierten Montagesystemen in der industriellen Produktion. Montagestudie,* Schriftenreihe 'Humanisierung des Arbeitslebens', vol. 61 (Düsseldorf: Campus).

Benz-Overhage, K., Brumlop, E., v. Freyberg, Th., Papadimitriou, Z. (1983). *Computergestützte Produktion, Fallstudien in ausgewählten Industriebetrieben* (Frankfurt: Campus).

Beynon, H. (1973) *Working for Ford* (London: Penguin Books).

Braverman, H. (1977) *Die Arbeit in modernen Produktionsprozeß* (Frankfurt: Campus).

Bright, J. R. (1958) *Automation and Management* (Cambridge/Mass.: Harvard University Press).

Brighton Labour Process Group (1977), 'The Capitalist Labour Process, *Capital and Class,* 1, 3–26.

Brodbeck, B. *et al.* (1981) *Handhabungssysteme, Entscheidungshilfen und Einsatzerfahrungen aus technischer Sicht* (Düsseldorf: VDI-Verlag).

Cole, R. E. (1979) *Work, Mobility and Participation: A Comparative Study of American and Japanese Industry* (Berkeley, Los Angeles, London: University of California Press).

Deutschmann, Ch. (1985) *Der Weg zum Normalarbeitstag. Die Entwicklung der Arbeitszeiten in der deutschen Industrie bis 1918* (Frankfurt: Campus).

Dore, R. (1973) *British Factory – Japanese Factory* (Berkeley and Los Angeles: University of California Press).

Dostal, W., Köstner, K. (1982), Beschäftigungsveränderungen beim Einsatz numerisch gesteuerter Werkzeugmaschinen. *Mitteilungen aus der Arbeitsmarkt- und Berufsforschung,* 15, 443–9.

Edwards, R. C. (1979) *Herrschaft im modernen Produktionsprozeß* (Frankfurt und New York: Campus 1979).

Form, W. H. (1986) *Blue-collar Stratification. Autoworkers in Four Countries* (Princetown: Princetown University Press).

Friedman, A. (1977) *Industry and Labour* (London: The Macmillan Press).

Gallie, D. (1978) *In Search of the New Working Class* (Cambridge: Cambridge University Press).

Gensior, S. (1984) 'New Technologies – Possibilities for a New Valuation of Women's Work' in A. Olerup, I. Schneider, E. Monod (eds), *Women, Work and Computerization. Opportunities and Disadvantages,* pp. 171–80 (Amsterdam: North Holland).

Gensior, S. (1986) *Mikroelektronik – Anwendung und ihre Bedingung für die Qualifikationen: ein Literaturbericht.* Berlin, WZB-Discussion Papers, no. 7.

Heinrich, K. -D., Schäfer, D. (1982) *Menschengerechte Arbeitsgestaltung in der Elektroindustrie* (Frankfurt: Campus).

Jones, B. (1982) 'Destruction or Redistribution of Engineering Skills? The Case of Numerical Control', in S. Wood (ed.), *The Degradation of Work? Skill, Deskilling and the Labour Process,* pp. 179–200 (London: Hutchinson).

Jürgens, U., Naschold, F. (ed.) (1984) *Arbeitspolitik. Materialien zum Zusammenhang von politischer Macht, Kontrolle und betrieblicher Organisation der Arbeit* (Opladen: Westdeutscher Verlag).

Kalmbach, P., *et al.*, (1980) *Bedingungen und soziale Folgen des Einsatzes von Industrierobotern. Sozialwissenschaftliche Begleitforschung zum Projekt der Volkswagenwerk AG, Wolfsburg: Neue Handhabungssysteme als technische Hilfen für den Arbeitsprozeß* (Bremen: Universität).

Kern, H., Schumann, M. (1984) *Das Ende der Arbeitsteilung? Rationalisierung in der industriellen Produktion* (München: Verlag C. H. Beck).

Kern, H., Schumann, M. (1974) *Industriearbeit und Arbeiterbewußtsein. Vol. 1 und 2* (Frankfurt: Europäische Verlagsanstalt).

Kittner, M. (ed.) (1985) *Gewerkschaftsjahrbuch* (Köln: Bund-Verlag).

Knights, D., Willmott, H., Collinson, D. (eds) (1985) *Job Redesign* (Aldershot: Gower).

Kornblum, W. (1974) *Blue Collar Community* (Chicago und London: University of Chicago Press).

Lappe, L. (1981) *Die Arbeitssituation erwerbstätiger Frauen* (Frankfurt und New York: Campus).

Lappe, L. (1985) *Neue Technologien und ihre Auswirkungen auf die Tätigkeit der Beschäftigten in der Metallindustrie. Ein Literaturüberblick.* Paderborn: Arbeitskreis Sozialwissenschaftliche Arbeitsmarkforshung (SAMF), No. 2.

Lappe, L. (1984) The Advance of Microelectronics in Assembly Operations. New Opportunities for Working Women? in A. Olerup, I. Schneider, E. Monod (eds), *Women, Work and Computerization. Opportunities and Disadvantages* pp. 161–70 (Amsterdam: North Holland).

Lappe, L. (1985) 'Berufsverlaufsmuster und Reproduktions-interessen junger Facharbeiter' in E. -H. Hoff, L. Lappe, W. Lempert, *Arbeitsbiographie und Persönlichkeitsentwicklung,* pp. 179–99 (Bern: Huber).

Lappe, L. (1986a) *Frauenarbeit und Frauenarbeitslosigkeit. Eine empirische Überprüfung geschlechtsspezifischer Arbeitsmarktsegmentation,* Paderborn: Arbeitskreis Sozial-wissenschaftliche Arbeitsmarktforschung (SAMF), no. 2.

Lappe, L. (1986b) Kontrolle des Arbeitsprozesses. Ein Beitrag zur Labour-Process Debatte in: *Journal für Sozialforschung,* 4, 418–42.

Lappe, L. (1986c) Technologie, Qualifikation und Kontrolle: Die Labour-Process Debatte aus der Sicht der deutschen Industriesoziologie in: *Soziale Welt,* 213, 310–30.

Littler, C. R. (1982) *The Development of the Labour Process in Britain, Japan and the USA* (London: Heinemann Educational).

Marglin, S. A. (1974) What do Bosses do? The Origins and Functions of Hierarchy in Capitalist Production. *Review of Radical Political Economics,* 6, 60–112.

Mickler, O. (1981) *Facharbeit im Wandel. Rationalisierung im industriellen Produktionsprozeß* (Frankfurt: Campus).

Mickler, O., Dittrich, E., Neumann, U. (1976) *Technik, Arbeitsorganisation und Arbeit. Eine empirische Untersuchung in der automatischen Produktion* (Frankfurt: Aspekte Verlag).

264   *The Labour Process in German Industrial Sociology*

Mickler, O., Mohr, W., Kadritzke, U. (1977). *Produktion und Qualifikation. Bericht über die Hauptstudie im Rahmen der Untersuchung von Planungsprozessen im System der beruflichen Bildung* – Eine empirische Untersuchung zur Entwicklung von Qualifikationsanforderungen in der industriellen Produktion und deren Ursachen, Teil I und II. Göttingen: Soziologisches Forschungsinstitut (SOFI).

Moldaschl, M., Weber, W. (1985) Flexible Fertigungssysteme: Arbeitsorganisation. Qualifikation und Belastung. Eine prospektive Arbeitsplatzbewertung. Berlin: *Diplomarbeit an der Technischen Universität Berlin.*

Nichols, Th., Armstrong, P. (1976) *Workers Divided* (Glasgow: Fontana).

Otto, P. (1983) *Wie schnell kommen die Roboter? Prognoseprobleme technischer Entwicklungen, Veröffentlichungsreihe des internationalen Instituts für vergleichende Gesellschaftsforschung* (Berlin: Wissenschaftszentrum, WZB).

Penn, R. (1982) Skilled Manual Workers in the Labour Process, 1856–1964, in S. Wood (ed.), *The Degradation of Work? Skill, Deskilling and the Labour Process* pp. 90–108 (London: Hutchinson).

Schmiede, R., Schudlich, E. (1976) *Die Entwicklung der Leistungsentlohnung in Deutschland. Eine historisch-theoretische Untersuchung zum Verhältnis von Lohn und Leistung unter kapitalistischen Produktionsbedingungen* (Frankfurt: Aspekte Verlag).

Sorge, A., Hartmann, G., Warner, M., and Nicholas, I. (1982) *Mikroelektronik und Arbeit in der Industrie* (Frankfurt: Campus).

Stone, K. (1975) 'The Origins of Job Structures in the Steel Industry', in R. C. Edwards *et al.* (eds), *Labor Market Segmentation* (Lexington, Mass: D. C. Heath).

Thompson, P. (1983) *The Nature of Work (an Introduction to Debates on the Labour Process)* (London: Macmillan).

Turner, H. A. *et al.* (1967) *Labour Relations in the Motor Industry* (London: Allen & Unwin).

Wobbe-Ohlenburg, W. (1982) *Automobilarbeit und Roboterproduktion. Eine Fallstudie zum Einsatz von Industrierobotern im Volkswagenwerk* (Berlin: Verlag Die Arbeitswelt).

Wood, S. (1982) *The Degradation of Work? Skill, Deskilling and the Labour Process* (London: Hutchinson).

Zimbalist, A. (ed.) (1979) *Case Studies on the Labour Process* (London: Monthly Review Press).

Index

Kelly, J. E. 4, 43, 68, 96-7, 166,
    199, 211, 212, 214-15, 219,
    220, 221, 222, 225 n1
Kelly, Pete 193 n28
Kern, H. 234, 235, 236-7, 238,
    242, 243, 245, 253
Kiesler, Sara 33, 43
King, J. L. 32, 42, 43, 44
King, W. R. 34
Kling, R. 30, 31
Knights, David 1, 4, 8, 119, 144,
    147, 166
knowledge
    professional 35-6
    shop floor 181, 182
knowledge engineering 36
Konsynski, B. 35
Koopman, P. L. 42
Kornblum, W. 232
Kostner, K. 243
Kraft, Philip 20, 198, 218, 224

Labor-Management Committees
    174
Labor-Management Services
    Administration 174
labour
    co-operation 6, 172-5, 183
    compliance with new technology
        7-8
    control 119-22
    degradation 66, 69, 77, 85, 87,
        214
    surveillance 10
labour costs 178
labour force, non-manual 1
labour process 1, 5-7, 8, 97, 144,
    165-7
labour solidarity, weakening 189
Land, F. 209
Lappe, Lothar 16-17, 230, 234,
    246, 248
Larson, M. S. 38
Lash, S. 6
Laudon, K. C. 40
Lawrence, P. R. 4
layoffs, impact of automation
    251-2

Learmonth, G. P. 35
Leavitt, H. J. 119
Lee, D. J. 69
Lee, Gloria L. 11-12, 91
Leone, W. C. 66
Likert, R. 4
line management 179
Littler, C. R. 1, 4, 68, 234
Lockyer, K. G. 68
long-range planning 188
Lorsch, J. W. 4
Loveridge, R. 110
Lucas, H. C. 34

McFarlan, F. W. 34
McGregor, D. 4
machine operators, numerically
    controlled machines 242
machine tool companies 52, 61
machine tool operators 10-11
machine tools 71, 239-43
machining centres 75-8
McKenney, J. L. 34
Mackenzie, D. 5
McKesson Pharmaceutical
    Company 35
McLean, E. R. 30, 32, 34
McLoughlin, I. P. 118, 124, 132
maintenance activities 245, 256,
    260 n3
man-machine interface 203
management
    control 52-4, 67, 101, 106, 107,
        119-22, 172, 189-90, 209, 212
    implications of TOPS 137
    Japanese style 172-3, 193 n36
    predefining systems design 218
    response to organisational
        change 179-80
    restructuring 188
    views on job redesign 219-20,
        223
Management Advisory Services 38
management by objectives 177
management consultants 38, 189
management information systems
    27-8, 169, 175-6, 177, 200
management process, QWL as
    187